W9-CIH-083

THE COMPLETE GUIDE
TO DIVORCE

How to Win and Hold a Mate

The Legal Encyclopedia for Home and Business

Your Legal Advisor

THE
COMPLETE GUIDE
TO DIVORCE

by SAMUEL G. KLING

PUBLISHED BY **BERNARD GEIS ASSOCIATES**

DISTRIBUTED BY RANDOM HOUSE

CARNEGIE LIBRARY
LIVINGSTONE COLLEGE
SALISBURY, N. C. 28144

© 1963 by Samuel G. Kling

All rights reserved under International and Pan American Conventions. Published by Bernard Geis Associates; distributed by Random House, Incorporated, in New York and simultaneously in Canada by Random House of Canada, Limited

Library of Congress Catalog Card Number: 63-18457

Manufactured in the United States of America

Third Printing

346.0166
K 65

*This book is dedicated to all those who
seek a second chance at happiness*

The author is grateful to the many clients
who have contributed questions to this book.

111030

Table of Contents

Leonard L. Greif, Jr.

SAMUEL G. KLING

tributed reviews to the Sunday editions of *The New York Times* and the New York *Herald Tribune,* and he has had articles published in *Look, Better Homes and Gardens,* and many other magazines. *Your Marriage,* Mr. Kling's nationally syndicated column, appeared in the New York *World-Telegram,* the Chicago *Daily News,* and fifty-five other leading newspapers for eight years.

Two of Mr. Kling's previous books, *Your Legal Advisor,* a layman's handbook of law, and *The Legal Encyclopedia for Home and Business* have sold almost two million copies.

PUBLISHED BY

BERNARD GEIS ASSOCIATES

Printed in the United States of America

A Note
to the Reader

The aim of this book is to supply basic information about current divorce laws, practices, and procedures throughout the United States as well as Canada, Mexico, and certain other foreign countries.

Addressed to laymen, this is a guidebook by a divorce lawyer for those who seek or contemplate annulment, separation, or divorce. It is my earnest hope that the reader will find in these pages the answers to the hundreds of questions that arise before, during, and after divorce litigation—questions busy lawyers frequently find they cannot answer simply because they lack the necessary time for study and research. However, a book cannot replace legal advice, and I urge the reader who considers divorce to consult his lawyer.

The Complete Guide to Divorce is based on the practical experience of the author. In the thirty years I have actively engaged in the practice of law I have handled thousands of divorce cases of practically every type and description. I have read and studied extensively in the fields of marriage counseling, psychiatry, and psychoanalysis. In addition, I wrote a nationally syndicated daily column on the subject of marriage for more than eight years called "Your Marriage" which appeared in the New York *World-Telegram* as well as in fifty-four other leading newspapers.

Equally important, from the day I first began the practice of law I have consistently attempted to effect reconciliations between those who came to see me about divorce, and I have been successful in a gratifying proportion of the cases. My bent has ever been toward saving marriages whenever possible, not in destroying them. I am convinced, however, that a divorce is preferable to an unhappy marriage and that a divorce can often be the only constructive solution to an impossible domestic situation.

By this I do not mean that divorce is a panacea, or that it automatically and routinely guarantees marital happiness the second time around. It does not. Some people are divorce prone and would be unhappy no matter whom they married. Emotionally immature, these men and women carry over their neurotic personalities into their second, third, and fourth marriages with equally sad results. The simple truth is that having been emotionally deprived of love since childhood, such persons find themselves unable to give love to others.

But there are tens of thousands of men and women who are able to profit by their marital mistakes and for whom a reshuffling of the marriage deck affords a second chance at happiness. These are the people for whom divorce is therapeutically sound and who are successful in achieving lasting wedded happiness with new mates.

Finally, I should like to call special attention to two unique chapters of the book. The first: "Can the Marriage Be Saved?" is a valiant attempt to probe behind the legal façade of divorce into the real causes of marital breakups. Stated briefly, I have tried to evaluate which marriages can be saved and which are beyond redemption, and to indicate what marriage counseling can and cannot do.

The other chapter about which I would like to comment is: "After Divorce—What?" Every divorce poses problems and requires more or less difficult adjustments. To gather information for this chapter I have interviewed hundreds of divorced persons, discussed their problems, and gleaned insights that may be helpful to those faced with the crushing, disturbing question: After divorce—what?

If my book allays the reader's fears and anxieties about divorce, if it encourages the preservation of those marriages that *can* be saved, if it helps clarify the minds of those who feel that divorce is inevitable as to the proper course to pursue, and if it answers all the questions he or she would like answered about the legal aspects of annulment, desertion, separation, and divorce, then the thirty years that went into the preparation of this comprehensive guide will have been well spent indeed.

SAMUEL G. KLING

Baltimore 2, Maryland

Can
1
the Marriage
Be Saved?

For whom is this book intended?

This book was designed for those who have made up their minds to get a divorce. However, since divorce is so serious a step we urge you to consider first the possibility of saving your marriage, as suggested in this chapter, or to consider one of the alternatives to divorce as discussed in Chapters 2 and 3.

Can *all* marriages be saved?

No. Despite the women's magazines, television, and the movies, not all marriages can or should be saved. Many should never have been contracted in the first place. Hasty marriages, for example, on the part of young, immature people account for a disproportionately large number of divorces. Again, many men and women are simply not good marriage material. Their marriages would fail no matter whom they married or how often. Moreover, some men and women wed for the wrong reasons and find that, after the first flush of sexual enthusiasm has waned, there is really nothing to hold the marriage together.

At what point, if any, should a marriage be considered hopeless?

When the pain of continuing the marriage so far exceeds the benefits or pleasures that an ordinarily prudent person would not hesitate to call it quits. Obviously, this is an individual decision, for what is painful to one person may be tolerable to another. Whenever possible, however, a decision should be reached with the help of a skilled marriage counselor, psychologist, or psychiatrist.

Can married love be rekindled?

Much depends on what caused the love to die in the first place. If the marriage withered because of serious personality clashes on the part of either or both parties, the solution will lie in attempting to resolve the conflicts by modifying personality behavior. This requires considerable professional assistance over an extended period of time, and even so is only moderately successful. Most marriages fail because of a basic incompatibility. The incompatibility may be sexual, intellectual, or temperamental. Whatever the reason, getting at the source of the difficulty instead of merely treating symptoms is always indicated. This does not necessarily mean that all such marriages are hopeless and should be quickly dissolved. Some of these marriages can be reclaimed by providing psychological insight and re-education. But here again skilled professional help is called for.

Does the length of time of the marriage affect the chances of saving it?

Yes. The longer a marriage is allowed to deteriorate the harder it is to salvage, since hostility, indifference, pride, and inertia become increasingly difficult to dislodge. The prognosis is usually more favorable for a couple married only a few years than it is for a couple married twenty years, where behavior patterns have become so rigid that neither marriage counseling nor psychiatry can do much good. But even such cases are not always hopeless. For it does happen that, given insight and understanding, older couples can sometimes alter their behavior sufficiently for the marriage to function again.

When is a marriage really worth saving?

When there is still some residual affection between husband and wife and when both earnestly seek to improve the marriage. Without such a strong desire little can be done. All marriages produce problems. In a successful marriage the pipelines of communication are kept open. Being reasonably mature, the husband and wife will discuss the areas of conflict as rationally and as objectively as possible. If they find they are not making satisfactory progress on their own, they won't hesitate to call in the aid of a marriage counselor. On the other hand, for either party to refuse to discuss the basic problem suggests an immaturity and hostility that makes saving the marriage impossible.

Is the husband or wife generally more eager to save the marriage?

The wife, usually. Despite their emancipation, women still have a greater stake in marriage and the family. On the other hand, the ego and pride of men often prevents them from seeking professional help. As a rule the more interested and mature the individual the more eager he will be to explore the possibilities of a reconciliation.

Are interfaith marriages especially prone to failure?

Yes, since often more than the religious convictions of the parties are involved. Marriage research reveals that the more a couple have in common the greater the likelihood of marital success. When a couple are too different in background, personality, outlook, or religion, the gloomier the outlook. Statistically, marriages between Catholics and Jews are most hazardous, those between Protestants and Catholics have a high risk potential. Those between Jews and Protestants are most successful.

How do children affect an interfaith marriage?

A failing interfaith marriage without children is one thing; a failing interfaith marriage with youngsters is quite another. Many interfaith marriages do succeed, however, even where there are children. All other things being equal, a couple can resolve its religious difficulties provided there are other compensatory satisfactions. For example, each party can continue with his own church, or a couple may decide to attend a third church. One party may convert to the other's religion. Or both husband and wife can give up their religion. The problem of religious training for the children is often a formidable one and usually a source of friction. A couple may reach an understanding on this issue as on others. If irreligious or only mildly religious, a couple may send a child to an Ethical Culture school or have him attend a Unitarian church, where greater emphasis is laid on ethics than on theology. Or some other compromise may be arrived at. Each case is an individual one. Provided there are sufficient compensatory factors the religious question is not necessarily an insoluble one. It is only when the marriage provides little or no satisfaction that conflicting religious views often become the straw which breaks the marital back.

Can a "second honeymoon" revive a failing marriage?

Rarely. More important than the second honeymoon is the attempt to resolve the difficulties which suggest the need for a second honeymoon. If the couple has a deep-seated sexual problem or is otherwise basically incompatible a second honeymoon will only succeed in further embarrassing the husband or wife. By itself, therefore, a second honeymoon accomplishes nothing. But where marital conflicts are resolved beforehand a "second honeymoon" may be an admirable way of celebrating an already improved marriage.

In a failing marriage, is it helpful to seek the advice of friends or relatives?

Not as a rule. Friends and relatives are apt to be biased in favor of the one seeking advice. Lacking objectivity, they often tend to place the entire blame on one person. Also the one seeking advice tends to give a biased and distorted version of what really happened, so that friends and relatives are likely to be influenced by what they are told. More basic still, friends and relatives often lack the insight and scientific understanding to make a real contribution toward either improving or dissolving the marriage.

What about clergymen?

In recent years many clergymen have become interested in pastoral counseling, have read widely in the fields of psychology and psychiatry, and can be helpful to couples who come before them. Many clergymen, however, have not been trained in the art and science of marriage counseling and are not versed in the techniques of psychotherapy.

Are separate vacations helpful in saving a marriage?

On the contrary separate vacations are often an excuse to escape from a dull or intolerable marriage. A husband and wife genuinely fond of each other don't seek ways and means of avoiding each other. Instead they do things together, sharing whatever pleasures are available. It is only when the marriage becomes irksome that the husband or wife will suggest a separate vacation which then becomes a mere evasion or failure to face the problems at hand.

Is there such a thing as an impossible or hopeless marriage?

Yes. Many marriages which end in divorce, as well as many marriages which don't end in divorce, are of this nature. But here too what constitutes an impossible or hopeless marriage is largely subjective. A marriage to a sadist may seem quite hopeless to an outsider but tolerable, if not pleasurable, to the spouse involved.

What are the chances of saving a marriage where there is a considerable age difference between husband and wife?

In marriage what is important is not the chronological but the emotional age of the parties. People marry for various reasons and to fulfill various psychological needs, often of an unconscious nature. A young girl may marry a much older man because she seeks a substitute father or because he symbolizes strength and power. The older man may marry a young girl because to do so bolsters his ego, feeds his vanity, or because he finds growing old intolerable and hopes that some of the girl's youth will rejuvenate him. If the desires of both parties are fulfilled the marriage may be a good one. It is only when the unconscious reasons which prompted the marriage are unfulfilled that trouble appears.

What are the chances of saving a marriage where one of the parties is an alcoholic?

Poor. Not every heavy drinker is an alcoholic, however, though the ranks of alcoholics come from the heavy drinkers. Alcoholism is a disease and alcoholics are sick. A true alcoholic is so heavily dependent on liquor that he is mentally disturbed and unable to function efficiently, either at his work, his marriage, or in his social life. Another distinguishing characteristic in contrast to the merely heavy drinker is that the true alcoholic becomes a compulsive morning drinker and often has blackouts accompanied by loss of memory of events which occurred while drinking.

Why do people become alcoholics?

Usually to relieve an anxiety which has become intolerable. Alcoholism is thus primarily an escape from a world which the alcoholic is unable to cope with, in which he finds himself threatened and overwhelmed.

What is the treatment for alcoholism?

Medically it is divided into two parts: tranquilizers to relieve tension or anxiety, and antabuse drugs to eliminate the desire for liquor.

Can alcoholics be cured?

Yes, with the rate of cure depending on the desire of the alcoholic. The stronger the motivation the better the chance for a cure. About half of all alcoholics can be rehabilitated with prompt medical treatment. Where the alcoholic evinces a strong desire to be helped, the odds are 90% in his favor.

Is Alcoholics Anonymous really helpful in effecting a cure?

Yes. The quicker an alcoholic is brought into contact with this organization the better for the individual and for the prospects of saving the marriage. It is only when the alcoholic refuses treatment, either medical or through AA, that a separation or divorce should be contemplated. But rehabilitating an alcoholic does not necessarily mean that the marriage will be preserved or that it is worth saving. It is merely the indispensable first step toward salvaging the individual with the ultimate hope of reclaiming the marriage.

Can a marriage be saved when the husband is a gambler?

Yes, provided the gambler is willing to undergo psychological treatment. A distinction must again be drawn between the man who plays cards for reasonable stakes, who can afford to lose, and the man who persistently plays for stakes he can ill afford. In the first case the security of the family is not threatened. In the latter case it often is. Heavy, habitual gambling is a disease. Seeking the underlying reasons for the gambling is a first step. Unfortunately, few gamblers request such help. If they do, there are often good results.

What about drug addiction?

The World Health Organization's Committee on Addiction-Producing Drugs has suggested the following definition of drug addiction: ". . . a state of periodic or chronic intoxication, detrimental to the individual and to society, produced by the repeated consumption of a drug (natural or synthetic). Its characteristics include: (1) an overpowering desire or need (compulsion) to continue taking the drug and to obtain it by any means, (2) a tendency to increase the dose, and (3) a psychic (psychological) and sometimes

11

a physical dependence on the effects of the drug." Contrary to popular belief, drug addiction isn't as widespread as is commonly thought. According to the United States Public Health Service there are now approximately 60,000 addicts, mostly men, who suffer from some form of personality disorder compounded frequently with a complex system of habit patterns that add to the difficulty of treatment.

What are the chances of curing a drug addict?

On a statistical basis less than 25% are permanently cured. Whether a given individual can be rehabilitated will depend on the nature of the anxieties, conflicts, and neuroses which drove him to drugs in the first place. Treatment consists of removal of the addict to an institution where the activities of the patient and the sources of the drug can be controlled.

Can a marriage be saved where one of the spouses has been unfaithful?

Yes, though much depends on the nature and extent of the infidelity. According to Kinsey half of all husbands stray at one time or another and so do about a fourth of all wives. Since these figures were released more than ten years ago the probabilities are that there has been greater promiscuity in the intervening decade. One of the harsh facts of life, therefore, is that both men and women have varietist or straying tendencies, apparently inherited from their simian ancestors. A sharp distinction, however, must be drawn between a casual, occasional infidelity and one where the husband or wife is emotionally involved over a long period of time. The prospects for the future success of the marriage are much better for the former than for the latter. Much more important are the reasons for the infidelity. Did the husband stray because the wife was frigid? Because she failed to provide him with ego satisfaction? Was he unfaithful to prove his virility? Did the wife succumb because she was unable to derive sexual satisfaction from her husband? Because she lacked companionship? Because he humiliated and degraded her? Uncovering the real, often unconscious, motives for the infidelity is the first step in rehabilitating a marriage. Here again a willingness to discuss the basic issue is of paramount importance. If this doesn't help, professional aid should be promptly sought.

Can a marriage be saved where the wife resents her role as a house-wife?

Much depends on the reason for the resentment. A wife who rebels at being a housewife may do so because she unconsciously resents being a woman. Envying the male, she seeks to ape him, becomes aggressive and belligerent, and often seeks to humiliate and degrade him. Being a housewife, to her, is equivalent to being a menial, a role she detests. Marriage to such a wife does not represent a partnership with a division of labor and responsibility, but dependence and enslavement. Obviously such a wife is not a prime candidate for a successful marriage until she shows a marked change in attitude and behavior, a change which usually comes, if at all, only with some deep therapy such as psychoanalysis.

Can a marriage be saved where a couple is sexually incompatible?

Again much depends on the nature and extent of the incompatibility and the willingness of both parties to seek professional help. Sexual incompatibility in a married couple may result from a falling out of love by one or both spouses, fear, ignorance, or indifference. A distinction should be drawn between a couple who were sexually incompatible from the beginning of a marriage and a couple who after some years find that the sex side of their life has deteriorated to a point where one or both spouses no longer enjoy it. In the first case, the sexual incompatibility may be due to carryovers of sexual feelings and experiences from early childhood. The young husband or wife may conceive of sex as something obscene or sinful, ideas inherited, perhaps, from the parents. In such cases re-education on a deep level is often indicated, for the incompatibility is not directed toward the mate but to the sex act itself. The case is somewhat different in a couple who were originally com-

13

patible sexually but who after some years of married life no longer find pleasure in the sex act. There may be many reasons for the subsequent incompatibility. The marriage itself may have deteriorated which is reflected in sexual indifference. The husband or wife may be having an affair, with neither the energy nor desire for sex relations with the mate. Or they may no longer be attractive to each other physically or mentally.

What if the wife is frigid?

A frigid wife is one unable to enjoy sexual intercourse or reach an orgasm with any man. A wife capable of reaching an orgasm with another man is not frigid. Frigidity in a wife is one of the commonest complaints of husbands and a frequently disturbing factor in a marriage. Since sexual feelings and desires are the barometer of a marriage it often happens that a wife is unwilling to have sex relations with her husband not because she is frigid, but because she is hostile or resentful. She may, and often does, resent her husband's treatment of her in other aspects of the marriage.

Is frigidity often due to physical factors?

Rarely. A small vagina or an unusually large penis may cause difficulty but the combination of these two factors in a couple is uncommon. If this is a source of trouble a physician should be consulted.

What are the real causes of frigidity in wives?

One is adult experiences and conscious thoughts; the other childhood experiences and their aftereffects.

How do adult experiences and conscious thoughts affect frigidity?

An early sexual experience may have produced such an emotional shock that it left permanent scars which affect the marriage. Sexual relations on the honeymoon performed by a clumsy or inept husband, resulting in pain, may also leave emotional scars which may make subsequent sexual pleasure impossible. A fear of pregnancy may also foster frigidity.

How do carry-overs from childhood affect frigidity?

A wife may become frigid because of a childhood fear that her vagina will be damaged, a fear that is carried over into adulthood. She may have learned this from her mother or sisters who told her that men are predatory, coarse, and brutal. As a child, the wife may have witnessed her father attacking the mother sexually with residually painful results. Or she may have imagined such was the case when actually there was no rape at all. The causes of psychological frigidity are generally of an unconscious nature, with the wife unaware of her early childhood experiences.

Can a marriage be saved where the wife is frigid?

Only if the psychological reasons behind the sexual unresponsiveness are uncovered. Psychotherapy by a marriage counselor, psychiatrist, or analyst is usually required to do this effectively. It should be said that frigidity in a wife often leads to philandering on the part of the husband, which may terminate the marriage itself, or to adultery on the part of the wife to prove she is not frigid.

How does impotency affect the marriage?

Impotency in the male is equivalent to frigidity in the female. A husband is impotent when he is unable to have an erection with any woman. The causes are generally psychological. A husband may unconsciously fear damage to his penis as a result of childhood masturbation, even though childhood masturbation is quite harmless. He may have been instilled with a fear of sex by his mother. Or he may have regarded her as so good and pure that in identify-

15

ing his wife with his mother the sex act becomes an impossible desecration. There are many, many causes.

Is premature ejaculation on the part of the husband a form of impotency?

Yes. Though there are no absolute standards, a normally potent husband is able to maintain an erection from three to five minutes. Where there is premature ejaculation the orgasm comes within a few seconds with consequent frustration on the part of the wife. Continued sexual failure on the part of the husband leads to increased fear and anxiety and thus to further failure. The best way to break the chain is to undergo psychological treatment, either at the hands of a marriage counselor, psychiatrist, or analyst. Without such treatment the marriage usually ends in failure, with or without divorce.

Is a marriage doomed because of a lack of money?

Not necessarily, though the lack of it makes marriage increasingly difficult. Actually the high cost of living has compelled many wives to enter the labor market in order to support the family unit, with often dire consequences to the family. But a family living on a limited budget can nevertheless have a rewarding marriage provided there are other compensatory factors. What is important is the couple's attitude toward money and how it should be spent. If the wife is extravagant and the husband parsimonious—or vice versa—difficulties are likely to arise which may well affect other aspects of the marriage.

Is a marriage affected where the wife earns or has the greater income?

Not necessarily, with much depending on the attitude and basic maturity of the couple. A wife who earns more than her spouse and makes him uncomfortably aware of it imperils the marriage. A husband who earns less than his wife may feel that his masculinity and traditional role of provider are threatened. The husband may react by becoming impotent in order to punish his wife. He may become hostile or aggressive or behave in some other way detrimental to the marriage. Only if he is able to overcome his hostility can such a marriage be preserved. For her part, the wife will have to bolster her husband's ego by making him feel that he is the most important person in her life.

Is marriage to a career woman extra-hazardous?

In many cases, yes. It takes an unusual woman to combine the talents of wife, mother, and career, and there are not too many such women. In the typical case the wife is more likely to make a career out of her job or profession than of her marriage. Many husbands with strong egos find their "career" wives no threat to their own security. Other husbands, however, may find this an impossible situation.

Can a marriage be saved where a couple discover that they now have much less in common than they originally thought?

Yes. In the first place, there are no ideal marriages. In the second place, a marriage does not consist merely of peaks of ecstasy but also of valleys of despair. In the third place, the individuals in a marriage have varied patterns of growth. Sometimes it is the husband who expands his intellectual and emotional horizons. Sometimes it is the wife. It is rare for them to grow at the same rate, however. In the typical marriage it is not unusual for a couple to discover that they now have less in common than formerly. The novelty may have worn off sexually. The husband may have become so absorbed in the business of making money that he has little time or inclination for companionship with his wife. Having more time on her hands, the wife may further her education by taking courses, attending book reviews and lectures, visiting museums in the afternoon, all of which may make her a more interesting person. The husband, preoccupied with getting ahead in his job or career, may have less time and energy for such extracurricular activities.

The solution lies in finding some special new interest which both husband and wife can share. This might be golf, bridge, music, or visiting and taking an interest in the local art museum. The important thing is planning and doing things together.

What can be done to save a marriage where either the husband or wife is emotionally immature?

Without expert help, very little. Even with such help the prognosis is doubtful since it is difficult to modify or change basic personality structure.

What is emotional maturity?

Maturity in an individual means living up to one's chronological age. The grown man who behaves like a spoiled child is immature. So is the wife who is unable to make the slightest decision by herself. Maturity means that the individual lives in accordance with the actual facts of life, no matter how harsh, rather than in hopes and fears. If a wife is relatively free from illness she does not act like a hypochondriac with all sorts of imaginary ailments. If the husband has a prosperous business he is not overwhelmed by the fear of bankruptcy. A second criterion of maturity is the willingness to give up short-term pleasures for longer-term values. A mature husband will give up the pleasure of a casual affair in favor of preserving a marriage which has greater long-term value. A wife may forgo the pleasure of buying a fur coat and other luxuries if she knows the family as a whole will suffer. Maturity consists in being independent, in being able to make decisions without running to everyone for help. "No man," said John Donne, "is an island entire of itself." And no man is completely independent. There is a difference, however, between a man who, when he has to make a decision, does so on the available facts and a man who has decisions forced upon him by others. A fourth aspect of maturity is the ability to love someone other than oneself. Many marriages are wrecked by emotionally immature couples. These are husbands and wives who from early childhood have been blocked in their capacity to love. Being highly narcissistic, such people can only take without being able to give.

A mark of maturity paradoxically is the capacity to be dependent on others. A clinging vine type of wife is immature. So is the Caspar Milquetoast type of husband. These examples, however, are extreme. By a mature type of dependence is meant the capacity to accept advice when necessary, as well as the capacity to accept love. Marriage is an interpersonal relationship with the husband and wife being dependent on each other. The wife depends on the husband for financial and emotional security. The husband depends on the wife for ego support and sexual satisfaction. Finally, maturity is the willingness to accept responsibility, pleasant or unpleasure, because the job has to be done.

Can in-laws break up a marriage?

Not if the couple present a united front and are mature in their approach to the problem. Many mothers-in-law are unable to let go of their offspring. Unhappy in their own marriages, they cling desperately to their children, living vicariously through them. They attempt to guide and direct the lives of their married sons and daughters. Some expression of interest, however, is both natural and normal. A good husband or wife will continue to be a good son-in-law or daughter-in-law.

Can a marriage be saved if both husband and wife are unduly aggressive?

Probably not. A husband and wife who are both aggressive are constantly at war with each other, with each determined to maintain a superior position. Such marriages are explosive. It is much more "normal" for a husband to be aggressive than a wife, since he has to get along in a competitive world. A wife's aggression, on the other hand, may reflect her resentment at being a woman or her attempt to castrate or otherwise humiliate her husband. A marriage is more likely to be successful where only the husband is mildly aggressive, with the wife more dependent and submissive.

It may also be successful if the wife is aggressive, provided the husband is willing to be dominated. Too much aggression on the part of the male, however, may indicate neurotic feelings of inferiority, insecurity, and inadequacy for which he is trying to compensate.

Can a marriage be saved if there is unequal participation in family discussions?

Yes, if the wife doesn't mind being dominated. But a mature husband will not impose his views even on a dependent wife. Instead, he will take her feelings into consideration even if she is unable or unwilling to express them. Many wives, in fact, are unable to express themselves because unconsciously they fear their husband's opposition. In a good marriage there is a willingness to compromise on issues, to take each other's welfare and happiness into consideration.

Can a marriage be saved if the husband or wife doesn't want children?

Yes, provided both parties are in agreement in their desire not to have them. It is only when one of the partners desires children and the other doesn't that trouble is likely to follow. The husband may fear that a child will no longer make him the center of his wife's interest or attention. A wife may not want youngsters because she is too narcissistic or because she has a neurotic fear of pregnancy.

Can having children help save a marriage?

Rarely. Having a child is a normal accompaniment of a good marriage. But where a marriage is already on the rocks, having a child usually serves only to hasten the process of deterioration. This is true not only because more problems are likely to arise because of the child but also because the husband or wife may feel that he or she is trapped, so that making an exit from the marriage becomes more difficult.

Should a marriage be preserved for the sake of the children?

Certainly a greater attempt should be made to save such a marriage since the welfare and happiness of more than the husband and wife are involved. The available evidence indicates however that children would be no worse off (and possibly better off) if the parents were separated. A divorce in fact can be therapeutically helpful to a child since it removes him from an emotionally disturbing environment. In the final analysis the total situation must be considered.

Can a marriage be saved if one of the parties is jealous?

Some jealousy is both normal and desirable. A marriage without some degree of jealousy indicates an indifference or lack of real love. Jealousy becomes neurotic or pathological where either the husband or wife is jealous without any basis in fact. In such cases the pathology should be treated by expert help if the marriage is to continue successfully.

Can a marriage be saved if a reconciliation is made on a trial basis?

Yes, since a solution may be reached either through discussion or by seeking competent professional help.

Is a marriage worth saving for reasons of financial security?

Much depends on the needs of the individuals involved. A wife who knows that her finances will be drastically reduced if she obtains a divorce may prefer to continue with the marriage even though it is a bad one, especially if there are children. Another possible reason for the continuance of such a marriage would be the case of a middle-aged or elderly wife unable to work or otherwise fend for herself financially.

How successful is self-analysis in improving a marriage?

Two people who are reasonably mature and genuinely care for each other can, through honest discussion and self-analysis, go a long way toward rehabilitating a failing marriage. Many married people, however, are neither mature nor reasonable. For such individuals self-analysis is apt to be futile. For one thing they find it difficult to be objective about the areas of conflict. For another they tend to avoid honest discussion, with both husband and wife maintaining fixed and unyielding positions.

What is a marriage counselor?

A marriage counselor is a specialist exclusively concerned with people and their marriages. His chief function is to make the marriage work or, where this isn't possible, to provide such insight that the couple will take voluntary steps to dissolve the marriage.

What is a psychiatrist?

A psychiatrist is first of all a physician. In addition, a psychiatrist has had special training and experience in the diagnosis and treatment of nervous and mental disturbances, such as obsessions, compulsions, hysteria, and depressions. The focus of his attention is the disturbed individual who may not even have a marriage problem. He may treat the patient by drugs, electric shock treatment, suggestion, re-education, or by any other psychological technique.

How does a psychiatrist differ from a psychoanalyst?

A psychoanalyst is a psychiatrist who has had special training in the techniques first developed by Sigmund Freud. He deals with patients mainly on an unconscious level, striving to make them aware of what was formerly hidden or repressed. There are also lay analysts without medical degrees who call themselves psychoanalysts.

Do psychiatrists engage in marriage counseling?

To some extent, yes. A husband may be depressed by a lack of potency which is affecting the marriage. If the husband's potency is restored the marriage may be improved. While this may not be marriage counseling in a strict sense, the net result is the same. Unlike marriage counselors, both psychiatrists and analysts work with either the husband or wife rather than with both.

What are the qualifications of a good marriage counselor?

First, he should have some training and experience in marriage counseling; he should have a broad background in some profession such as psychology, psychiatry, law, or medicine. Third, it is desirable that he himself be happily married in order to have a standard by which to judge his client's. Fourth, that he have some training in the field and that he be a member of the American Association of Marriage Counselors, the only recognized body of professional marriage counselors in the country. (For a qualified marriage counselor in your community write to the American Association of Marriage Counselors, Inc., 27 Woodcliff Drive, Madison, New Jersey.) Such qualifications, of course, are not always a guarantee of competence or that the counseling will be successful. But it is almost a certainty that the counselor will be neither a quack nor a fraud. Fifth, the marriage counselor should be thoroughly familiar with the available knowledge in his field, including a grasp of the fundamentals of psychiatry and psychoanalysis as well as some understanding of sociology, ethics, law, and philosophy.

What other traits should a marriage counselor possess?

He should be a man of character. A marriage counselor may have a brilliant mind, but if he is unscrupulous the counseling can end in disaster for him and his client. Marriage counseling is a highly charged emotional process; it is relatively easy, for example, for an emotionally disturbed wife to fall in love with her counselor. Hence it takes character on the part of the counselor to resist such temptation. A marriage counselor moreover should be honest, both with himself and with his clients. If in his opinion the marriage seems hopeless he should not hesitate to say so, though in all

23

cases he should leave the ultimate decision and responsibility to his client.

To be successful in marriage counseling requires respect for the counselor as a person. Having a string of academic degrees is simply not enough. More important is that the counselor be patient, sympathetic, tolerant, and understanding; that he have a warm, engaging personality; and that he be sincere and objective.

With what problems are marriage counselors concerned?

With both premarital and postmarital problems. The former involves preparation for marriage, sex education, courtship, and engagement questions. Postmarriage counseling concerns such basic areas of conflict as money, in-laws, sex, religion, recreation, children, infidelity, and personality conflicts.

How does marriage counseling work?

Through interviews. The client talks and the counselor listens. Each interview lasts about fifty minutes. In that time the client has a chance to talk about his marital problems, his wife, and himself. Through insight and understanding, the counselor helps the client come to grips with the basic problem. Often this is no easy task, since clients tend to be evasive and often refuse to face their difficulties.

Do counselors see both parties together or separately?

The usual practice is to see the husband and wife together for at least the initial interview and perhaps the final one; they are then seen separately.

What do marriage counselors charge?

Experienced marriage counselors, engaged in private practice, charge anywhere from $10 to $25 an hour, a not unreasonable fee considering the time involved, the background of the counselor, the issues at stake, and the fact that divorce is considerably more expensive. For those who cannot afford the services of a private counselor there are family agencies which charge considerably less. Fees may range from nothing at all to $10 or $15 an hour depending on the income of the client. Many communities have a branch of the Family Service Association, where help can be obtained. These are usually staffed by trained social workers with or without previous training in the specific field of marriage counseling.

Marriage clinics are special counseling centers dealing specifically with marital problems. Their work is primarily that of diagnosis and treatment through counseling. They also engage in research and educational activities. Unlike the private marriage counselor, the marriage clinic is a team effort employing the services of a number of specialists: psychiatrists, psychologists, sociologists, urologists, and gynecologists. Marriage clinics devote full time to a solution of marital problems with the added advantage of staff consultation. Best known of the marriage clinics are the American Institute of Family Relations in Los Angeles, and the Marriage Council of Philadelphia, under the direction of Emily H. Mudd.

How long does marriage counseling take?

Some couples are successfully counseled in one or two sessions where the imparting of simple information is all that is required. In more difficult cases ten or more interviews may be necessary. Much depends on the nature and extent of the problem as well as the age and personality of the client. In general, the younger the client the more hopeful the prognosis. More important than mere age, however, is the determination of the couple to save the marriage.

Is it necessary for the counselor to see both husband and wife?

For best results, yes. For one thing it indicates that both parties are interested in saving the marriage, an encouraging sign. For another it provides a more balanced picture of the marriage itself. Seeing only one party to the dispute, the counselor gets to know only one

25

side of the story which may or may not be the true story. When he sees both husband and wife he is in a better position to appraise the marriage.

This is the ideal situation. There are many times, however, when one of the spouses—usually the husband—refuses to see the counselor. The husband may feel that the counselor is too much of a threat to his ego and that counseling will expose his weaknesses; or he may not want to save his marriage for one reason or another. But even in such cases it may still be advisable for the wife to seek professional help. It may be that the wife is really at fault and that with the insight that she receives she will be better able to cope with her husband and improve the marriage. On the other hand, the insight she obtains from the counseling process may convince her that the marriage is really hopeless and suggest the need for a separation or divorce. Finally, it not infrequently happens that the counselor is able to persuade the reluctant spouse to come in and present his side of the story.

When should a couple see a marriage counselor?

Just as soon as there is an awareness on the side of either spouse that the marriage is threatened with collapse. Unfortunately, too many couples conceal their marital difficulties for years before coming to a counselor. This is like suffering the pains of a stomach ulcer without bothering to go to a physician for prompt treatment. In general, the longer the delay the less hopeful the prognosis. This doesn't mean that every casual or occasional quarrel should send the husband or wife rushing to the counselor. No marriage— no matter how good—is without its ups and downs, its stresses and strains. It is only when those stresses and strains are severe and persistent that outside professional assistance is indicated and when the services of a qualified marriage counselor become imperative.

How successful is marriage counseling?

Estimates vary, but the usual figures range from 25% to 50%. Marriage counseling is no panacea. Neither is psychiatry nor psychoanalysis. Whether a given case ultimately ends in success or failure depends on the qualifications and skill of the counselor, the age of the couple involved, the nature and depth of their problem, and how anxious they really are to save the marriage. The last is probably the most important consideration of all. Problems dealing with frigidity and impotency are so deep-seated that they often require more treatment (or of a different nature) than that of the marriage counselor. In many cases psychiatry is indicated.

2 *The Background of Divorce*

Are divorces more frequent today than they were fifty years ago?

Yes. Today marriage has a breakup rate three times that of a half century ago.

About how many marriages end in divorce each year?

Approximately one out of every four. This figure does not take into account the large number of married couples who are emotionally divorced but who, for one reason or another, prefer to remain legally wed.

Why are there more divorces today than a half century ago?

There are many explanations. Probably the basic one is the emancipation of women—economic, legal, sexual, and intellectual. One of the consequences of such emancipation is that wives have become increasingly aggressive so that the war between the sexes has become more overt and real instead of disguised and subtle as before. Because of their new freedom wives today demand a great deal more from marriage than they did fifty years ago—demands their husbands are often unable to meet. Another powerful reason for the increase in divorce is the breakdown of religion. Divorce was formerly considered an affront to God, justified for only the gravest of reasons. The reward for an unhappy marriage, presumably, was a life of perpetual bliss after death. Today many people insist on marital happiness now. They feel that there is only one life and that is on earth, and they wish to make the most of their time while they still live. Hence when the marriage does not work out after a reasonable number of years many husbands and wives want out. They no longer wish to remain unhappily wed to fight continuously and venomously throughout their lives.

In which year of marriage is divorce most likely to occur?

The second year.

What is the average length of a marriage which ends in divorce?

Roughly about six years.

What are the psychological reasons for divorce?

Many psychiatrists and psychoanalysts believe that divorce arises from factors deeply ingrained in the personalities of the husband and wife. These factors stem from early childhood experiences and were heavily influenced by the parents of both the man and woman, influences which the adults have never been able to shake off. A mother, for example, may have raised her son to be completely dependent on her. If that son marries a woman who was taught to be neurotically dependent on her parents, conflicts result which may lead to a marital rupture. To assure a reasonable amount of marital happiness, the dependent son should have married a strong woman upon whom he could lean. Similarly the overly dependent girl should have married a strong husband upon whom she could lean. Since the basic emotional needs of both husband and wife were not met, a divorce is likely to follow.

Are marriages which end in divorce similar to unhappy marriages which do not end in divorce?

To some extent, yes. The appreciable difference is that in marriages which end in divorce there is not only a strong desire to escape but a willingness to pay the price of divorce. In marriages which are equally bad but which do not end in separation or divorce there is an unwillingness to pay the price. A couple who are emotionally divorced may refuse to terminate the marriage legally because of children, status, finances, religion, inertia, or even cowardice. There may even be a neurotic satisfaction in remaining unhappily wed. The husband, for example, may be a sadist who enjoys inflicting pain. The wife, for her part, may be a masochist who enjoys having pain inflicted on her. So long as the emotional needs of both individuals are met the marriage will continue.

Are there any other reasons why some husbands and wives desire to escape from marriage?

Yes. One possible explanation is that a person desires to escape because for the first time he has the feeling he can get along without his spouse. The spouse who does think this way sooner or later becomes irritable, impatient, and frustrated. He feels that his wife blocks him from the freedom for which he yearns. Obtaining a divorce thus often becomes an obsession. This may account for the fact that many married individuals fall in love with outsiders—the outsider serving to crystallize the spouse's feeling that he can get along without his mate. It may also account for the hostility which often accompanies a divorce action—a bitterness which often disappears after the divorce is granted.

How do people arrive at the idea of divorce?

A couple whose marriage is about to end usually go through a number of steps before the actual legal termination.

1. Since sex is often the barometer of a marriage, there comes a time when one of the spouses begins to withdraw from the sexual life of the other. The husband may, at first, be a bit more reluctant to make the necessary sexual overtures. He may plead fatigue, ill health, or business worries. He may tell himself that too much sex is bad for his health or that his wife is too dowdy. Gradually the process of withdrawal increases. Sex relations with his wife become less and less frequent until weeks, months,

or even years go by without intercourse. During this period the husband may decide to sleep in twin beds, then gradually, and with some embarrassment proceed to separate rooms. A similar process takes place with the wife. In the end there is virtually no sex life between the husband and wife.

2. In addition to changes in the sexual behavior of the couple, other changes begin to take place. The couple become increasingly estranged from each other, find it more difficult to talk to each other. The home is embarrassingly heavy with silence, or if the husband and wife are still on formal speaking terms, the conversation lacks warmth and depth. In still other cases, however, there is communication between the couple but it is likely to be violent and abusive. There is no meeting of the minds and even less meeting of the hearts. Tension, anxiety, aggression, and hostility are the key words in the faltering interpersonal relationship. For the first time the husband or wife, or both, understand that something is drastically wrong with the marriage and that the process is irreversible.

3. Next comes the first overt mention of the word divorce. Either party to the marriage may have thought about the possibility of a separation or divorce but suppressed the notion in the hope that the marriage would spontaneously improve and that the areas of disagreement which had plagued the couple would or could be reduced or minimized while the areas of agreement would or could be expanded. When time fails to bring about any satisfactory improvement the aggrieved party announces that he or she wants a divorce. If both parties are basically convinced that the marriage is hopeless there is likely to be agreement that a divorce is desirable. If only one of the parties is convinced, further pleas for additional reconciliations, marriage counseling, psychiatric treatment, or whatnot are likely to be made, but with little success. For one psychological reason or another, the aggressor who first suggests divorce wants out, and he wants out as quickly and as painlessly as possible.

4. The breach is further widened and the appearance of marital solidarity shattered when one or both parties begin to discuss their marriage difficulties with outsiders. Before this they had

31

kept their trouble more or less to themselves, nursing their domestic wounds in private. Now comes a new phase when the public is taken into the couple's confidence. Sexual intimacies, or the lack of them, which neither person would have dared share with any outsider are now confided to friends and relatives. For the first time the husband is openly accused of being a philanderer, a penny pincher, a domestic dictator or whatever other accusations occur to the wife which will humiliate and degrade him. For his part, the husband now freely confides that his wife was a shrew and a nag, that she spent his money extravagantly, that she neglected the children, and that she was frigid sexually and dull mentally. Once the marital linen is aired publicly there is rarely any turning back, for to do so would involve loss of face.

5. Next comes the actual separation. This may take the form of separate beds or separate rooms. Or either the husband or wife, usually the former, moves into a separate apartment. The breach is thus widened and hurts multiplied. The eroding process of self-justification and vindication continues apace with the good years of the marriage quickly forgotten. All that is remembered is the pain and humiliation of the period immediately preceding the separation.

6. Finally comes the divorce itself, which presumably once and for all spells the end of the marriage. But this too is often more appearance than reality. It is not always easy to erase the memory of five, ten, or twenty years of a marriage. And even if we succeed in suppressing conscious memories of a marriage, unconscious memories have a disturbing habit of rising to the surface and playing havoc with our nervous system. All marriage is based in part on illusion and in part on rationalization. The tendency is to close one's eyes to reality, to refuse to see ourselves as we really are. This is illusion. To rationalize is to adopt an acceptable explanation for basically unacceptable behavior. In marriage, as in life, our real motives for our behavior are often concealed and disguised. The aggressive wife justifies her behavior by declaring that her husband is a spoiled child. The miserly husband rationalizes his behavior by asserting that his

wife does not know how to use money wisely. Both practice self-deception and both avoid the deeper, more meaningful reasons for their conduct.

Which occupational groups are most prone to divorce?

Most vulnerable to divorce are unskilled laborers who have a divorce rate more than three times that of those engaged in the professions and owners of businesses.

Is there any relation between divorce and income?

Yes. All studies indicate that the higher the income tax bracket of the husband the less likely there is to be a divorce in the family. On the other hand, divorce or separation are uncommonly high among the low income groups who are usually also the least educated.

What connection is there between education and divorce?

The more education a couple have the less likely are they to divorce. College educated couples have a lower divorce rate than couples who have graduated from high school only. High school graduates have a lower divorce rate than those who have merely graduated from grammar school.

Are working wives a hazard to marital stability?

Yes. Few wives are able to combine successfully a job or career with a home, a husband, and children. Yet one-third of all wives work. Some do so because of a need to find fulfillment outside of marriage, some because it would be difficult to manage without the combined incomes of both husband and wife. Whatever the reasons for a wife's working, the chances are that some phase of the marriage and family will be neglected. Rearing a child by baby sitter or proxy is at best a poor substitute for a mother's love and attention. Nor is working all day and coming home exhausted at night calculated to make a wife a pleasant companion. Finally,

33

many husbands resent having their wives work in the first place, even when the husband is unable to support the household alone.

Does the length of engagement have any bearing on susceptibility to divorce?

Yes. In one study 70% of those divorced were engaged for six months or less. Couples engaged for two years or more, on the other hand, were divorced in only eight per cent of the cases. What is important, however, is not so much the length of the engagement but the total period of acquaintance. The longer the period the better the opportunity the man and woman have of really knowing each other, especially in discovering each other's personality defects.

Which are the most frequent legal grounds for divorce?

Cruelty and desertion. Together these constitute more than 80% of all divorces granted. Adultery is the legal cause for divorce in about 5% of the cases though it is a ground for divorce in all fifty states.

Who usually gets the divorce, the husband or wife?

The wife. Approximately 73% of all divorces are granted to the wife and 27% to the husband. In part this is due to the husband's somewhat outmoded sense of chivalry, whereby the man assumes the burden of guilt and the "little woman" goes scot free. Moreover, since it is the male who is usually the breadwinner he is more apt to supply legal ammunition in the form of nonsupport and desertion. And he is probably more given to adultery—and has more opportunity—than his wife.

When does divorce occur?

More divorces occur in the second year of marriage than in any other. More than 6% of those which do break up do so before the first anniversary, and nearly 10% before the second.

Is divorce an urban or rural phenomenon?

Urban. City life, on the whole, is more conducive to divorce than rural life since the former provides much more temptation for straying.

Are childless couples more or less prone to divorce than couples with children?

60% of all divorces are granted to childless couples. This does not necessarily prove anything one way or another, since the heaviest concentration of divorces occurs in the early years of marriage when childlessness is at its height. Available studies, however, suggest that the mere presence of children is not a deterrent to divorce. For the married population as a whole, the childless are about twice as prone to divorce as those with both education and children. The decision to have youngsters is for many a decision that the marriage is good enough to continue. Stated another way, the decision to postpone children suggests that the marriage isn't going well.

What are the most common complaints leading to divorce?

1. Basic personality conflicts
2. Excessive drinking
3. Desertion
4. In-law problems
5. Another woman
6. Sexual incompatibility
7. Inadequate finances
8. Disinterest in the home or children
9. Over-aggressiveness on the part of either the husband or wife

Who usually wants to break up the marriage, the husband or wife?

The husband. The male seems to tire of the female more frequently than the female tires of the male. What is true among humans is also true among man's animal ancestors, the apes. There also seems to be a certain strategy leading to divorce. In the usual case it is the husband's overt behavior which often compels the wife to seek a divorce in order to save face. For example it is the husband's adultery which forces the wife to take legal steps to sever the marriage, even though it may have been the wife's actual behavior which prodded the husband into infidelity.

Is the decision to seek a divorce usually a hasty one?

No. Long before legal steps are taken a more or less serious deterioration in the marriage has taken place. Divorces, in fact, are usually preceded by a long period of conflict, tension, and anxiety. The final decision to file for a divorce is the result of a process that lasts on the average about two years prior to the actual filing of the suit.

Do the anticipated effects of the divorce on the children or the prior approval or disapproval of friends or relatives speed or retard the decision to get a divorce?

Apparently neither children nor the prior approval of friends or relatives has any effect on the prospective divorcee arriving at a decision.

Are older women more or less reluctant to obtain a divorce than younger women?

More reluctant. The older the wife the more time she is likely to take in deciding on a divorce. For one thing, she may have less energy and decisiveness. For another, she may be less optimistic about the future, either to support herself or to find another husband. She may also be reluctant to be replaced by a younger, more attractive woman. In addition, with increasing duration of the marriage more time is required to move from serious consideration of divorce to the actual filing of the suit.

Do most divorcees receive marriage counseling before divorce?

No. Of the nearly million husbands and wives who obtain divorces each year, only a handful seek the services of a marriage counselor. To begin with there are probably no more than a few hundred qualified marriage counselors throughout the United States so that even if prospective divorcees availed themselves of every available qualified marriage counselor there simply wouldn't be enough to go around. In addition, the number of those who actually seek marriage counseling is minimal.

In preparing for divorce, what questions are most likely to be discussed by husband and wife?

Details most likely to be discussed are:
1. Division of property
2. Effect of divorce on the children
3. Support or alimony
4. Remarriage to others
5. Seeing each other

Do husbands and wives agree on divorce terms before or after filing suit?

Most couples agree on divorce terms before filing suit. In one study 79% of the couples agreed on a division of property, 68% agreed on support payments and 63% agreed on custody and visitation rights of children.

Are agreements made before the divorce usually kept afterwards?

No. After divorce with its succeeding months of adjustment, the lives of the ex-spouses grow so far apart that prior arrangements become not only impossible but often irrelevant.

Is separation or the actual divorce a greater emotional strain?

The final separation seems to produce the greater trauma. It is then that there is difficulty in sleeping, poorer health, greater loneliness, low work efficiency, memory difficulties, increased smoking, and increased drinking.

Do divorcees think they would have been better off if they had not obtained a divorce?

When asked this question, 66% of those queried said they would have been better off financially if there had been no divorce, 57% thought they would have been better generally, 53% said their health would have been worse, 50% said it would have been better for the children, 41% declared that if there had been no divorce they would have been unhappier, and 37% declared they would have been worse off financially if the decree had not been granted.

Do divorcees have much property to divide?

No. Most divorces occur in economic strata where there is little income. In one survey 40% of the divorcees had no property to divide, 5% had between $1 and $249, 16% had between $250 and $999, 14% had between $1,000 and $1,999, 8% had between $2,000 and $3,999, and 18% had over $4,000 to divide at the time of divorce.

Who is more likely to receive the property, the husband or wife?

The wife. However, the more property there is to be divided, the more likely there is to be an equal division.

3 *Alternatives to Divorce*

What are the alternatives to divorce?

1. Remain unhappily wed
2. Obtain an annulment
3. File criminal proceedings
4. Institute a suit for separate maintenance, if a woman
5. Separate, either voluntarily or involuntarily

Under what circumstances should a couple remain unhappily wed?

A husband may decide to suffer the slings and arrows of an outrageous marriage for a variety of reasons. He may be sexually or emotionally dependent on his wife. He may be convinced that he can't afford a divorce, that his wife's terms would ruin him financially. Or he may decide to have his cake and eat it too by remaining married and philandering on the side. A wife may also prefer to remain unhappily wed. She may decide that a divorce would seriously reduce her standard of living. She may be old or infirm. She may want to punish her husband by not allowing him to marry the "other woman." Or, like her husband, she may feel that she can have the best of two worlds by having an occasional affair. Religion, fear of public opinion, and children are other reasons by which couples, emotionally divorced, justify their remaining together.

Is it desirable to remain unhappily wed and have affairs on the side?

Not as a rule. For one thing, being a philanderer is by no means as simple or as glamorous as it sounds. Some men—and women—seem to be born with a talent for adultery. Others acquire it at an early age and some never at all. For some having an affair or a series of affairs is as easy as rolling off a log, since they are able to deceive both themselves and their spouses without too many qualms. In short, they possess two main requisites for adultery: an elastic conscience and a talent for deception.

But for the so-called average man—or woman—having an affair is fraught with difficulties. In the first place he simply has no talent for it. Whether through fear, habit, or whatnot, he is unable to get emotionally involved with another woman. In the second place, even if he does get himself involved he is likely to suffer from such pangs of conscience that he becomes emotionally ill. Hence the sleepless nights with increasing resort to tranquilizers and alcohol. For such an individual an affair is not so much an alternative as a disaster, and the sooner he disabuses himself and realizes that he is not a Don Juan or a modern-day Casanova, the better for all concerned.

In what way is an annulment an alternative to divorce?

It may be the only way of severing the marital tie in states where the client has no ground for divorce. New York, for example, has the highest annulment rate in the nation, largely because it grants divorces only on the ground of adultery. The term "fraud" has been so loosely applied by the courts there that New York has become known as the "annulment mill."

What exactly is an annulment?

An annulment is a legal proceeding which declares that a marriage never lawfully existed, declaring it void from its very inception. A divorce merely ends a marriage as of the date the decree was signed.

What are some of the practical consequences of an annulment as compared with a divorce?

1. A divorce has no effect on the legitimacy of the children. An annulment, unless changed by the law of the state, makes the children of a marriage illegitimate, losing for them a right to inheritance. In most states, however, children are now legitimized and can inherit property, much like children of a divorced couple.

2. In a divorce a wife may obtain alimony and support for her children. In an annulment, which in effect declares that the marriage never legally existed, the wife can neither obtain alimony nor support for the children unless the state law expressly allows it, which is rare.

3. In some states the right to remarry after divorce is sometimes restricted; the "guilty" party is in this way punished for his or her unlawful behavior.

4. After an annulment or decree of nullity a woman may sue for seduction and wrongful habitation.

5. Communications between the parties made after the marriage and prior to the decree are not treated as confidential and are freely admissible in evidence.

6. In an annulment the man acquires no rights in the woman's property.

7. The woman is not entitled to homestead exemption, given by some statutes, to a divorced individual.

8. There are no restrictions on the right to remarry, as there sometimes is in divorce.

Which are the most liberal annulment states?

California and New York.

When are annulment proceedings the preferred method of ending a marriage?

1. When at the time of the ceremony there was some defect, impediment, or lack of capacity which stood in the way of a valid marriage.

2. When the marriage was of relatively brief duration.

3. When, as in New York, the parties are otherwise unable to terminate their marriage. In New York adultery is the only ground for an absolute divorce. Since not all couples wish or can afford to obtain divorces on adultery, with its techniques of hotels, hired detectives, and collusion between the parties, annulment may be the preferred method of dissolving a marriage. In New York there are said to be more than a hundred grounds for obtaining an annulment, most of them revolving around fraud. Obtaining an annulment in New York, therefore, is much easier than obtaining a divorce, and hence much more popular.

What are the grounds for annulment in the various states?

Alabama

1. Incest
2. A previously existing marriage not dissolved by divorce or death
3. Being under the age of parental consent (17 for male, 14 for female with parental consent, 21 for male, 18 for female without parental consent.)
4. Miscegenation, or marriage between a white and Negro

Alaska

1. Insanity at the time of the ceremony
2. Fraud
3. Force or duress
4. Being under age (18 for M, 16 for F with parental consent; 21 for M, 18 for F without parental consent)
5. Incest

Arizona

1. Incest
2. Miscegenation

Arkansas

1. Insanity at the time of marriage
2. Fraud
3. Impotency
4. Being under the age of consent (18 for M, 16 for F with parental consent; 18 for M, 16 for F without parental consent)

California

1. Insanity at the time of the ceremony
2. Either party being unable to consummate the marriage
3. Fraud
4. The use of force
5. The existence of a previous marriage not dissolved by divorce or death
6. Being under age (18 for M, 16 for F with parent's consent; 21 for M, 18 for F without parent's consent)

Colorado

1. Lack of age
2. Fraud
3. Force
4. Either party unable to consummate the marriage, that is, to have normal sexual relations.

Connecticut

1. Conviction of a felony, that is, being sentenced for such serious crimes as murder, manslaughter, arson, burglary, robbery, rape, sodomy, mayhem, and larceny, among others
2. Incest
3. Where the marriage ceremony has not been solemnized by the proper authority

Delaware

1. Fraud
2. Force
3. Impotency
4. Incest

5. A previously existing marriage not dissolved by divorce or death
6. Being under the age of consent (18 for M, 16 for F with parental consent; 21 for M, 18 for F without parental consent)

Florida

Although there are no specific statutes, annulments are usually granted on such grounds as fraud, duress, and impotency. A marriage is also void by reason of incest and miscegenation.

Georgia

1. Being under age (17 for M, 14 for F with parental consent; 21 for M, 21 for F without parental consent)
2. The existence of a previous marriage not dissolved by divorce or death
3. Incest
4. Insanity
5. Impotency
6. Fraud

Hawaii

1. Being under age (18 for M, 16 for F with parental consent; 20 for M, 20 for F without parental consent)
2. Insanity at the time of the marriage
3. Where either party is unable to consummate the marriage
4. Incest
5. A previously existing marriage not dissolved by divorce or death
6. Venereal disease
7. Leprosy
8. Force
9. Fraud

Idaho

1. Being under age (15 for M, 15 for F with parental consent; 18 for M, 18 for F without parental consent)
2. Insanity at the time of the marriage
3. Fraud
4. Force

5. A previously existing marriage not dissolved by divorce or death
6. Where either party is unable to have normal sexual relations

Illinois

1. Fraud
2. Incest
3. Insanity

Indiana

1. Fraud
2. Incest
3. Insanity at time of marriage
4. Being under age (18 for M, 16 for F with parental consent; 21 for M, 18 for F without parental consent)

Iowa

1. Fraud
2. Incest
3. Being under age (16 for M, 14 for F with parental consent; 21 for M, 18 for F without parental consent)
4. Insanity at time of marriage
5. Impotency
6. Incest
7. A previously existing marriage not dissolved by divorce or death

Kansas

1. Incest
2. Insanity at time of marriage
3. Being under age (18 for M, 16 for F with parental consent; 21 for M, 18 for F without parental consent)

Kentucky

1. Fraud
2. Force
3. Being under age (18 for M, 16 for F with parental consent, 21 for M, 18 for F without parental consent)
4. Insanity at time of marriage
5. A previously existing marriage not dissolved by divorce or death

45

6. Miscegenation
7. Marriage contract not solemnized by proper authority

Louisiana

1. Incest
2. Force
3. Previous existing marriage
4. Miscegenation
5. Accomplice in adultery

Maine

1. Incest
2. Insanity at time of marriage
3. A previously existing marriage not dissolved by divorce or death
4. Under age (16 for M, 16 for F with parental consent; 21 for M, 19 for F without parental consent)

Maryland

1. Incest
2. A previously existing marriage not dissolved by divorce or death
3. Miscegenation

Massachusetts

1. Incest
2. Under age (18 for M, 16 for F with parental consent; 21 for M, 18 for F without parental consent)
3. Insanity at time of marriage

Michigan

1. Insanity at time of marriage
2. Under age (18 for M, 16 for F with parental consent; 18 for M, 16 for F without parental consent)
3. Incest
4. Certain infectious diseases

Minnesota

1. Epilepsy
2. Insanity at time of marriage

3. Fraud
4. Force or duress
5. Under age (16 for M, 15 for F with parental consent; 21 for M, 18 for F without parental consent)
6. Incest

Mississippi

1. Incest
2. Miscegenation

Missouri

1. Fraud
2. Force
3. Either party unable to consummate the marriage
4. A previously existing marriage not dissolved by divorce or death
5. Incest
6. Miscegenation

Montana

1. Insanity at time of marriage
2. Fraud
3. Force
4. Under age (18 for M, 16 for F with parental consent; 21 for M, 18 for F without parental consent)
5. A previously existing marriage not dissolved by divorce or death
6. Either party unable to consummate the marriage

Nebraska

1. Insanity at time of marriage
2. Under age (18 for M, 16 for F with parental consent; 21 for M, 21 for F without parental consent)
3. Fraud
4. Force
5. Incest
6. Miscegenation
7. Venereal disease
8. Either party incapable of consummation of the marriage

Nevada

1. Under age (18 for M, 16 for F with parental consent; 21 for M, 18 for F without parental consent)
2. Insanity at time of marriage
3. Fraud
4. Incest
5. Miscegenation
6. A previously existing marriage not dissolved by divorce or death

New Hampshire

1. Insanity at time of marriage
2. Under age (14 for M, 13 for F with parental consent; 20 for M, 18 for F without parental consent)
3. A previously existing marriage not dissolved by divorce or death
4. Incest
5. Epilepsy or some other similar disease

New Jersey

1. Under age (18 for M, 16 for F with parental consent; 21 for M, 18 for F without parental consent)
2. Insanity at time of marriage
3. Either party unable to consummate the marriage
4. Impotency
5. Incest
6. Fraud
7. A previously existing marriage not dissolved by divorce or death

New Mexico

1. Incest
2. Under age (18 for M, 16 for F with parental consent; 21 for M, 18 for F without parental consent)

New York

1. Insanity at time of marriage
2. Under age (16 for M, 14 for F with parental consent; 21 for M, 18 for F without parental consent)
3. Either party unable to consummate the marriage

4. Fraud
5. Force
6. Incurable insanity for five years
7. Desertion for five successive years

North Carolina

1. Under age (16 for M, 16 for F with parental consent; 18 for M, 18 for F without parental consent)
2. Insanity at time of marriage
3. Either party unable to consummate marriage
4. Incest
5. A previously existing marriage not dissolved by divorce or death
6. Miscegenation

North Dakota

1. Under age (18 for M, 15 for F with parental consent; 21 for M, 18 for F without parental consent)
2. Insanity at time of marriage
3. Fraud
4. Force
5. Impotency
6. Incest
7. A previously existing marriage not dissolved by divorce or death

Ohio

1. Incest
2. Under age (18 for M, 16 for F with parental consent; 21 for M, 21 for F without parental consent)
3. Force
4. Insanity

Oklahoma

1. Under age (18 for M, 15 for F with parental consent; 21 for M, 18 for F without parental consent)
2. Insanity at time of marriage
3. Incest
4. Miscegenation

Oregon

1. Incest
2. A previously existing marriage not dissolved by divorce or death

Pennsylvania

1. A previously existing marriage not dissolved by divorce or death
2. Incest
3. Insanity

Rhode Island

Note: There are no annulment statutes in this state. Divorce is the proper remedy.

South Carolina

1. Incest
2. Miscegenation
3. A previously existing marriage not dissolved by divorce or death

South Dakota

1. Under age (18 for M, 15 for F with parental consent; 21 for M, 18 for F without parental consent)
2. Fraud
3. Force
4. Insanity at time of marriage
5. A previously existing marriage not dissolved by divorce or death
6. Either party incapable of consummation of the marriage

Tennessee

1. Incest
2. Miscegenation
3. Insanity at time of marriage

Texas

1. Impotency
2. Incest
3. Miscegenation

Utah

1. Insanity at time of marriage
2. Under age (16 for M, 14 for F with parental consent; 21 for M, 18 for F without parental consent)
3. Incest
4. Either party unable to consummate the marriage
5. Infectious diseases
6. Fraud
7. Miscegenation
8. Force

Vermont

1. Under age (18 for M, 16 for F with parental consent; 21 for M, 18 for F without parental consent)
2. Incest
3. Either party unable to consummate the marriage

Virginia

1. Insanity at time of marriage
2. Incapacity to understand
3. Incest
4. A previously existing marriage not dissolved by divorce or death

Washington

1. Insanity at time of marriage
2. Fraud
3. Force
4. Incest

West Virginia

1. Insanity at time of marriage
2. Under age (18 for M, 16 for F with parental consent; 21 for M, 21 for F without parental consent)
3. Impotency
4. Incest
5. A previously existing marriage not dissolved by divorce or death

CARNEGIE LIBRARY
LIVINGSTONE COLLEGE
SALISBURY, N. C. 28144

6. Miscegenation
7. Wife pregnant by person other than husband and without his consent
8. Prostitution

Wisconsin

1. Under age (18 for M, 16 for F with parental consent; 21 for M, 18 for F without parental consent)
2. Insanity at time of marriage
3. Fraud
4. Force
5. Incest
6. A previously existing marriage not dissolved by divorce or death
7. Either party incapable of consummating the marriage

Wyoming

1. Insanity at time of marriage
2. Under age (18 for M, 16 for F with parental consent; 21 for M, 21 for F without parental consent)
3. Incest
4. A previously existing marriage not dissolved by divorce or death
5. Fraud
6. Miscegenation

What constitutes force to entitle one to an annulment?

Force is another word for duress. A marriage contract entered into under coercion of mind or will makes it void. Duress to void a marriage must be actual violence or a threat which destroys consent. It must be of such a nature that instills a fear of grievous wrong, death, great bodily injury, unlawful imprisonment, or loss of good name. It must overcome the will of the party imposed upon and lead him to do what he otherwise would not do.

Can a marriage be annulled if the girl's father threatened to kill the man because the latter had sexual relations with the daughter, and the man reluctantly married the girl?

Yes, since this would constitute duress. However, if the husband continued to live with his wife for more than a few weeks, the chances are he would forfeit his right to have the marriage ended by annulment.

Can an annulment be obtained by a husband who, after making a girl pregnant, consents to marry her after the girl threatens him with exposure?

Many courts deny the right of annulment under such circumstances. The reasoning is that the man only did what he should have done in the first place.

Can the courts compel a man to marry a woman he has made pregnant?

Rarely. Cases where this is most likely to occur are where the man has been convicted of rape or seduction. He may then be given the alternative of marrying the woman or facing a prison term. If he marries the woman, chances are he will not be able to have the marriage subsequently voided.

Can a woman compel a man to marry her when the latter has made her pregnant?

No. Except in the rare cases mentioned above, no one can force another into marriage. Where a woman has become pregnant she can, after the birth of the child, compel the father, through the courts, to support the child until the latter attains his majority.

Can an annulment be obtained if the only purpose of the marriage is to give the child a name and not for the parents to live together as man and wife?

Yes. According to a Connecticut court "there can be no marriage without the consent of the parties and . . . though parties go through the form of a marriage contract, if both understand that neither intends to assume a contractual obligation, no real contract is created and . . . no marriage ever came into existence."

53

Can an annulment be procured where one of the parties to the ceremony was intoxicated?

Yes, if the person was so intoxicated that he or she did not know the nature, meaning, and consequence of the marriage contract. To obtain relief, proceedings should be instituted promptly, usually within a few days or weeks. The right to relief may be forfeited if the person entitled to such relief continues with the marriage.

Can an annulment be obtained where both parties are under the age of parental consent?

Yes. In such a case either party, or the parents of either party, may institute proceedings to obtain an annulment.

Suppose only one of the parties is under the age of parental consent?

In this case the party under the age of parental consent can procure an annulment. The person over the age of parental consent, usually the boy, will not generally be allowed to successfully file annulment proceedings.

Suppose a runaway couple flees to a state where the statutory requirements for marriage are less than in the state in which they were originally married?

An annulment probably would be granted on the theory that the marriage without parental consent was repugnant to the public policy of the home state.

Can an annulment be procured where a couple marry in violation of the state law requiring written consent of the parents?

Not as a general rule, assuming both parties are above the minimum age requiring parental consent. Such a provision requiring the written consent of parents does not make a marriage illegal where it is performed without such written consent. Only the officials issuing such licenses, as well as those performing the ceremony, will be held to account. California, however, has held such marriages valid.

Is marriage to a mentally defective person a ground for annulment?

Yes. To validate a marriage the law requires that both parties know and understand the nature and consequences of the marriage contract.

Can an annulment be procured where one of the parties was in a mental institution before the ceremony but concealed the fact from the other party who discovered it after the marriage?

Yes, provided the wronged party took prompt action after learning the fraud.

What is meant by impotency to form the basis of an annulment?

Impotency is the inability to have normal sexual intercourse, largely psychological in origin. In women the condition is known as frigidity. The impotency or frigidity must have been unknown to the other party at the time of the marriage.

Suppose it could be proved that the wife's frigidity could be corrected by minor surgery. Would the annulment still be granted?

Probably not, for the evidence must show that the frigidity or impotency is incurable. Since in this case the frigidity might be corrected the annulment would probably be denied.

Can an annulment be procured where a middle-aged or elderly couple enter into marriage solely for reasons of companionship?

No. A couple may marry for any reason it wishes. Having married for that reason neither party can later change its mind and claim he or she was not getting what had been bargained for.

Can a marriage be annulled if as a result of an accident or disease the husband becomes impotent?

No. Since the impotency must have existed at the time of the marriage. The proper remedy would be a divorce in those states where impotency is a ground for divorce.

What must be shown to end a marriage on the basis of fraud?

Since marriage is a contract, any misrepresentations that go to the very essence of the contract may be used to annul the marriage. To end a marriage on the basis of fraud it must be shown:

1. That there was a false representation.
2. That the plaintiff had no knowledge that the representation was false.
3. That the defendent intended that the representation be relied upon.
4. That the party suing relied on the representation and that he would not have married the defendant had he known the true facts.
5. That there was resulting damage.

Can a marriage be annulled if a man is persuaded to marry a woman on the latter's representation that the former made her pregnant when actually she was made pregnant by another man?

Yes. This is the kind of fraud that goes to the essence of the marriage contract.

Can a marriage be annulled if the wife conceals from her husband that her pregnancy was induced by another man?

Yes.

Is it ground for annulment if a woman tries to pass off an illegitimate child as one born in lawful wedlock?

Yes, provided the husband instituted proceedings promptly after discovering the facts.

Is lesbianism or homosexuality a ground for annulment?

Yes, if the facts were unknown at the time of the marriage.

Is the refusal to have children a ground for annulment?

Yes, provided there was an understanding before marriage that the couple would have children afterward. The law assumes that marriage is entered into for, among other things, sexual intercourse so that children may be born. The refusal of one of the parties to go ahead with the promise would be sufficient to void the marriage. This is one of the more popular grounds for annulment in New York.

Can a husband have a marriage annulled when, after the marriage, he learns that his wife has misrepresented her age?

No. Misrepresentations as to age, character, temperament, social standing, and fortune are not generally considered such important frauds as to void a marriage. The law takes the view that in courtship some puffing is both allowable and inevitable, with the principle of *caveat emptor* (let the buyer beware) applying. Thus a fortune hunter who marries a woman in the belief that she's wealthy and that she will turn over a portion of her property to him will not be able to annul the marriage if the lady fails to keep her side of the bargain. Nor will a woman be able to have the marriage annulled if she entered wedlock under the false impression that the man was a member of a socially prominent family.

Does this mean that if a woman marries under the impression that her husband is a law-abiding person when as a matter of fact he has served a term in prison for a felony, she cannot have the marriage annulled?

No. Where the character defect is so flagrant most courts would not hesitate to grant relief.

Can a marriage be annulled when before marriage the couple agree to have both a civil and religious ceremony and after the civil ceremony one of the parties refuses to go ahead with the religious ceremony?

Yes.

Can a marriage be annulled where a man and woman enter into a written agreement in which the man consented to turn Catholic, his wife's religion, and to rear the children in his wife's faith, the man later repudiating the agreement after the children are born?

Yes, since most courts would agree that such a fraud goes to the very essence of the marriage contract.

Can a marriage be annulled where a woman marries a man under the belief he is a Democrat when actually he is a Communist?

Yes. Virtually all states would allow the wife to annul such a marriage.

What constitutes an incestuous marriage so as to provide the basis of an annulment?

An incestuous marriage is one banned either because the parties are related by blood (consanguinity) or by marriage (affinity). Under our present laws all states ban marriages between mothers and sons, fathers and daughters, grandfathers and granddaughters, grandmothers and grandsons, sisters and brothers, and between uncles and nieces, and aunts and nephews.

Is the marriage of first cousins considered incestuous?

Yes, in about half the states; no, in the others. In six states even first cousins once removed are forbidden to marry.

May a man marry his stepmother?

Half the states, including Pennsylvania, forbid such marriages. In such states a man may not only not marry his stepmother, but is forbidden to marry his daughter-in-law, stepdaughter, or step-granddaughter. A woman may not marry her stepfather, son-in-law, stepson, or stepgrandson.

What is miscegenation?

Miscegenation is the intermarriage of whites and other races, especially Negroes. All Southern states forbid such marriages, not only making them void and so a basis for an annulment action, but criminal as well. A number of Western states have laws restricting marriages between whites and Orientals, as well as whites and Negroes.

May a husband have a marriage annulled when, unknown to him at the time of the marriage, the wife either had no ovaries or lacked the capacity to have children?

No. In almost every state all the law requires is the capacity to have sexual relations, not the ability to have children.

Can you describe the mechanics of a typical case where an annulment might be granted?

A couple in New York find a few weeks after the marriage that they are basically incompatible. Both want to end the marriage as quickly and as painlessly as possible. Since adultery is the only ground for an absolute divorce in New York and they are unwilling to obtain one on this ground, the husband convinces himself that he has objected to the use of contraceptives from the beginning of the marriage, that they in fact thwart his desire to have children. He is also able to produce a friend or relative willing to testify to a crucial conversation that he had with his wife in which the latter admitted that she did not want children and refused sexual relations unless the husband used contraceptives. If the court believed such testimony and the wife did not contest the suit, the chances are the annulment would be granted.

In what way are criminal proceedings an alternative to divorce?

A criminal proceeding against either husband or wife does not legally dissolve a marriage. It may be indicated when the husband makes a punching bag of his wife, when he fails to support his wife and children, when he is habitually drunk, and when he abuses or mistreats the youngsters. It is a remedy frequently resorted to by those in the lower income brackets.

What are some of the disadvantages of instituting criminal proceedings?

One is that it usually tends to so embitter the husband that continuation of the marriage becomes virtually impossible. Another disadvantage is that a husband receiving a jail sentence for beating his wife is hardly in a position to support his wife and children. In many cases the wife after swearing out a warrant for her husband's arrest and hearing him sentenced to thirty days in jail, urges the magistrate to release him so that she often defeats the very end she sought in the first place. Sometimes, however, the effect is sobering on the husband and he does make some attempt to reform.

What are the advantages of instituting criminal proceedings?

One is that it may prevent a recurrence of incidents. A husband who is arrested and tried—even if he is later dismissed by the magistrate—may be less likely to indulge in violent temper tantrums. He may be more cautious about assaulting his wife or children or even in getting drunk, knowing that the magistrate will be much more severe with him the second time he appears. Another advantage is that a criminal proceeding often serves as a foundation for a future bill of divorce.

In what way does a criminal proceeding serve as a foundation for a divorce?

If the husband is convicted of assault and battery against the wife it may lay the foundation for a divorce action on the ground of cruelty in those states where cruelty is a ground for divorce. If the husband or wife is convicted of habitual drunkenness the other party may institute divorce proceedings if the state allows alcoholism as a ground for divorce. A husband who deserts his wife and small children and refuses to support them may be arrested and compelled to support the family. He may even be brought back if he has fled to another state.

Suppose a husband deserts his wife and small children and flees to another state. Is it necessary to have him extradited in order to compel him to contribute to the family?

No. The Uniform Support of Dependent's Act, adopted in all states, now makes it possible for an abandoned wife to obtain help without going to the trouble of having the errant husband extradited. Under this act the wife goes to the prosecuting attorney in her home city and states the basis of her complaint. The court will then hold a hearing to determine all the facts and circumstances of the case, including the amount of money necessary to support the family unit. The court in the community in which the husband is located files proceedings against the deserting spouse. If the husband agrees to pay the amount stipulated by the court in the wife's home state, the threat of extradition with its possible jail sentence is dropped. If the husband refuses to pay the amount so stipulated the chances are he will be extradited and compelled to stand trial.

Can a wife compel her husband to support her and the children even if she leaves the home?

Yes, provided she is legally justified in leaving the home. She may be so justified where the husband is a habitual drunkard, where he physically assaults the wife or children, or where he refuses to support the family.

What is a suit for separate maintenance?

This is a civil proceeding instituted by the wife, awarding her alimony without obtaining a divorce.

61

Under what circumstances will separate maintenance be awarded?

Usually in those cases where the husband has forced his wife to leave the home because of his outrageous behavior. The husband may be a habitual drunkard. He may have threatened the lives of the wife and children. He may refuse to support them. Unable to tolerate conditions at home, the wife leaves and finds an apartment or home for herself and the children. Not wanting a divorce, she may engage an attorney to file a suit for separate maintenance. If after a hearing the court is satisfied that the facts are as the wife sets them forth, an order will be granted allowing the wife a certain amount of money for the support of herself and the children. In all cases, however, the wife must prove by satisfactory evidence that she herself was not at fault in breaking up the marriage.

May a wife request separate maintenance if she remains in the home or apartment, but lives apart from her husband?

Yes, if she can prove there is such an acute housing shortage that she can find no other place in which to live. It is exceptional, however, for courts to grant separate maintenance where the husband and wife continue to live under the same roof, although apart.

Can a separate maintenance suit be successfully maintained if the wife has sufficient funds of her own?

Not usually. A prime requisite for a separate maintenance suit is that the wife is unable to support herself and her children. If it can be proved that just before leaving, the wife cleaned out the joint checking account which provided her with adequate funds, the action will be defeated. It will also be defeated if the wife is financially independent, has a private income of her own, or holds a job which pays her a salary adequate enough to support herself and the children.

4 *Separations*

Aside from those already mentioned, what other alternatives are there to an absolute divorce?

The most frequent alternative is to seek a separation, either voluntary or involuntary.

What is an involuntary separation?

An involuntary separation is an act of desertion on the part of either husband or wife with the intent not to return. If the husband deserts and neglects to provide for his wife and children, criminal proceedings may be instituted against him. The wife may also file for either a partial or absolute divorce, depending on the length of the desertion in her particular state. She may, alternatively, have a right to file a suit for separate maintenance without even asking for a divorce. For the wife to have such rights the husband must have been legally at fault, that is, the abandonment must have taken place without any legal justification.

What is a partial divorce?

A partial divorce is the same as a legal separation. The husband and wife live separate and apart. Neither can remarry until an absolute divorce is granted.

63

Is a wife justified in leaving her husband because some deliberate act on his part forced her to leave?

Yes. This is known as "constructive" desertion. A wife may leave because the husband refuses to support her and the children, because he falsely accused her of being an adulteress, because he threatened her life or physically assaulted the children, because he refused to have sex relations with her, or for a variety of other reasons.

Can there be a voluntary separation without a written agreement?

Yes. A couple can agree verbally on any terms they see fit. The wife, for example, may refuse to accept support from her husband though this is the rare exception rather than the rule.

Are there any advantages to entering into a voluntary separation without a written agreement?

No. A verbal agreement is apt to be loose, ill-defined, and vague, and most important of all, difficult to enforce because of lack of proof of what the parties really intend. In this respect it is very much like any other verbal contract. Moreover, a verbal separation agreement, entered into without benefit of legal counsel, is apt to be disadvantageous to one or both parties.

What is a voluntary separation?

Where a husband and wife agree to live separate and apart, without going into court, the separation is said to be voluntary. Spouses living apart under such circumstances may enter into a separation agreement arranged by respective counsel. Such an agreement may contain any terms agreed upon by the parties. If the contract is violated, the wife may bring the husband into court and have the agreement enforced. For the husband's refusal to pay the judgment, however, the wife cannot have him sent to jail as she can in a legal separation.

What is a legal separation?

A legal separation is the result of litigation in court brought by one spouse against the other. Its terms are embodied in the court's decree. For violation of those terms the husband may be committed to jail. A legal separation is similar to a partial divorce. Either party may procure a separation upon showing just cause. Under such a separation the parties, though living apart, remain man and wife and may not remarry. Where the wife procures the legal separation, the husband, by court order, is usually under an obligation to support her and the children. Where the husband obtains the decree, since he is viewed as the "innocent" party, he is usually under no such obligation to support the wife, but is compelled to support the children until they attain their majority. The husband, in fact, is always obliged to support the children, regardless of the fact that he or his wife obtained the separation or divorce.

While voluntarily living separate and apart, one of the spouses commits adultery. What can the innocent party do about it?

He or she can file suit for an absolute divorce. If the innocent party is the husband he will be relieved of paying further alimony. If there are children involved the guilty party may lose custody of the children.

After marriage a couple enter into an agreement whereby they plan to live separate and apart for six months after the signing of the contract. Is such a pact valid?

No, the separation must take place at the time of the agreement or immediately following it.

A husband and wife voluntarily live separate and apart. To forestall the wife's running up debts, the husband inserts the following advertisement in the local newspaper: "I will not be responsible for my wife's debts." A grocer sells the wife some canned goods, butter, and meat. Is the husband responsible for such items?

Yes. Such advertisements are usually worthless. Under the law a husband is responsible for his wife's necessaries, despite the fact they are living apart. Such necessaries include food, medical and dental care, clothes, and shelter.

How does a legal separation differ from an absolute divorce?

In a legal as well as a voluntary separation, the parties are unable to marry any third person. The name of the wife cannot be changed.

May a husband and wife resume living together during a legal separation?

Yes. If they do, the parties forfeit whatever rights they may have had during the separation.

Do all states provide for a legal separation?

No. Georgia, Mississippi, Missouri, New Mexico, Ohio, South Dakota, Texas, and Washington do not recognize legal separations or partial divorces.

Why do couples seek a limited divorce or legal separation rather than an absolute divorce?

Because:
1. It allows the couple time to adjust to the idea of divorce.
2. It provides an opportunity to effect a reconciliation.
3. It conforms to their religious faith, as in the case of Catholics.
4. The husband or wife may not have sufficient grounds for an absolute divorce.
5. It provides the wife with certain advantages if she suspects her husband intends to run off to Nevada, in order to get rid of the wife.

What are such advantages?

The chief ones are that it fixes the husband's obligations in terms of alimony and support as well as custody of the children, in case she does not wish to contest the out-of-state divorce.

What are the grounds for a legal separation or partial divorce in the various states and territories?

Alabama

1. Cruelty or for any other cause if plaintiff desires a separation only (*See* grounds for divorce in Alabama)

Alaska

Legal separations are not recognized in this state

Arizona

1. Any ground for absolute divorce or such conduct as may render it unsafe or improper for wife to cohabit with husband

Arkansas

1. Adultery
2. Nonsupport
3. Mental or physical cruelty
4. Habitual drunkenness
5. Living apart for five years without having sexual relations
6. Refusal to have sexual intercourse

California

1. Adultery
2. Desertion
3. Abandonment
4. Nonsupport
5. Mental or physical cruelty
6. Habitual drunkenness

Colorado

1. Adultery
2. Impotency
3. Desertion
4. Abandonment
5. Nonsupport

6. Mental or physical cruelty
7. Habitual drunkenness
8. Conviction of felony

Connecticut

1. Adultery
2. Desertion
3. Abandonment
4. Mental or physical cruelty
5. Habitual drunkenness
6. Postmarital insanity
7. Conviction of felony

Delaware

1. Adultery
2. Desertion
3. Mental or physical cruelty
4. Habitual use of drugs
5. Postmarital insanity
6. Conviction of felony
7. Being under age

District of Columbia

1. Adultery
2. Desertion and abandonment
3. Mental or physical cruelty
4. Living apart for five years without sexual relations

Florida

1. Adultery
2. Impotency
3. Desertion and abandonment
4. Mental or physical cruelty
5. Habitual drunkenness

Georgia

No legal separations, or partial divorces

Hawaii

1. Adultery
2. Desertion for six months
3. Nonsupport
4. Physical and mental cruelty
5. Habitual drunkenness
6. Habitual use of drugs
7. Postmarital insanity
8. Conviction of felony

Idaho

No legal separations, or partial divorces

Illinois

1. Adultery
2. Desertion
3. Desertion and abandonment
4. Nonsupport
5. Mental or physical cruelty
6. Habitual drunkenness
7. Venereal disease
8. Conviction of felony

Indiana

1. Adultery
2. Desertion and abandonment
3. Nonsupport
4. Mental or physical cruelty
5. Habitual drunkenness or use of drugs

Iowa

1. Adultery
2. Desertion
3. Mental or physical cruelty
4. Habitual drunkenness

5. Venereal disease
6. Conviction of felony

Kansas

1. Adultery
2. Impotency
3. Abandonment and desertion
4. Nonsupport
5. Mental or physical cruelty
6. Habitual drunkenness
7. Postmarital insanity
8. Conviction of felony
9. Fraud

Kentucky

1. Adultery
2. Impotency
3. Abandonment
4. Mental or physical cruelty
5. Habitual drunkenness
6. Venereal disease
7. Postmarital insanity
8. Conviction of felony

Louisiana

1. Adultery
2. Desertion and abandonment
3. Nonsupport
4. Mental or physical cruelty
5. Habitual drunkenness or drug addiction
6. Conviction of felony
7. Living apart for one year without sexual relations

Maine

1. Desertion

Maryland

1. Desertion or abandonment
2. Physical cruelty

Massachusetts

1. Desertion or abandonment
2. Nonsupport

Michigan

1. Desertion
2. Nonsupport
3. Mental or physical cruelty
4. Habitual drunkenness

Minnesota

1. Adultery
2. Impotency
3. Desertion
4. Mental or physical cruelty
5. Habitual drunkenness
6. Postmarital insanity
7. Conviction of felony

Mississippi

No grounds for legal separation, or partial divorce

Missouri

No grounds for legal separation, or partial divorce

Montana

1. Adultery
2. Desertion or abandonment
3. Nonsupport
4. Mental or physical cruelty
5. Habitual drunkenness or addiction to drugs

6. Postmarital insanity
7. Conviction of felony

Nebraska

1. Desertion
2. Nonsupport
3. Mental or physical cruelty

Nevada

1. Adultery
2. Impotency
3. Nonsupport
4. Mental or physical cruelty
5. Postmarital insanity
6. Conviction of a felony
7. Living apart for three years without sexual relations

New Hampshire

1. Adultery
2. Impotency
3. Desertion or abandonment
4. Nonsupport
5. Mental or physical cruelty
6. Habitual drunkenness
7. Living apart for three years without sexual relations

New Jersey

1. Adultery
2. Desertion or abandonment
3. Physical cruelty

New Mexico

No specific grounds for legal separation or partial divorce. On permanent separation, either spouse may institute suit in the district court for division of property, for disposition of children, or for alimony without asking for dissolution of the bonds of matrimony. In such suit the court may restrain the use or disposition of the property of either spouse, may provide for the support of the wife during pendency of the suit and for expenses of the suit in behalf of the wife, and on final hearing, allow to the wife a portion of the husband's property, as well as alimony. The court may also provide for the care, custody, and maintenance of the minor children, setting aside portions of the property of the parties for such purposes.

New York

1. Adultery
2. Cruel and inhuman treatment
3. Unsafe and improper conduct
4. Abandonment
5. Failure to support wife

North Carolina

1. Desertion or abandonment
2. Mental or physical cruelty

North Dakota

1. Adultery
2. Desertion or abandonment
3. Nonsupport
4. Mental or physical cruelty
5. Habitual drunkenness or drug addiction
6. Postmarital insanity
7. Conviction of felony
8. Refusal to cohabit

Ohio

No grounds for legal separation or partial divorce

Oklahoma

1. Adultery
2. Impotency
3. Postmarital insanity
4. Conviction of felony

5. Being under age
6. Refusal to cohabit

Oregon

1. Abandonment
2. Nonsupport
3. Mental or physical cruelty
4. Habitual drunkenness

Pennsylvania

1. Abandonment
2. Mental or physical cruelty

Rhode Island

1. Adultery
2. Abandonment
3. Nonsupport
4. Physical or mental cruelty
5. Venereal disease

South Carolina

1. Adultery
2. Desertion
3. Physical cruelty
4. Habitual drunkenness or drug addiction

South Dakota

No grounds for a legal separation or partial divorce

Tennessee

1. Abandonment
2. Nonsupport
3. Mental or physical cruelty

Texas

No grounds for legal separation or partial divorce

Utah

1. Desertion or abandonment
2. Nonsupport

Vermont

1. Adultery
2. Desertion or abandonment
3. Nonsupport
4. Mental or physical cruelty

Virginia

1. Desertion or abandonment
2. Mental or physical cruelty

Washington

No grounds for legal separation or partial divorce

West Virginia

1. Desertion or abandonment
2. Nonsupport

Wisconsin

1. Desertion
2. Nonsupport

Wyoming

1. Nonsupport

What is a separation agreement?

This is an agreement entered into by the husband and wife, usually as a prelude to an absolute divorce, which settles such important questions as the division of property, alimony, support for the children, and their custody.

Is it necessary to have an attorney draw up such an agreement?

Although not absolutely essential, it is highly advisable that both parties be represented by counsel in order to protect their respective interests.

Can one lawyer represent both husband and wife?

No, since there is a conflict of interests between the couple. Such representation moreover is a violation of legal ethics and may be punishable by disbarment of the attorney.

What are the advantages of a separation agreement?

It allows the couple to settle for themselves the important questions concerning the liquidation of the marriage rather than have them settled through the costly and time-consuming process of fighting it out in the courts.

What are the mechanics of a separation agreement?

In a marriage about to be liquidated, one or both parties engage counsel to draw up such an agreement which is then submitted to the other party by counsel. Usually, a number of conferences take place between respective counsel for both husband and wife before the final agreement is hammered out. In practice, attorneys often advise their clients to attempt to come to some agreement between themselves as to who will get the house or apartment, how the furniture and other household objects will be divided, who will get the automobile, stocks, and bonds, if any, how much alimony will be given to the wife and how much support provided for the children, who will have custody of the children, and arrangements for visitation privileges. The wife will usually be asked by her counsel to draw up a detailed budget for her children and herself. The husband will be asked to give a detailed account of his income and assets. All such data form the basis of the separation agreement finally signed by both parties.

What specific information will an attorney want to know before preparing a separation agreement?

He will want to know the names and addresses of the parties, the date and place of the marriage, the date of birth and name of each child, the division of personal property and household effects.

What specific items does personal property include?

It will include furniture, furnishings, rugs, household appliances such as refrigerators and washing machines, television, radio, and hi-fi sets, records, silverware, glassware, china, linens, books, works of art, stocks and bonds, promissory notes, bank accounts, club memberships, charge accounts, automobiles and boats, jewelry and furs, cameras, sports equipment. The attorney will want to know whether insurance has been taken out on any of these items and in whose name, and who pays the premiums. Often the husband and wife will have arrived at some rough division of these items even before consulting an attorney.

What else will the attorney want to know?

He will want to know whether the husband owes any money to his wife and how the indebtedness is to be treated; that is, does the wife expect repayment or is she willing to cancel the indebtedness. He will want to know the amount of the mortgage due on the home, who is to continue payments, and what disposition is to be made of the property when the mortgage is paid. He will also want to know whether the wife has any interest in the husband's business, what that interest is, and how it is to be disposed of either during the separation or after the divorce. He will want to know if the wife holds in her name property belonging to the husband, or if the husband holds in his name any property belonging to the wife. If the couple live in an apartment, the attorney will want to know whether there is a lease, who is to occupy the apartment, and who is to pay the rent. He will want to know about any community property and what disposition is to be made of it.

What will the attorney want to know about children and visitation rights?

He will want to know whether there is an agreement as to the custody of the children and whether there are to be rights of visitation and if so when and under what circumstances. He will want to know with whom the children are to spend their summer vacations, weekends, and holidays. He will want to know which parent is to make the ultimate decision as to the child's education, from kindergarten to college, including summer camps. He will want to know if there is to be mediation in case the agreement is to the effect that both parents are to have an equal voice in the matter, and who is to be the mediator. He will want to know if the mother or father is to be permitted to take the children out of the state and under what circumstances, and whether there is to be any notice in case of illness.

What will the attorney want to know about support for the wife?

He will want to know if the husband and wife have reached an agreement as to the amount of support for the wife, and how and under what circumstances it is to be made. He will want to know whether there is to be a lump sum settlement and if so is the sum to be fixed and certain or will it vary with the husband's income; he will want to know what is to happen to the amount of support in the event the wife remarries after obtaining a divorce. He will want to know what provision is to be made for the children's support and education and whether or not there will be additional payments by the husband in case of emergencies and medical, hospital, and dental bills. He will want to know about any insurance policies for the benefit of the children, and whether the couple have Blue Cross, Blue Shield, health and accident insurance, and what disposition is to be made of them. He will want to know about any life insurance policies, who are the beneficiaries, who pays the premiums, whether there are any loans on the policies, whether the spouse is to have the right to borrow on them in the future, whether the husband or wife is to maintain the policies in force, or, if there is no insurance in force, whether the husband will bind himself to take out a policy, or policies, and what provisions will be made as to income taxes.

What does a separation agreement look like?

A sample agreement might read as follows:

"Memorandum of Agreement made and entered into this 1st day of June, 1955, by and between Jane Doe, party of the first part and Richard Doe, party of the second part.

Whereas the parties hereto are husband and wife, having been married in the city of Baltimore, state of Maryland, on May 7, 1943, and

Whereas unhappy differences have arisen between the said parties, by reason of which they have agreed to live separate and apart from each other for the future, and

Whereas there are two children of said marriage, John, born July 4, 1945, and Mary, born June 26, 1947, and

Whereas the parties hereto desire to enter into an agreement for the maintenance and support of the wife and for the maintenance and support and education of the children, and for the fulfillment of such other obligations as under the law exist between the parties;

Now, therefore, in consideration of the premises and of the mutual promises and covenants hereinafter contained, the parties hereto have agreed as follows:

1. It shall be lawful for each of the parties hereto at all times hereafter, to live separate and apart and free from the interference, authority, and control of the other as fully as if each of the said parties were unmarried, and for each to conduct, carry on, and engage in any employment, business, or occupation for his or her own sole and separate use and benefit, and free from any control, restraint, or interference, direct or indirect, by the other party as if each were single and unmarried.
2. Neither of the parties shall molest the other or compel or seek to compel the other party to cohabit or dwell with him or her by any proceedings for restoration of marital rights, or otherwise.

3. The wife agrees that she will not, except as herein provided, at any times hereafter contract any debt or debts, charge or liability for which the husband or his estate shall or may be or become liable or answerable.

4. The wife further agrees that she, her executors and administrators will, except as herein provided, at all times hereafter keep the husband, his heirs and executors, and administrators, indemnified from all debts and liabilities hereafter contracted or incurred by the wife and from all actions, proceedings, claims, demands, costs, and expenses whatsoever in respect hereto.

5. The wife further accepts the provisions made in this agreement in full satisfaction of any and all rights or claims on her part against the husband, his property or his estate for support and maintenance.

6. Each of the parties releases and forever discharges the other party hereto, his or her executors, administrators, and assigns, from every type of action and cause of action, suits, debts, dues, sums of money, accounts, bonds, bills, specialties, covenants, controversies, agreements, promises, variances, trespasses, damages, judgments, executions, claims, and demands, whether in law or in equity, which one has against the other, or which the heirs, executors, administrators, and assignees of each party hereafter can, shall, or may have against the heirs, executors, administrators, or assignees of the other party hereto, by reason of any matter, cause or thing whatsoever, from the beginning of the world to the date of this agreement, except as to the terms and conditions of this agreement.

7. That the wife shall have the care and custody as well as control of the children, but that the husband shall have the following rights:

    A. That the husband shall have the right at all reasonable times to visit the said children.

    B. That the husband shall have the right of custody of the children during half of each Christmas season, the wife retaining the right to have the children on Christmas Eve and Christmas day.

C. That the husband shall have the additional right to have the custody and control of the children for at least one month during the summer vacation, said month to be chosen by the wife by giving him at least two weeks notice.

D. During the time when the children are living with the wife, the husband shall have, at all reasonable times, the right of visitation to the said children, provided the husband shall give to the wife at least twenty-four hours advance notice of such visit. Such visit or visits shall take place at such place or places as are convenient to the children and the visiting parent. It is expressly agreed, however, that neither of the parties shall, without the express consent of the other, visit or enter the residence of the other, except in case of the illness and inability to leave the premises of the children so visited.

E. It is further agreed that neither party will attempt to alienate the affections of the children from the other party and will not permit any person to do so, insofar as they can control or prevent the actions of any such person. Each of the respective parties further agrees that he or she will not belittle or disparage the other, either in public or in private, and will not seek to influence the children as to which of the parties the said children may care to live with.

F. The provisions of this agreement conferring benefits upon the children shall, in addition to the rights of the respective parties hereto to enforce such provisions, be enforceable only and on behalf of the said children as third party beneficiaries of this agreement.

8. The husband shall pay to the wife, for her care and support, the sum of $300 per month, in equal installments of $150 each in advance on the first and fifteenth day of each month at such places as the wife may, from time to time, designate. These payments shall not be reduced or changed in any manner by reason of the fact that the wife may work from time to time, have other sources of income, whether from work done by her, or otherwise. The husband shall continue such payments during the lifetime of the wife or, in the event the parties shall be

legally divorced, until the wife shall remarry. The said payments shall not be increased or decreased by reason of any change in circumstances of either wife or husband.

9. In addition to the stipulations in paragraph eight, the husband further agrees to pay an additional sum of $200 a month for the support and maintenance of the two children of the parties. Such payments shall be made in equal installments of $100 at the first and fifteenth day of each month and shall be in lieu of all doctors, hospital, nursing, drug, and dental bills incurred by either the wife or the children. The husband shall pay and make full payment of all school, tuition, and camp bills or charges incurred in the case of or on behalf of the said children, including all charges for camp uniforms and clothing and school equipment and fees. On reaching college age each child shall be sent, if he or she desires, to a college or colleges mutually agreed by the parties hereto, but the expense shall be borne by the husband.

10. The furniture, linens, household items, etc., now part of the household residence shall be equally divided between husband and wife.

11. The husband agrees to keep in full force and effect his $25,000 life insurance in which his children are the beneficiaries until such children attain the age of 21 or marry, whichever comes first.

12. Each party hereby waives and releases any and all rights which each may have under inheritance or other statutes to any personal or real property hereafter acquired or owned by either of them, and each waives any right of election to take against any last will and testament made by either of them. Each party shall be free to acquire, accumulate, use and enjoy, and dispose of any property, real or personal, as though each were unmarried.

13. Should either party obtain an absolute divorce against the other, the provisions of this agreement may be incorporated in the text of such decree at the request of either party. Despite such incorporation, however, this agreement and all the terms thereof shall survive and be separate from such decree and the

parties hereto shall be bound to the performance of this agreement in accordance with the terms thereof.

14. Both parties hereby agree that they will, promptly and upon request, make, execute, and deliver to the other any and all necessary documents, deeds, transfers, assignments, or other papers required to carry out the intent of this agreement.

15. This agreement and all the terms thereof shall be binding upon the heirs, executors, administrators, personal representatives, assigns, and estate of both parties.

16. This agreement and the terms and conditions thereof and the rights, privileges, duties, and liabilities of the parties under it, shall be construed in accordance with the law of the state of Maryland as it exists on the date of the making of this agreement.

17. Dated this 10th day of June, 1961.

_____	_____
Witness for husband	Husband
_____	_____
Witness for wife	Wife

After a separation agreement has been signed, can either of the parties date other individuals?

Yes, if such dating does not lead to sexual relations with a third party. Even after the separation agreement is signed, the parties remain husband and wife until an absolute divorce is obtained. To prove adultery it is not essential to be caught in the act. All that must be proved is that the husband or wife had an adulterous disposition and the surrounding circumstances were such as to lead a reasonable person to believe that the act did take place.

What is the effect of the husband or wife committing adultery after a separation agreement is signed?

While the agreement would still be enforceable, the innocent party would have the right to seek an absolute divorce on the ground of adultery. In addition, the wife's rights to her husband's property

83

may be adversely affected. A clause in the separation agreement voiding the agreement in case of adultery is enforceable.

Is it wise to entertain in your home during a legal separation?

No. Some such entertainment may make one party feel that the other party had both the disposition and the opportunity to commit adultery. Should this be proved, the innocent party may be able to obtain an absolute divorce.

Does the husband or wife have the right to change the lock of the apartment or house after a separation agreement is signed?

Yes.

What can be done if only one of the parties desires a separation?

The other party may decide to remain wed and attempt to adjust to the marriage as well as possible. If he or she has grounds for at least a partial divorce, the other party may file a suit for separate maintenance. Or a bill for an absolute divorce may be instituted, provided there are grounds.

Can the husband have his payments to his wife reduced during a separation?

Only if there is no written separation agreement. If the agreement is merely verbal the husband can reduce his payments to nothing. The wife can then, through her legal counsel, attempt to negotiate a written agreement with the husband's attorney; failing that, the wife can resort to the courts for legal redress.

Is it desertion if the husband or wife leaves the house to sleep elsewhere after a domestic quarrel?

Not necessarily. To constitute desertion there must be an abandonment without any intent to return, with the desertion being continual. Of course, if the husband or wife committed adultery—

that is, had sexual relations with some other person—a ground for divorce would arise.

Is it desertion if the husband or wife willfully chooses to sleep in another bedroom other than the one they share?

Not necessarily. It is not the fact that the parties sleep in separate bedrooms that is important, but that they refuse to have sexual relations. The unjustified refusal to have sexual intercourse with each other for the statutory period (18 months in Maryland, for example), may entitle the wronged party to a divorce on the ground of desertion. If the refusal to have sexual intercourse is for a period less than the 18 months (as in Maryland, for example), the innocent party may be entitled to either a suit for separate maintenance or a partial divorce.

When a sum of money for support has been decided upon by a couple, can it be raised or lowered by either party?

No, if there has been a written separation agreement in which both parties were represented by legal counsel. If only the husband had an attorney, the wife, by retaining counsel, may seek to have the agreement changed if she can show that it was unfair, in that the husband failed to make a full and fair disclosure of his assets, or that the agreement was entered into as a result of fraud, duress, or ignorance.

Can either the husband or wife demand that the other leave the house before the separation has been made legal?

Not if the house is in the names of both husband and wife. If it is, both parties have equal rights with neither being able to force the other out.

Must the husband or wife obtain the other's permission to take the children out of the state for a vacation during a separation?

A written separation agreement usually contains—or should contain—a clause providing for such a contingency. If there is no written separation agreement either party may take the children out of town without first obtaining the permission of the other parent.

During a separation does all property, savings accounts, stocks, etc. —though in the husband's name only—belong to both husband and wife?

No. They belong exclusively to the husband unless the wife can prove that the property, money, and stocks were actually paid for with her funds or that she contributed as much as her husband.

If the husband or wife receives an inheritance during the separation would it be considered part of his income?

If there is a written separation agreement, no subsequent inheritance would modify it. If the agreement were merely a verbal one or not yet reduced to writing, the fact that the husband or wife had inherited a sum of money would be taken into consideration either by the lawyers negotiating a settlement, or by the court.

During a separation can either party, without the consent of the other, move to another city?

Yes, if the separation is a voluntary one. However, if the husband leaves the city with the intent not to support his wife and children he may—if circumstances so warrant—be returned by way of extradition. Or the wife can go to the city to which the husband has fled and swear out a warrant for nonsupport if she is legally justified in so doing. Or she may institute proceedings under the Uniform Support of Dependents' Act by seeing the prosecutor in her own community.

If the husband and wife have sexual relations during the separation, does this void the proceedings?

Yes. To resume cohabitation and have sexual relations terminates the separation as of the date of the intercourse.

How Divorce Proceedings Are Begun

5

---

ow are divorce proceedings begun?

sually by retaining a lawyer.

always necessary to retain counsel in a separation or divorce eeding?

s, if you are the party suing for a divorce. If you are the defend-
t and do not wish to contest the divorce it may not be absolutely
ential to retain counsel, but it is always advisable in order to
tect your legal rights. It is also wise that both parties to separa-
proceedings be represented by separate attorneys.

loes one go about selecting an attorney?

way is to make inquiries of friends or relatives. A good idea
ask questions about the nature of the services performed by
attorneys. Were they satisfied? Are the attorneys experienced
atrimonial law? Do they enjoy good reputations among their
lawyers? Are their fees reasonable?

e lawyers who specialize in divorce?

specially in the larger cities. However, a lawyer engaged in
l practice is often competent to handle a divorce matter.

Is a written separation agreement voided if the husband mits adultery after the agreement is signed?

No. To void the agreement there must be evidenc duress as to the agreement itself, not to some extra as adultery committed by either party.

How does a court determine the amount of money f children during a separation?

The amount is determined by the husband's inco the financial resources of the wife. Usually the are allotted—depending on the number of one-third and one-half of the husband's net incor

How can a written separation agreement be termi

1. By the husband and wife mutually agreein agreement.
2. By the parties again living together as man
3. By either party showing that there was f agreement was entered into.

When attempting to reach a settlement must records to prove his exact income?

An experienced lawyer will usually insist duce a sworn statement of his net worth t tax returns for the past three years.

Are there some attorneys who will not handle divorce matters?

Yes, just as there are some lawyers who do not handle tax matters or criminal law.

Are there special qualities one should look for in a divorce lawyer?

In general the qualities that distinguish a divorce lawyer are those that stamp any good attorney, with the notable difference that he is experienced in the field of divorce or matrimonial law. The first characteristic of a good divorce lawyer is honesty. He tells a client whether or not the latter can meet the divorce requirements of his particular state and whether the client has sufficient evidence to win the case in the event it is contested. If the attorney has any doubts or reservations about the outcome he will not hesitate to mention them.

Will a divorce lawyer guarantee success in a specific case?

No, since he is aware that the trial of a contested divorce matter is by its nature highly speculative. At most, counsel will offer a reasoned opinion as to the client's chances of winning or losing a case.

What are other characteristics of a good divorce lawyer?

1. He is thorough. He takes copious notes, prepares his legal documents and cases with care and deliberation, examines all witnesses before trial, so that no hitch is likely to develop that might have been foreseen.
2. He is alert and resourceful.
3. He can shrewdly appraise the strengths and weaknesses of his opponent's case as well as his own.
4. He is a good talker. He speaks convincingly and what he has to say makes sense. His arguments before a judge are clear and persuasive, so that he is likely to be given the benefit of any doubt.
5. He is tenacious. He does not give up easily and sees a divorce case through to a conclusion.

6. He is mature. He does not fly into a rage or indulge in temper tantrums when things do not go his way, nor is he easily irritated by what may appear to be his client's thoughtless or even senseless behavior.

7. A good divorce lawyer is in the best sense of the term an expert in human relations. He is aware that his client is going through a difficult and upsetting period and he is as reassuring as any good psychologist or psychiatrist.

8. A good lawyer is a man of infinite patience. Knowing that his client is likely to be upset and confused, and that he will want many answers to many questions, he will be neither brusque nor curt. He will answer queries as honestly and as straightforwardly as possible. He will not be too disturbed when the client regales him with legal advice he has gotten from friends and relatives. In every divorce matter well-meaning but uninformed friends and relatives offer counsel. Some of it may be good, other, bad or irrelevant. It is for the lawyer to decide, not for friends or relatives. The basis of a good attorney-client relationship is confidence. The confidence must be reciprocal, not one-sided. The client must believe that his attorney has the client's best interests at heart. If he does not, the client has the right to discharge the attorney, after he has paid him for his legal services, and employ another. If, however, the client does believe that the attorney is both competent and honest he should allow him to make the decisions. That is why he employed him in the first place.

9. A good lawyer is psychologically sophisticated. He will not be easily shocked by anything the client tells him, including an account of his past or present infidelities. If he is experienced, he will have heard many such stories before. He will set the client at ease and avoid giving him the crushing feeling that he has either sinned or been a miserable failure as a husband or wife.

10. A good lawyer holds a client's confidences inviolate. The relationship between attorney and client is a privileged one. A good lawyer is discreet. He is not a name dropper. He does not discuss his cases, except in the most general terms, with either

his wife or his friends. He conducts himself with dignity and discretion, avoiding cheap publicity instead of inviting it.

May one lawyer represent both parties to a divorce?

No. To do so is a violation of legal ethics, since there may be—and often is—a conflict of interests between husband and wife.

What does a divorce cost?

The total cost of a divorce is divided into legal fees and actual court expenses. A fee for handling a divorce case may range from $250, in the case of a client who may earn no more than $100 a week to $25,000 or more, in the case of an extremely wealthy client. For the client in the $10,000 a year bracket the fee generally runs to $500. For the client who earns $25,000 a year the fee may run to $2,000 or more.

On what does a lawyer's fee depend?

What a lawyer will charge ultimately depends on a number of factors: The difficulty of the legal questions involved; the number of witnesses to be questioned and interviewed; whether the case is to be contested or not—and if the former, how long the trial is likely to last; whether a separation agreement is to be drawn between the parties—and, if so, the number of conferences necessary to consummate the settlement; the wealth of the parties concerned; the reputation and experience of the attorney; the amount charged by other lawyers in the community for similar services; and whether a case will be taken to a higher court in the event it is lost.

What about court costs?

In addition to the attorney's fee, there will be court costs that will have to be paid. Where a divorce is uncontested the court costs should be $100 or less.

Where the case is contested the court costs may run into hundreds of dollars.

Where the case is appealed to the state's highest appellate court, the court costs, including the stenographic transcription of the lower court's proceedings, will run considerably more.

Does a lawyer's fee include court costs?

Yes, usually. It all depends, of course, on the contractual arrangement made between attorney and client. As a rule, the fee charged will include the usual court costs in an uncontested case, but not the court costs in either a contested one or a case appealed from the lower court to the state's highest court. The best arrangement is for the client to ask his attorney at the first interview exactly what his fee will include, so that there will be no mistake later on. If the fee is to be $500 in the average uncontested case, do not hesitate to ask if it will include the court costs. Better still, a client should ask the attorney to give a written statement or letter as to what the fee will include so that there will be no misunderstanding. Many clients are too timid or too apprehensive to ask the necessary questions beforehand. If they did there would be fewer disputes later on.

What is a retainer?

A retainer is a portion of the total fee the client deposits with his attorney which binds the latter to represent the former. Given a retainer, the attorney can no longer represent anyone whose interests are in conflict with the client's. Suppose, for example, both the husband and wife are friends of a certain attorney. By going to the attorney and giving him a retainer to represent him, the husband precludes the wife from being represented by the husband's counsel.

How much of a retainer do attorneys require?

Usually about a third of the total fee. If the fee is to be $500 the attorney may require a retainer of $150 or so. But there is really no hard and fast rule. A great deal depends on the individual practice of the attorney. Some lawyers will require more, some less.

When will the balance of the fee have to be paid?

Generally, before testimony is taken in an uncontested divorce case, or before the actual trial in a contested one. Where the case, having been lost, is taken to the state's highest court of appeal, the remainder of the agreed fee is usually paid before argument is made in the appellate court.

What can a client do to either institute or defend divorce proceedings when he or she is without funds to employ counsel?

There are several possibilities. If the husband has an adequate income of his own, the attorney representing the wife may be able to secure a fee from the husband's counsel, after he has filed a bill for a divorce. He may do this by entering into an arrangement with the husband's attorney, if the case is uncontested, say for a $500 fee. If the husband's attorney refuses to agree on the amount of a fee or on any fee at all, the wife's counsel may still agree to take on the case and obtain his fee later by having the judge who is hearing the case award him one.

In other words, the wife's counsel may petition the court to award him a fee which may be smaller or larger than what he may have gotten if he had been able to agree on one with the husband's counsel. Most lawyers prefer to work out their own fee arrangements with their clients rather than rely on opposing counsel or on the judge hearing the case.

What if you have no funds at all?

A second possibility where the client has no funds is to seek legal assistance from one of the many Legal Aid Societies throughout the country.

To be eligible for Legal Aid, a client must prove that his income and assets are so inadequate that he can't afford to pay *any* fee at all. Legal Aid services are free. (For a complete list of Legal Aid Societies throughout the country see Appendix I.) There is no charge for advice or counsel. Most Legal Aid Societies are community service agencies, supported by contributions from the city or state.

What is the difference between Legal Aid and Lawyers' Referral?

Legal Aid is a free, charitable service provided by the community. The stated reason of the Lawyers' Referral service is to provide a means whereby any person who needs the services of an attorney and can afford to pay for one, but does not have one and is too unsophisticated to find one on his own, may be referred to an attorney through the Bar Association. Typically, the applicant pays a registration fee of $1 for the referral and pays the attorney a fixed fee of $5 for the initial consultation of up to thirty minutes. The attorney makes a normal charge for any additional services. Periodic reports are required of the attorneys.

In case of dispute, both attorney and client agree to arbitration by the Lawyers' Referral Committee. Lawyers' Referral is a sort of halfway house between free legal aid and private legal counsel. Legal fees charged for divorce are usually much less than normal because clients who use Lawyers' Referral are apt to come from low-income groups. Many come to Lawyers' Referral from Legal Aid because their incomes suggest that they can afford some fee rather than no fee at all.

How does Lawyers' Referral actually work?

Lawyers' Referral is a rotating service or pool of lawyers, providing a sort of pot luck of legal help. A client cannot have the lawyer of his choice, but must take the one whose name currently heads the list. If the client is dissatisfied with the lawyer chosen, he is eligible, by paying another consultation fee, to use the services of the attorney next in line.

Suppose a wife agrees to pay a fee to her attorney but the latter also collects one from the husband's counsel or is awarded one by the court. Will the wife's attorney return her original fee?

The usual practice is for the wife's attorney to deduct any fees received either from husband's counsel or from the court from the wife's fee.

In either case the wife's attorney whenever he files a petition for a fee makes a full disclosure to the court as to what fee, if any, he has already received.

What takes place at the first conference between attorney and client?

The first conference between attorney and client is most important. Let us assume a client has made diligent inquiries and that he has finally made a choice of attorneys, someone, preferably, who has had wide experience in matrimonial matters. The client's first step, obviously, is to phone the attorney's office and request an appointment. This may be made with his secretary or with the attorney directly. At the first conference the client tells his story in order to determine whether he has legal grounds for divorce. Naturally the client will be nervous, upset, and perhaps even embarrassed. It is not always easy to unburden oneself to a comparative stranger. But if the lawyer inspires confidence, if he is sympathetic and understanding, the client should have little trouble in filling in the details of the decline and fall of his marriage. A good lawyer will set him at ease. He will not insist on a perfectly coherent, logical account of the marital breakup. Instead, he will allow the client to proceed at his own pace, with as much time as he requires. Some clients have a knack for being mentally tidy and objective. They can provide a concise summary of all a lawyer needs to know in thirty minutes or less. Other clients require much more time, are much less coherent, stammer and stumble through their story a half dozen times until the patience of even the best lawyer is almost exhausted. But the good lawyer's patience is never quite exhausted. He is aware that people differ sharply and react differently to more or less similar situations.

What can a client do if he is dissatisfied with the lawyer at the first conference?

If he concludes that the lawyer is not for him, he should not hesitate to consult someone else. After all it is the client's money and his problem, and he is entitled to counsel of his choice. But he must not be unreasonable, either. Lawyers are human and they are busy, and a client must not expect to take all day to discuss his domestic situation—two hours should be sufficient for a detailed sketch of the marriage and how it reached the point of no return. If, after the first conference, the client decides that he and the attorney are not compatible, good manners require that the client call or write counsel advising that he has changed his mind. The client should not be surprised to receive a bill for the time consumed in the initial conference, since a lawyer's time and advice are his chief stock in trade, and he has a right to make reasonable charges.

What information will the attorney require at the first conference?

He will want to know, among other things, the client's full name and address, his business and residence phones, the type of business or profession engaged in (if the husband), his income, the amount of insurance he carries, his total net worth (including stocks and bonds), the date of the marriage and where it took place, the length of his residence in the state, the number of children, if any, the date the wife left the husband or the date the husband left the wife, and/or the reasons for the adultery, desertion, or other potential ground for divorce. If the client is the wife, he will want to know whether or not she is employed, what training or occupational skill she possesses, whether she has any independent income or property, whether it is her first, second, or third marriage. He will want to know whether she has been previously divorced, the state of her physical and mental health, and finally, whether there is any chance or desire for a reconciliation. In sum, what the client has to do is satisfy the attorney that he can meet the necessary requirements for a divorce in his or her particular state. If the lawyer has a social conscience he will also want to explore the possibilities of a reconciliation, even though the client may have already seen a marriage counselor or psychiatrist.

What else will the lawyer want to know?

He will want to know whether the other spouse will contest the divorce. The vast majority of divorce cases are uncontested. Some are fought to the bitter end. Although a client cannot guarantee that his spouse will not fight the case he should be able to express an opinion as to the probabilities so that the attorney will be prepared for any eventuality. In either event, he will want to know what witnesses will be available to prove the case. Finally he will want to discuss how much money will be needed to support the wife and minor children, that is those under 21. To this end, it is extremely helpful if at the first interview the client brings in a detailed budget to indicate how much money she will require for food, clothing, shelter, medical and dental care. The budget should be based not so much on past expenditures but rather on what the wife can reasonably get along with at the present time.

Is there anything else an attorney will advise a client during the first interview?

Yes. An experienced divorce lawyer will deliver two preliminary cautions to every client: one is to avoid behavior that may be suspicious or incriminating; the other to avoid discussing the case with other persons.

What is meant by suspicious or incriminating behavior?

By incriminating behavior is meant any action that may lead to an accusation. For example, pending divorce proceedings, the attorney should warn his client against going out with members of the other sex, or receiving them in the home. Until the divorce decree is signed by the judge a couple is considered legally married. Hence if the client is not to be penalized, he or she should avoid all behavior that may lead the average person to conclude that adultery has been committed.

Is there a practical reason for this?

Yes. Let us assume the spouse left for the required statutory period without sufficient legal reason. Based on the information the client has supplied the attorney, the latter files a Bill of Complaint asking for an absolute divorce on the ground of desertion. A few weeks later the client receives a cross-bill of complaint alleging that he committed adultery during the separation. Actually, the client did not commit adultery, though he was seen repeatedly in cocktail lounges with members of the other sex and had had them in his apartment. But even though the client is innocent he may not be able to defend himself successfully against the charges and may lose the divorce suit—together with all the monetary advantages he might have had, had he received the divorce rather than his spouse. No lawyer can force a client to do anything, just as no physician can compel a patient to take the medication he prescribes. But this doesn't mean the advice or the medication isn't worth taking. And the best possible advice, pending divorce proceedings, is to avoid any behavior that may be suspicious or incriminating.

Does this mean that a client should not go out at all?

No. There is no reason why a client cannot attend anything he likes, just as long as the finger of suspicion can't be pointed at him. He can attend concerts, movies, theater, and even parties, as long as he goes alone or with members of his or her own sex.

Why shouldn't the client discuss the case with friends and relatives?

Friends and relatives are not trained lawyers, nor are they in possession of all the facts. Lacking objectivity, they tend to view the case from the point of view of the friend or relative, forgetting that a divorce case is not always black and white, but has various shades and nuances.

Nor do they remember that each case, though similar, is different from every other, not so much in the law but in the applicable facts. More important from a legal point of view, is that promiscuous gossip may actually serve as a boomerang and prove damaging in court. In one case, after the couple separated the husband began to boast of his amatory conquests. It wasn't long before word got around to the wife's lawyers who promptly subpoenaed several witnesses. Brought into court the witnesses helped the wife obtain a divorce she might not otherwise have procured.

Are there any other matters an attorney is likely to discuss at the first conference?

Yes. One that he will almost certainly mention is the Bill of Complaint that he will file after he has assured himself that the client has a sufficient cause of action.

What is the Bill of Complaint?

A Bill of Complaint is a formal legal statement, prepared by the plaintiff's attorney (that is, the complaining party or the party bringing an action) requesting that a marriage be dissolved by a decree of divorce, either partial or absolute. A simple Bill of Complaint would look as follows:

John Doe Complainant	:	
	:	In the Circuit Court
vs.	:	of
	:	Baltimore City
	:	
Jane Doe Defendant	:	

To the Honorable, the Judge of Said Court
Your complainant says:

1. That he and the defendant were married July 15, 1958 in Baltimore, Maryland, in a religious ceremony.
2. That both the complainant and the defendant have resided in the City of Baltimore, State of Maryland, for more than one year prior to the filing of this bill of complaint.
3. That one child was born of said marriage, whose name is John Doe, Jr., who is one year old.
4. That ever since their said marriage your complainant has behaved himself as a faithful, affectionate, and kindly husband toward the said defendant.
5. That the said defendant on or about September 15, 1962 did commit adultery with a person whose name will be revealed at the hearing of the above-named cause and that said adultery took place in the City of Baltimore, State of Maryland.

6. That your complainant has not lived nor cohabited with the said defendant since he discovered the said adultery, nor has he condoned, connived, nor forgiven such adultery.

TO THE END THEREFORE:

(1) That the complainant may be divorced a vinoculo matrimonii (absolute divorce) from the defendant.
(2) That the complainant may be allowed to have the custody of said infant child.
(3) That the complainant may have such other and further relief as his case may require.

And as in duty bound, etc.

John Doe	Samuel G. Kling
Complainant	Solicitor for Complainant.

Is the Bill of Complaint the legal means by which divorce proceedings are begun?

Yes. They are the papers which, through the sheriff's office, will be served on the defendant. In this case the relief requested was relatively simple because the complainant, through her counsel, might have asked for alimony *pendente lite* (pending litigation), permanent alimony, support for the child, as well as counsel fee for himself as her attorney or solicitor. It should be pointed out too that each allegation will have to be supported or corroborated by evidence and by at least one witness.*

Does the client have to sign the Bill of Complaint?

Yes. Most experienced lawyers require their clients to sign the Bill of Complaint. One reason is to make the client—not the attorney—responsible for the allegations as well as the consequences which may flow therefrom. In the anxiety to obtain a divorce, a client may give her attorney false and misleading information. If the law requires that she be a resident for one year she may tell her attorney that she has been a resident that long when actually

* See Chapter 10 for proof required.

she has only resided in the state ten months. To swear falsely to a material fact in a divorce proceeding may lead to criminal prosecution for perjury. By signing the Bill of Complaint the client declares that the allegations are true, thus affording the attorney some protection against a dishonest client.

How many conferences are there likely to be between a client and the attorney?

A simple divorce case that is uncontested may require no more than two or three conferences, one of which may be devoted to interrogating the client's witnesses to determine whether their testimony is legally sufficient. A complicated, contested divorce may call for a score or more conferences. A great deal depends on the individual case.

How long does it take to obtain a divorce?

Much depends on the type of divorce and the particular state. A court-contested divorce case, with many witnesses appearing on both sides, may take from a few days to a few weeks in actual trial. This is in addition to the time it takes to get the case on the trial calendar, which may require anywhere from a full month to a year or more.

An uncontested divorce case, where *both* parties are represented by counsel, may not take much more than a month or two, sometimes even less. To relieve any doubts, the client should ask his lawyer at the conclusion of the first interview, about how long it will take to dissolve the marriage legally. Sometimes there are difficulties in serving the defendant with legal papers, as well as other delays for which the attorney may not be responsible.

Should a wife resume her maiden name after divorce?

If there are children the wife will most likely want to retain her married name. If there are no children she probably would want to use her maiden name. This is a matter which should be discussed with the attorney, preferably at the first conference.

6 Grounds for Divorce

What are the grounds for an absolute divorce in the fifty states?

Alabama

1. Incapacity
2. Adultery
3. Physical violence
4. Abandonment for one year
5. Imprisonment in penitentiary for two years under sentence of seven years or more
6. Habitual drunkenness or drug addiction contracted after marriage
7. Five successive years in insane asylum after marriage; spouse so confined being hopelessly and incurably insane when divorce is filed
8. Final decree of partial divorce or final decree of separate maintenance in effect for more than four years
9. Husband may obtain divorce on the ground of wife's pregnancy at time of marriage without his consent or knowledge
10. Wife may obtain divorce for nonsupport for two years

What are the residence requirements in Alabama?

Alabama is no longer one of the easy divorce states. Courts do not have jurisdiction to grant a divorce if neither party is domiciled in Alabama. Personal appearance by both parties does not confer jurisdiction to grant divorce. Plaintiff must have resided in state at least one year if defendant is a nonresident, except that no particular period of residence is required where defendant is a nonresident. A wife seeking divorce because of nonsupport must have lived in state for two years and husband and wife must have been separated during such time.

Alaska

1. Impotency at time of marriage, continuing until divorce proceedings are begun
2. Adultery
3. Conviction of felony
4. Willful desertion for one year
5. Cruelty impairing health or endangering life, or personal indignities making life burdensome
6. Incompatibility of temperament
7. Drunkenness, habitual and gross, contracted after marriage and continuing for one year
8. Willful neglect by the husband to provide common necessaries of life for the wife for 12 months when able to do so, or when failure to do so is because of his idleness, profligacy, or dissipation
9. Incurable mental illness when spouse confined to an institution for at least 18 months prior to the filing of the divorce
10. Addiction, after marriage, to habitual use of drugs

What are the residence requirements in Alaska?

Plaintiff must have been a resident of the state when the application for divorce is filed for one year prior thereto.

Are there any restrictions on remarriage in Alaska?

No.

Arizona

1. Adultery
2. Physical incompetence at time of marriage, continuing until time of suit
3. Conviction of felony and sentence of imprisonment but no divorce can be instituted until one year after conviction which must not have been on plaintiff's testimony
4. Willful desertion for one year preceding commencement of suit
5. Habitual intemperance
6. Extreme cruelty
7. Husband's neglect to provide wife with common necessaries of life for one year, he having the ability to do so, or failing to do so because of idleness or dissipation
8. Conviction of felony before marriage, the fact being unknown to the other party at the time of marriage
9. Wife's pregnancy by another man at time of marriage which was unknown to husband
10. Failure of husband and wife to cohabit for five or more years for any reason

What are the residence requirements in Arizona?

One year for the plaintiff.

Are there any restrictions as to remarriage?

Yes. Either party may remarry after expiration of one year after divorce decree. However, a marriage performed outside the state within the year period is not void.

Arkansas

1. Adultery
2. Impotency at time of marriage continuing until divorce proceedings are begun
3. Desertion for one year without reasonable cause

4. Husband or wife by former undissolved marriage, living at time of marriage
5. Conviction of felony or infamous crime
6. Habitual drunkenness for one year
7. Cruel and barbarous treatment endangering life of innocent party
8. Indignities to person, making his or her life intolerable
9. Parties living apart for three consecutive years without co-habitation, whether or not by mutual consent
10. Willful nonsupport
11. Insanity in which the spouse must have been continuously confined in an institution for at least three years or have been adjudicated insane for more than three years before filing of suit

What are the residence requirements in Arkansas?

Plaintiff or defendant must have lived in the state for at least sixty days before the filing of the divorce and for at least three months after the decree is signed. A nonresident establishing residence must prove bona fide residence to exist at the time suit is filed and at the time the decree is signed.

Are there any remarriage restrictions in Arkansas?

No.

California

1. Adultery, when action is begun within two years after discovery of the infidelity
2. Extreme cruelty, either mental or physical
3. Willful desertion
4. Willful neglect
5. Habitual intemperance
6. Conviction of a felony when action is begun within two years after completion of sentence or pardon
7. Incurable insanity where insane person has been incurably in-

sane for a continuous period of three years preceding the filing of the divorce and has been confined to an institution, or under the jurisdiction of the institution for at least three continuous years immediately preceding the filing of the action and upon the testimony of the medical staff of the institution that such spouse is incurably insane

8. Willful desertion, willful neglect, or habitual intemperance for at least one year before the filing of the divorce bill

What are the residence requirements in California?

Plaintiff must have been a resident of the state for one year, and of the county in which the bill is filed, for three months before legal action can be brought. This provision does not apply to cross complaints where the defendant denies the allegations of the plaintiff and brings divorce charges of his or her own, asking that the plaintiff's bill be dismissed and that a divorce be granted the defendant.

Note: Every final divorce in California requires both an interlocutory and a final decree.

An interlocutory decree is entered after trial if the court finds that a divorce should be granted. The function of the interlocutory decree is to declare that the party in whose favor the court decides is entitled to a divorce. This decree stands for one year, during which time the parties are still husband and wife, but neither party alone may dismiss the action. Appeals may be taken and motions for new trial made upon the interlocutory decree. Final judgment may not be entered until final disposition of such motion or appeal, or in the event the motion is granted, or the decree reversed.

A final judgment may be entered one year after the entry of the interlocutory judgment, or on the motion of either party, or on the court's own motion. The final judgment restores the parties to the status of single persons. After the date of a final judgment or decree the parties have the right of remarriage.

Are there any remarriage restrictions in California?

No.

Colorado

1. Impotency existing at the time of the marriage or resulting from immoral conduct after marriage
2. Adultery
3. Desertion for one year
4. Cruelty
5. Failure to support for one year
6. Habitual drunkenness for one year or drug addiction
7. Conviction of felony
8. Adjudication of insanity for not less than three years before commencement of action, provided such insanity is shown to be incurable (However, the party obtaining the divorce on this ground must continue to support the divorced party)
9. Living separate and apart for three consecutive years before the filing of the suit

What are the residence requirements in Colorado?

One spouse must have been a bona fide resident and citizen of the state for at least one year prior to the filing of the divorce, except where the ground is adultery or extreme cruelty and such offense was committed in the state.

Are there any remarriage restrictions in Colorado?

No.

Connecticut

1. Adultery
2. Fraudulent contract
3. Willful desertion for three years with total neglect of duty
4. The absence of a spouse for seven years where he or she has been unheard from
5. Habitual intemperance
6. Intolerable cruelty
7. Sentence to imprisonment for life

8. Any infamous crime involving a violation of conjugal duty and punishable by imprisonment in a state prison
9. Legal confinement because of mental illness for an accumulated period of at least five years within the six-year period preceding the filing of the divorce

What are Connecticut's residence requirements?

Plaintiff must have resided in the state for three years unless the cause of divorce arose after removal to state, or plaintiff was domiciled at time of marriage and returned with intention of remaining permanently, or where the defendant has lived in the state for three years and has been actually served.

Delaware

1. Adultery
2. Bigamy
3. Conviction of crime with imprisonment for two years
4. Extreme cruelty
5. Willful desertion for two years
6. Congenital or after-acquired inability and failure to support family
7. Habitual drunkenness for two years
8. Complaining party under age of consent at time of marriage and marriage not confirmed after reaching such age
9. Adjudication by commission appointed by Supreme Court that spouse is mentally ill and has been under supervision or care of a mental institution for five years
10. Voluntary three-year separation

What are the residence requirements for a divorce in Delaware?

Action may be brought for adultery or bigamy, if either party was a bona fide resident at the time the action arose. It may be brought on any other ground if either party has been a bona fide resident for two years prior to the filing of the divorce proceedings provided that if the cause arose out of the state and the residence began thereafter, the ground alleged in the jurisdiction of residence at the time the cause arose, as a ground for relief asked in Delaware.

District of Columbia

1. Adultery
2. Desertion for two years
3. Voluntary separation from bed and board for five consecutive years without cohabitation
4. Final conviction of a felony involving moral turpitude and sentence for not less than two years partly or wholly served
5. Where a partial divorce has been granted and separation has continued for two years since date of decree, it may be enlarged to an absolute divorce on application of the innocent spouse

What are the residence requirements in the District of Columbia?

One year; two years for any cause which occurred out of the District and prior to residence therein.

Florida

1. Relationship between parties within degree prohibited by law
2. Natural impotency
3. Adultery
4. Extreme cruelty
5. Habitual indulgence in violent and ungovernable temper
6. Habitual intemperance
7. Willful and obstinate desertion for one year
8. Divorce in any other state or country
9. Either party having a husband or wife living at the time of marriage
10. Voluntary three-year separation

What is the period of residence in Florida?

One year.

Georgia

1. Relationship between parties such that marriage is prohibited
2. Mental incapacity at time of marriage

3. Impotency at time of marriage
4. Force, duress, or fraud in obtaining marriage
5. Pregnancy at time of marriage unknown to husband
6. Adultery
7. Conviction of offense involving moral turpitude where penalty is two years or more in the penitentiary
8. Willful desertion for one year
9. Habitual intoxication
10. Mental or physical cruelty
11. Incurable insanity

What are the residence requirements in Georgia?

Either party must have resided in Georgia for at least six months prior to the filing of the divorce bill.

Hawaii

1. Adultery
2. Desertion for six months
3. Sentence of imprisonment for life or seven years or more
4. Extreme cruelty
5. Habitual intemperance or excessive use of drugs
6. Insanity lasting three years or more
7. Failure of the husband, having sufficient ability to do so, to support the wife for 60 days
8. Such mental cruelty, continued for not less than 60 days, as to make the life of the other burdensome and intolerable, and further living together insupportable

What are the residence requirements of Hawaii?

Two years.

Idaho

1. Adultery
2. Extreme cruelty
3. Willful desertion

4. Habitual intemperance
5. Conviction of felony
6. Willful neglect
7. Permanent insanity, provided insane spouse has been confined in an insane asylum in any state or foreign country for at least three years prior to the filing of the divorce bill
8. That parties have continuously lived separate and apart for five years or more

What are the residence requirements of Idaho?

Plaintiff must have been a resident for six full weeks before filing suit.

Illinois

1. Impotency
2. Another husband or wife living at the time of the marriage
3. Adultery
4. Desertion for one year without reasonable cause
5. Habitual drunkenness for two years
6. Attempt on life of spouse by poisoning or other means showing malice
7. Extreme and repeated cruelty
8. Conviction of felony or infamous crime
9. Communication of venereal disease

What are the residence requirements of Illinois?

One year, unless complaint or injury was committed within Illinois, in which case only six months residence is required.

Indiana

1. Adultery, unless it is committed with the connivance or consent of the other party or when it is followed by cohabitation with knowledge that adultery has been committed
2. Impotency existing at the time of the marriage
3. Abandonment for two years
4. Cruel and inhuman treatment

5. Habitual drunkenness
6. Failure of husband to support his family for two years
7. Conviction, after marriage, of an infamous crime
8. Five years commitment for incurable insanity in a hospital or asylum

What are the residence requirements of Indiana?

Period of residence required is one year; five years residence required for suits of divorce by reason of incurable insanity.

Iowa

1. Adultery
2. Desertion for two years
3. Conviction of felony
4. Chronic alcoholism
5. Extreme cruelty
6. When the wife at the time of marriage was pregnant by someone other than her husband, unless such husband has an illegitimate child then living which was unknown to the wife at the time of the marriage

What are the residence requirements of Iowa?

Except where the defendant is a resident of the state and served by personal service, the petition must show that the plaintiff has been for the last year a resident of the state, specifying the town and county in which he/she has resided.

Kansas

1. That either party had a former husband or wife living at the time of the remarriage
2. Abandonment for one year
3. Adultery
4. Impotency
5. That the wife at the time of the marriage was pregnant by someone other than her husband

6. Extreme cruelty
7. Fraudulent contract
8. Habitual drunkenness
9. Conviction of a felony and imprisonment therefor after the marriage
10. Insanity for a period of five years, the insane spouse having been an inmate of a state, federal, or private institution for such period and afflicted with an incurable type of insanity

What are the residence requirements in Kansas?

One year, unless the action is brought in the county where the defendant resides or is summoned. Neither party may remarry until six months after divorce decree has been signed by the court.

Kentucky

1. Such impotency or malformation as prevents sexual intercourse
2. Living apart without cohabitation for five consecutive years
3. Abandonment for one year
4. Living in adultery
5. Conviction of felony
6. Concealment from the other party of any loathsome disease existing at the time of the marriage or contracted afterward
7. Fraud, duress, or force in obtaining the marriage
8. Uniting with any religious society requiring renunciation of the marriage covenant or forbidding cohabitation
9. Habitual drunkenness of not less than one year's duration, accompanied by the wasting of the husband's estate, and without any suitable provision for the support and maintenance of the wife and children (A similar provision applies to the wife)
10. Habitual behavior toward the wife by the husband, for not less than six months, in such cruel and inhuman manner as to indicate a settled aversion to her
11. Such cruel beating or injury or attempted injury of the wife by the husband as indicates an outrageous temper in him, or probable danger to the wife's life, or great bodily injury (A similar

provision applies to husbands who are victims of their wives'
cruelty)

12. Pregnancy of the wife by another man unknown to the husband at the time of the marriage
13. Adultery
14. Habitual drunkenness for at least one year
15. Insanity of five years duration, provided the insane spouse has
been confined to an insane asylum, hospital, or other institution for not less than five successive years

What are the residence requirements of Kentucky?

One year.

Louisiana

1. Adultery
2. Conviction of felony and sentence to death or to imprisonment
at hard labor
3. Habitual intemperance, excesses, cruel treatment or outrages
if such conduct is of such a nature as to make living together
impossible
4. Public defamation
5. Abandonment
6. Attempt on the life of the other spouse
7. When one of the married persons has been charged with an infamous offense and has actually fled from justice, and the other
produces proof before the judge that the person accused was
actually guilty of such offense

What are the residence requirements of Louisiana?

None stated.

What are the restrictions on remarriage in Louisiana?

Where divorce is granted because of adultery, guilty party may
not marry his or her accomplice. A wife may not remarry until ten
months after dissolution of a preceding marriage.

Maine

1. Adultery
2. Impotency
3. Extreme cruelty
4. Desertion for three consecutive years
5. Gross and confirmed habits of intoxication from the use of liquors or drugs
6. Neglect to support wife and children, where husband is able to provide such support

What are the residence requirements of Maine?

Six months.

Maryland

1. Impotency at time of marriage
2. Any cause rendering marriage null and void *ab initio* under Maryland laws
3. Adultery
4. Abandonment for at least 18 months without reasonable expectation of a reconciliation
5. Voluntary separation without cohabitation for 18 consecutive months without reasonable expectation of a reconciliation
6. Conviction of a felony and sentence of at least three years in a penal institution, 18 months of which have been served
7. Permanent and incurable insanity, provided insane spouse has been confined in mental institution for not less than three years prior to filing of suit

What are Maryland's residence requirements?

The residence of either party gives the court jurisdiction. When the causes occurred out of Maryland, the plaintiff or defendant must have resided in Maryland one year prior to the filing of the divorce bill. Where the actual ground is insanity, the plaintiff must have resided two years in the state before he can file his bill.

Massachusetts

1. Adultery
2. Impotency
3. Desertion for three consecutive years prior to filing of suit
4. Gross and confirmed habits of intoxication caused by voluntary, excessive use of drugs or liquor
5. Cruelty
6. Nonsupport by the husband
7. Sentence to confinement for life or for five years or more in a penal institution

What are the residence requirements in Massachusetts?

If the plaintiff has lived in Massachusetts for five years preceding the filing of divorce bill, or if both parties have resided in the state at the time of their marriage, and the plaintiff has lived there for three years, a divorce may be decreed.

What are the marriage restrictions in Massachusetts?

Plaintiff may remarry after divorce, but defendant may not remarry for two years afterward if plaintiff is living.

Michigan

1. Adultery
2. Physical incompetence at time of marriage
3. Desertion for two years
4. Habitual drunkenness
5. Extreme cruelty
6. Nonsupport
7. Sentence to imprisonment for three years or more

What are Michigan's residence requirements?

Plaintiff must have resided in state for one year, unless marriage was solemnized in Michigan and plaintiff has resided in state from time of marriage until time he brings suit. One spouse must have resided in county where suit is filed for 10 days immediately preceding filing. If cause for divorce occurred outside state, one party must have resided in state for one year immediately preceding filing.

Minnesota

1. Adultery
2. Impotency
3. Cruel and inhuman treatment
4. Either party after marriage sentenced to any state or federal prison or reformatory
5. Willful desertion for one year
6. Habitual drunkenness for one year
7. Incurable insanity if insane party has been under regular treatment for insanity and confined in institution for at least five years preceding the filing of the divorce bill; however the divorce in such a case does not relieve plaintiff of obligation to support defendant
8. Continuous separation under a decree of a limited divorce for more than five years preceding the filing of the divorce bill
9. Continuous separation under order or decree of separate maintenance for two years preceding the filing of the divorce action

What are Minnesota's residence requirements?

Plaintiff must have resided in state for one year preceding filing of complaint, except in case of adultery while plaintiff is a resident of state.

What are Minnesota's remarriage restrictions?

Remarriage within six months after decree is forbidden except that the divorced persons may intermarry.

Mississippi

1. Natural impotency
2. Adultery

3. Sentence to penitentiary (unless pardoned before being sent there)
4. Desertion for one year
5. Habitual drunkenness
6. Habitual excessive use of drugs
7. Cruelty
8. Insanity or idiocy at time of marriage unknown to the other party
9. Prior undissolved marriage
10. Pregnancy by person other than husband at time of marriage, unknown to husband
11. Consanguinity within prohibited degree
12. Incurable insanity, if insane party has been under regular treatment and confined in an institution for preceding three years

What are Mississippi's residence requirements?

One year, for either party.

What are Mississippi's remarriage restrictions?

No legal restrictions except that in cases of adultery, court may prohibit remarriage of guilty party.

Missouri

1. Impotency at time of marriage continuing until divorce sought
2. Prior undissolved marriage
3. Adultery
4. Desertion for one year
5. Conviction of felony or infamous crime during marriage, or before marriage if innocent party was ignorant of fact before marriage
6. Cruelty, mental or physical
7. Husband's vagrancy
8. Pregnancy of wife by another man than husband at time of marriage, unknown to husband

What are Missouri's residence requirements?

No person who has not resided in state for one year prior to the filing of the divorce petition is entitled to a divorce. The exception is where the offense or injury occurred within the state, provided that if the plaintiff resided in the state one whole year before filing of petition and defendant pleads and proves facts entitling defendant to a divorce, the divorce will be granted despite defendant's nonresidence.

Montana

1. Adultery
2. Extreme cruelty, either mental or physical
3. Repeated publication or utterance of false charges against the wife's chastity
4. Willful desertion
5. Willful neglect or nonsupport
6. Conviction of felony
7. Incurable insanity, provided the insane spouse has been confined in an institution for the insane for five years prior to the filing of the divorce bill

What are Montana's residence requirements?

Plaintiff must have lived in state for one year before bringing action.

Nebraska

1. Adultery
2. Physical incompetency (impotency) at time of marriage
3. Sentence to imprisonment for life or for three years or more
4. Willful abandonment or utter desertion for two years
5. Habitual drunkenness
6. Incurable insanity where party has been confined to asylum for at least five years
7. Extreme cruelty
8. Refusal of husband to support wife

What are Nebraska's residence requirements?

If cause arose in state, plaintiff must have resided in Nebraska for at least one year before filing suit. If cause arose out of state, plaintiff or defendant must have resided in Nebraska for two years before suit is filed.

Nevada

1. Impotency at time of marriage
2. Adultery
3. Willful desertion
4. Conviction of felony or infamous crime
5. Habitual gross drunkenness, contracted since marriage, of either party, which prevents such party from contributing his or her share to the support of the family
6. Extreme cruelty
7. Nonsupport on the part of the husband, when such neglect is not the result of the husband's poverty which he could not avoid by ordinary industry
8. Insanity existing for two years prior to the commencement of the action
9. Husband and wife living apart for three consecutive years without cohabitation

What are Nevada's residence requirements?

Six weeks. No corroboration necessary except as to residence in Nevada.

New Hampshire

1. Impotency
2. Extreme cruelty
3. Conviction of a crime punishable by imprisonment for more than one year, and actual imprisonment under such conviction
4. Adultery
5. Extreme cruelty
6. Absence, unheard of for two years

7. Habitual drunkenness for two years
8. The joining of any religious society or sect which professes to believe that the relation of husband and wife is unlawful, and refusal to cohabit for six months
9. Willing absence of either party for two years without the consent of the other and refusal to cohabit
10. Nonsupport for two years
11. When the wife has left the state and remained absent and separate for ten years without the husband's consent, or without returning to claim her marriage rights
12. When the wife of any alien or citizen of any other state, living separate, has lived in the state for two years together, the husband having left the state to become a citizen of some foreign country, and not having come during that period into New Hampshire to claim his marital rights, and not having made suitable provision for his wife's support and maintenance

What are the residence requirements in New Hampshire?

Jurisdiction exists (1) where both parties were domiciled in the state when the action was begun; (2) where the plaintiff was so domiciled and the defendant was personally served within the state; (3) where the plaintiff was domiciled in the state for one year before the filing of the divorce bill.

Note: Whenever a divorce *nisi* or a petition for separation has been filed, the matter may be referred for marriage counseling, either on a compulsory or volunteer basis to an approved family agency within the jurisdiction of the court.

New Jersey

1. Adultery
2. Desertion for two years
3. Extreme cruelty, provided divorce on this ground is not filed until six months after last act of cruelty

What are New Jersey's residence requirements?

Two years.

New Mexico

1. Adultery
2. Impotency
3. Cruelty
4. Pregnancy of wife at time of marriage by someone other than her husband, without husband's knowledge
5. Abandonment
6. Conviction of a felony
7. Habitual drunkenness
8. Incurable insanity for five years
9. Incompatibility
10. Failure of husband to support wife according to his means, station in life, and ability

What are New Mexico's residence requirements?

One year prior to the filing of the action.

New York

1. Adultery

What are New York's residence requirements?

Action for divorce may be maintained (1) where both parties were residents of state at time offense was committed; (2) where both parties were married within state; (3) where plaintiff was a resident of state when offense was committed and is a resident when the divorce action was begun; (4) offense was committed in state and injured party is a resident when action was begun.

What remarriage restrictions does New York have?

Guilty party may not remarry during the life of the plaintiff unless the court granting the divorce gives permission after a lapse of three years and on proof of uniformly good conduct. Remarriage between divorced parties is permitted. Note: To get around this harsh provision against remarriage, parties frequently go out of the state to marry, such marriages being recognized as valid in New York.

North Carolina

1. Adultery
2. Impotency
3. Pregnancy of wife by another man at the time of the marriage without the knowledge of her husband
4. Separation for two years
5. Separation for five years or more without cohabitation by reason of incurable insanity of one person
6. Crime against nature

What are North Carolina's residence requirements?

Six months.

North Dakota

1. Adultery
2. Extreme cruelty
3. Willful desertion
4. Willful neglect
5. Habitual intemperance
6. Conviction of felony
7. Insanity for five years in which the insane person must have been confined in a state or government hospital for the insane for five years and be affected with incurable paranoia, paresis, dementia praecox, Huntington's chorea, or epileptic insanity

What are North Dakota's residence requirements?

One year, except in the case of insanity where the plaintiff must have been a resident for five years.

Ohio

1. That either party has a husband or wife living at the time of marriage
2. Desertion for one year

3. Adultery
4. Impotency
5. Extreme cruelty
6. Fraudulent contract
7. Any gross neglect of duty, usually nonsupport
8. Habitual drunkenness
9. Imprisonment in a penitentiary under sentence at the time of filing the petition
10. The procurement of an out-of-state divorce by which the party who procured it is released from the obligations of the marriage while the same remain binding on the other party

What are the residence requirements of Ohio before a divorce can be filed?

The plaintiff must be a resident of the state for one year, except in actions for alimony alone, and of the county 90 days preceding the filing of the petition.

Oklahoma

1. Abandonment for one year
2. Adultery
3. Impotency
4. Pregnancy of wife at time of marriage by another man other than husband
5. Incompatibility
6. Habitual drunkenness
7. Extreme cruelty
8. Fraudulent contract
9. Nonsupport
10. Imprisonment under sentence for felony at time divorce is filed
11. Procurement of final divorce decree outside of state which does not in Oklahoma release the other party from the obligations of marriage
12. Insanity for five years, after having been a patient of a mental institution for such period, in which case any two of three physicians, one being the superintendent of the institution, must agree that prognosis is poor

What are Oklahoma's residence requirements?

Six months residence required before petition can be filed. Petitioner must be a resident of county for thirty days.

What are Oklahoma's remarriage restrictions?

Remarriage while other party lives or cohabitation in Oklahoma with second spouse married outside the state, for six months after divorce decree and for thirty days after final judgment is bigamy, punishable by imprisonment.

Oregon

1. Impotency
2. Adultery
3. Conviction of a felony
4. Drunkenness contracted after marriage, which is continuous for one year
5. Desertion for one year
6. Cruelty, physical or mental
7. Permanent insanity where defendant is legally declared insane at least three years prior to suit and has been confined a major portion of the three years

What are Oregon's residence requirements?

One year.

What are Oregon's remarriage restrictions?

Neither party may remarry for six months after the divorce decree has been signed.

Pennsylvania

1. Incapability of procreation
2. Existing prior marriage
3. Adultery
4. Desertion for two years
5. Cruelty, physical or mental

125

6. Uncondoned force or coercion
7. Conviction of certain crimes in sentence of two years or more
8. Consanguinity or affinity

What are Pennsylvania's residence requirements?

Plaintiff must have been a resident within the state for at least one year prior to filing of suit; provided that if proceedings are begun in the county where defendant has been a bona fide resident for at least one year, residence of the plaintiff is not required.

What are Pennsylvania's remarriage restrictions?

Either party may remarry except that a defendant guilty of adultery may not marry the other party to the adultery during the lifetime of the plaintiff. Note: Such marriages when they take place do so outside the state after which the marriage is recognized as valid.

Puerto Rico

1. Adultery
2. Conviction of a felony which may invoke the loss of civil rights
3. Habitual drunkenness or the continued and excessive use of opium, morphine, or any other narcotic
4. Cruelty, physical or mental
5. Abandonment for over a year
6. Incurable impotency occurring after marriage
7. Attempt of the husband or wife to corrupt their sons or prostitute their daughters and connivance in such corruption or prostitution
8. Separation of the spouses for more than three years
9. Incurable insanity of either spouse for more than seven years

What are Puerto Rico's residence requirements?

Plaintiff must have lived in Puerto Rico for one full year preceding the action, unless ground for divorce occurred in Puerto Rico or while one of the spouses resided there.

What are Puerto Rico's remarriage restrictions?

Remarriage of divorced woman within 301 days after divorce is prohibited. No restriction on remarriage of divorced man. Spouse who remarries may be deprived by the court of parental rights as to the children.

Rhode Island

1. When the marriage was originally void or voidable by law
2. When either party is deemed to be or treated as if civilly dead
3. Impotency
4. Adultery
5. Extreme cruelty
6. Desertion for five years of either of the parties or for a shorter period in the discretion of the court
7. Drunkenness
8. Drug addiction
9. Nonsupport
10. Living separate and apart for ten years

What are Rhode Island's residence requirements?

Two years for both plaintiff and defendant.

South Carolina

1. Adultery
2. Desertion for one year
3. Physical cruelty
4. Habitual drunkenness or drug addiction

What are South Carolina's residence requirements?

Plaintiff must be resident for one year. Where plaintiff is non-resident and defendant has lived in state for one year immediately preceding action, divorce may be brought in county of defendant's residence.

South Dakota

1. Adultery
2. Extreme cruelty
3. Willful desertion for one year
4. Willful neglect for one year
5. Habitual intemperance for one year
6. Conviction of felony
7. Incurable chronic mania or dementia of either spouse having existed for five years or more, while under confinement

What are South Dakota's residence requirements?

Plaintiff must have resided one year in the state and three months in the county before he can file a divorce bill. However, where both parties live within state and plaintiff lived there from time of marriage until commencement of action, action may be begun at any time after plaintiff has resided in state for six months, three months of which he must have lived in the county where the bill is filed.

What are South Dakota's remarriage restrictions?

Where divorce is granted for adultery, guilty party may not re-marry any person except the innocent party, until the death of the other.

Note: If the guilty party marries outside the state and returns to South Dakota the marriage is usually recognized as valid.

Tennessee

1. Impotency
2. That either party has knowingly entered into a second marriage, a previous one still existing
3. Adultery
4. Willful or malicious desertion for one year, or absence for one year
5. Conviction of an infamous crime
6. Conviction of a felony and sentence to the penitentiary

7. Attempts on the life of the other, showing malice
8. Refusal by wife, without reasonable cause, to remove with husband to Tennessee and willfully absenting herself for two years
9. That woman was pregnant at time of marriage by another man without husband's knowledge
10. Habitual drunkenness contracted after marriage

What are Tennessee's residence requirements?

One year.

What are Tennessee's remarriage restrictions?

Defendant guilty of adultery may not marry person with whom act was committed during lifetime of former person.

Texas

1. Cruelty, physical or mental
2. Adultery
3. Voluntary separation for three years
4. When either party has been convicted after marriage of a felony and imprisoned in the state prison; provided that no suit for divorce may be sustained because of the conviction of either party for felony until one year after conviction; nor then if the Governor has pardoned the convict
5. Where the parties have lived separate and apart for seven years
6. Where either party has been adjudged insane and confined in an institution for five years prior to the filing of the divorce bill

What are Texas' residence requirements?

One year residence required in state and six months in the county in which the divorce is filed.

What are Texas' remarriage restrictions?

Neither party may remarry (except remarriage between parties) within twelve months after divorce for cruelty.

Utah

1. Impotency
2. Adultery
3. Willful desertion for more than one year
4. Nonsupport
5. Habitual drunkenness
6. Conviction of felony
7. Cruelty, physical or mental
8. Permanent insanity, legally adjudged
9. Separation for three years under decree of separate maintenance

What are Utah's residence requirements?

Plaintiff must have been an actual bona fide resident of state and county for three months before the institution of divorce proceedings.

Vermont

1. Adultery
2. Confinement at hard labor in the state prison for at least three years, if defendant is actually confined at the time the divorce bill is filed
3. Intolerable severity (cruelty)
4. Willful desertion for three consecutive years or absence of seven years without being heard of
5. Nonsupport
6. Insanity of either party with confinement in an institution for at least five years
7. Voluntary separation, without fault of plaintiff, for three consecutive years

What are Vermont's residence requirements?

Plaintiff must have lived in state for six months before commencement of proceedings, and one year before final action. Two years residence required before commencement of action for divorce on the ground of insanity.

What are Vermont's remarriage restrictions?

Party against whom divorce was decreed may not remarry (except former spouse) within two years after entry of decree, unless former spouse has died. Violation is punishable by fine or imprisonment or both. County court, however, may permit remarriage in shorter period.

Virginia

1. Adultery
2. Sodomy or buggery
3. Impotency
4. Sentence to a penitentiary
5. Conviction of an infamous crime before marriage, unknown to other party
6. Being fugitive from justice charged with felony and absent two years
7. Desertion for two years
8. Pregnancy of wife by another man at time of marriage unknown to husband
9. Prostitution of wife before marriage unknown to husband
10. Separation for three years

What are Virginia's residence requirements?

One of the parties must reside in and be a bona fide resident for at least one year prior to the filing of the suit.

What are Virginia's remarriage restrictions?

If ground for divorce was adultery, final decree may forbid guilty party to remarry; but for good cause, after six months, such part of decree may be revoked.

Virgin Islands

1. Impotency
2. Adultery
3. Conviction of felony
4. Desertion for one year
5. Cruelty, physical or mental
6. Insanity occurring after marriage
7. Habitual gross drunkenness contracted since marriage and continuing for one year prior to the filing of the divorce bill
8. Incompatibility

What are the residence requirements in the Virgin Islands?

Six weeks.

What are the Virgin Islands' remarriage restrictions?

Prohibited to either party until action heard and determined on appeal or until expiration of appeal time of 30 days.

Washington

1. Duress or force
2. Fraud
3. Want of legal age
4. Adultery, provided application for divorce is made within one year after it has come to the knowledge of the party applying for divorce
5. Impotency
6. Abandonment for one year
7. Nonsupport
8. Imprisonment if complaint is filed during the term of such imprisonment
9. Chronic mania or dementia existing at least two years prior to the filing of the complaint

What are Washington's residence requirements?

One year residence necessary.

West Virginia

1. Adultery
2. When either party has been sentenced to imprisonment for a felony, such sentence being final, and suit for divorce being started while such spouse is actually imprisoned or before both parties have actually cohabited
3. Cruelty, either physical or mental
4. Desertion for one year
5. Habitual drunkenness
6. Habitual addiction to drugs

What are West Virginia's residence requirements?

No period of residence required where ground for divorce is adultery. One year residence required in all other cases, if one of the parties was a bona fide resident when cause of action arose. Two years residence required after cause of action arose.

What are West Virginia's remarriage restrictions?

Neither party may remarry for sixty days from date of decree or pending an appeal. Guilty party may be forbidden to remarry for not more than one year.

Wisconsin

1. When either party after marriage has been sentenced and committed to imprisonment for three years or more
2. Desertion for one year
3. Adultery
4. Cruelty, physical or mental
5. Habitual drunkenness for one year
6. Where husband and wife have voluntarily lived separate and apart for five years
7. Nonsupport

What are Wisconsin's residence requirements?

Two years.

Wyoming

1. Adultery
2. Physical incompetency at time of marriage and continuing to divorce
3. Conviction of felony and sentence to imprisonment
4. Desertion for one year
5. Habitual drunkenness
6. Extreme cruelty, physical or mental
7. Nonsupport
8. Vagrancy of husband
9. Conviction of felony prior to marriage when facts were unknown to other party
10. Pregnancy of wife at time of marriage by another man unknown to husband
11. Incurable insanity and confinement in institution for at least two years before action is begun
12. Voluntary separation for two consecutive years

What are Wyoming's residence requirements?

Plaintiff must have lived in state 60 days immediately preceding time of filing petition, unless the marriage was solemnized in Wyoming and petitioner lived in the state until filing of divorce action. Where divorce is sought on the ground of insanity, plaintiff must have been a resident of state for one year.

Selected Foreign Divorce Laws

7

Canada

What are the grounds for divorce in Canada?

British Columbia, Alberta, Saskatchewan, Manitoba, New Brunswick, Nova Scotia, and Prince Edward Island have their own divorce laws. The rest of Canada's jurisdiction over divorce is assigned to the Canadian Parliament. In provinces other than those listed above, Parliament has authority to grant divorces for any reason it deems sufficient, but generally speaking the only ground recognized is adultery. There have been exceptional cases when other grounds such as impotency and malformation have been allowed as sufficient.

Alberta Province

1. Adultery
2. Sodomy
3. Rape of the wife
4. Bestiality

What are Alberta's residence requirements?

The only requirement is that the petitioner be domiciled in Alberta at the time the petition is filed, and that he or she resides there in good faith not merely for the purpose of obtaining a divorce.

British Columbia

1. Adultery

What are the remarriage restrictions in British Columbia?

Either party may remarry after the expiration of the 45 days allowed for an appeal.

Manitoba

1. Adultery

What are the residence requirements in Manitoba?

Domicile of the husband is necessary for either party to obtain a divorce. However, a married woman who has been deserted by and has been living separate and apart from her husband for two years or more may obtain a divorce in the province in which her husband was domiciled immediately prior to such desertion.

New Brunswick

1. Frigidity or impotency
2. Adultery
3. Consanguinity within prohibited degree
   Note: Although the above are the listed grounds for divorce, in practice only adultery is recognized as a ground for divorce. Frigidity, impotency and consanguinity are used to sever a marriage by way of annulment.

What are New Brunswick's residence requirements?

Essentially the same as those in Manitoba.

Nova Scotia

1. Adultery
2. Cruelty

What are Nova Scotia's residence requirements?

Residence of parties within the jurisdiction not required. The court has jurisdiction to decree a divorce only where the husband is domiciled in Nova Scotia, except that a deserted wife may sue in Nova Scotia if husband lived there immediately prior to desertion.

Prince Edward Island

1. Frigidity or impotency
2. Adultery
3. Consanguinity

What are the residence requirements on Prince Edward Island?

No specific residence required, except that the husband must be domiciled within the province at the time the divorce action is filed.

Bermuda

1. Adultery
2. Desertion for three years
3. Cruelty
4. Incurable unsoundness of mind with continuous treatment for three years immediately preceding divorce action
5. Husband guilty of rape or other unnatural offense

What are Bermuda's residence requirements?

The court may grant a divorce
(1) Where the husband is domiciled in Bermuda, or
(2) Being so domiciled, the husband has deserted his wife who has remained in Bermuda, or

(3) Being so domiciled husband has been deported and his wife has remained in Bermuda, or

(4) The husband's domicile is unknown or uncertain and the wife, prior to her marriage, was domiciled in Bermuda, or

(5) The wife petitioner has been a resident for three years preceding suit.

Costa Rica

1. Adultery of the wife
2. Scandalous concubinage of the husband
3. Attempt of either spouse against the life of the other
4. Attempt of the husband to prostitute the wife
5. Cruelty
6. At the request of either party when the spouses have been judicially separated for two years

What are Costa Rica's residence requirements?

No particular period of residence required. All the law requires is the showing that the plaintiff intends to establish a domicile in Costa Rica, even if, after the granting of the divorce, the plaintiff changes his mind.

Dominican Republic

1. Mutual consent
2. Incompatibility, but only after five years of marriage and provided there are no children
3. Formal declaration of absence of either party after four years
4. Adultery
5. Sentence for crime except for political offenses
6. Cruelty
7. Abandonment of the home for two years
8. Habitual drunkenness or narcotic addiction

What are the residence requirements of the Dominican Republic?

The residence requirements are similar to those of Costa Rica.

El Salvador

1. Pregnancy of wife in consequence of premarital illicit relations unknown to husband
2. Adultery of wife
3. Adultery of husband with public scandal or with abandonment of wife
4. Attempt of one spouse against the life of the other
5. Cruelty, physical or mental
6. Scandalous and habitual drunkenness
7. Abandonment for six months
8. Sentence for crime
9. Attempt of either spouse to corrupt the children, or complicity in their corruption
10. Separation of a year or more
11. Mutual consent

What are El Salvador's residence requirements?

These are similar to those of Costa Rica and the Dominican Republic, in that no special period of residence is required.

England

1. Adultery
2. Desertion for three years
3. Cruelty, physical or mental
4. Incurable unsoundness of mind where respondent has been continually under care and treatment for at least five years prior to the institution of divorce proceedings
5. Rape
6. Sodomy
7. Bestiality

What are England's residence requirements?

The only requisite is that the husband must have been domiciled in England at the time of the filing of the petition. No special period of residence is required.

France

1. Adultery
2. Violence
3. Gross insults
4. Cruelty
5. Conviction for infamous crime

> Note: France takes a liberal view as to what constitutes cruelty. It includes words or deeds or acts endangering life; humiliation and harshness and injuries which seriously reflect on the honor or name of the complaining party, including the refusal to resume or continue marital relations.

What are the residence requirements in France?

No specific period of residence is required. In the case of foreigners, however, both parties must appear before the court will act.

Japan

1. Mutual consent
2. Unchastity
3. Malicious desertion
4. Where the other spouse is not known to be either dead or alive for over three years
5. Incurable insanity
6. Any other grave reason for making difficult a continuation of the marriage

> Note: Japan has a liberal divorce law for its own citizens. As for foreigners resident in Japan, divorce is governed by the law of the husband's country at the time when the facts arose, but a divorce decree cannot be issued unless Japanese law also recognizes such grounds. No special period of residence is required.

Mexico

1. Birth of a child conceived by an act of the wife with another man before her marriage gives the husband the right to a

divorce, provided the child is judicially declared to be illegitimate

2. Adultery

3. Whenever one of the spouses becomes morally perverted (such perversion exists when the husband attempts to prostitute the wife, either directly or indirectly, by receiving remuneration of any kind for permitting another man to have illicit relations with her, or when the husband incites or by violence forces the wife to commit a crime, although not carnal, or an attempt of either spouse to corrupt the children, or the simple toleration of such corruption)

4. Any incapacity on the part of either spouse to fulfil the purpose of the marriage, or if either suffers from a loathsome or incurable disease, or is not mentally normal, if such disease is contagious or hereditary

5. Desertion for six months (if the husband leaves the home for more than one year and neglects to provide for his wife, the latter may divorce him)

6. Excessive cruelty, threats or grave injuries, or generally bad treatment of one spouse by another, if such treatment makes it impossible for the couple to live together

7. Any slander uttered by one against the other which, if true, would merit a punishment of more than two years in prison, or actual punishment for a crime, the penalty being more than two years in prison or exile, or habitual drunkenness, or any act against the person or property of another which would be a crime if committed by any party or parties in the same manner and punishable by imprisonment for no less than one year

8. Incompatibility of temperament

9. Mutual consent

Note: Adultery on the part of the wife is always a ground for divorce, but unless such act on the part of the husband is accompanied by one or more of the following circumstances, the husband cannot be divorced by the wife:

A. If the adultery is committed in the home

B. If there has been concubinage between the husband and the mistress, whether in the home of the married parties or not

C. If he publicly insults or mistreats his wife
D. If the legitimate wife has been mistreated by the guilty woman, in word or deed, or through the mistress, the wife has been mistreated in some way

What is the period of residence required in Mexico?

Since Mexico consists of a confederation of states similar to that of the United States, the laws of the various states making up the Mexican republic differ almost as widely as those in the various United States.

Which Mexican states have the most liberal divorce laws?

Sonora and Morelos.

Which are the leading cities in those states?

Cuernavaca, Morelos
Ciudad Obrégon, Sonora.

What are the residence requirements in Sonora and Morelos?

No residence requirements are necessary in either of these two Mexican states.

Under what circumstances does one obtain a Mexican divorce?

Such divorces are usually obtained when both parties agree on a divorce. The matter is most commonly handled by attorneys representing both parties in the United States who retain Mexican counsel to incorporate whatever property settlement and custodial questions are included in the divorce decree agreed upon by the American attorneys.

Is it necessary for both parties to appear in Mexico?

No. If the plaintiff appears in Mexico and the defendant is also represented by local Mexican counsel, Mexican requirements are complied with, and a divorce is usually granted within a matter of hours.

Are such divorces recognized in the United States?

Yes, under the principle of "comity of nations," which recognizes that a divorce valid in the country where it is procured is valid in other countries.

Is it necessary for the plaintiff to appear in a Mexican Court in order to obtain a divorce?

No. The usual practice is for the plaintiff, through his Mexican lawyer, to sign whatever legal papers are necessary.

How expensive is a Mexican divorce?

Mexican lawyers usually charge around $200 which includes court costs. In addition, the plaintiff will have to pay his American attorney, plus traveling expenses to Mexico and return.

How long does the plaintiff have to remain in Mexico?

The longer he stays the better. However, remaining in Mexico for 24 hours or more is usually sufficient to confer jurisdiction so that the subsequent divorce decree will be upheld in the United States.

8 *Explaining the Terms*

ADULTERY

What constitutes adultery so as to entitle the innocent party to a divorce?

Adultery is the act of sexual intercourse between a married person and a person other than his legal spouse.

Is a single act of adultery sufficient to maintain a divorce action?

Yes.

Does the plaintiff have to be caught in the act to maintain a divorce action?

No. Adultery may be proved by circumstantial evidence. Generally speaking all that is necessary is to prove that the defendant had both the disposition and the opportunity to commit adultery, so as to lead to an almost conclusive inference that sexual intercourse did take place.

Could an inference of adultery be drawn if the wife were caught petting with another man?

Mere petting by itself is insufficient to establish adultery.

A husband has sexual relations with a prostitute. Could the wife obtain a divorce on the ground of adultery?

Yes. It is the act of sexual intercourse that is important, not the fact that the woman had a previous reputation for unchastity.

A husband and wife agree to obtain a divorce. In furtherance of this plan, the husband agrees to be caught in adultery. Is such a divorce legal?

Not if the court hears about it. Both parties are guilty of a fraud on the court; should the facts later come out the divorce would be set aside. In New York state where adultery is the sole ground for an absolute divorce, decrees are often obtained by the husband and wife entering into a conspiracy, in which one of the parties agrees "to be caught" by either detectives or other third party.

A husband commits adultery. Confessing to his wife, the spouse forgives and continues to live with her husband, having sexual relations with him. Later, the wife changes her mind and seeks to obtain a divorce. Will she succeed?

No. In "condoning" or forgiving the adultery, the wife forfeits her right to a divorce on this ground.

Suppose that after the wife's forgiveness, the husband again commits adultery. May she then obtain a divorce?

Yes, since the forgiveness or condonation is merely conditioned on the husband's future good behavior.

A few years after marriage, the husband contracts a venereal disease. Would this be sufficient to justify a divorce on the ground of adultery?

No, not of itself. Venereal disease may be picked up innocently, without the husband having had intercourse with a woman. Where, however, the disease is transmitted through a woman and

145

her identity is discovered, a divorce may be had on the ground of adultery.

A wife sues her husband for divorce, charging adultery. The husband comes into court and admits the charge. Will the wife be successful?

No, not unless the wife produces a witness to corroborate her story. The husband's confession is insufficient.

Is a witness always necessary to prove adultery?

Yes. Some corroboration is always essential.

CRUELTY

What is physical cruelty so as to entitle the complainant to a divorce?

Physical cruelty is conduct that either actually or apparently endangers the physical safety or health of the other spouse to a degree making it physically impracticable for the endangered party to continue with the marriage.

Does the wife have to be actually assaulted for the act to be physical cruelty?

No. The mere threat to assault or beat the wife may be sufficient, provided there is some corroboration by a third party.

What evidence is required to establish physical cruelty?

Medical evidence, usually of treatments for the blows or lacerations, and/or photographs. Of course the testimony of a disinterested third party, undenied by the defendant, would carry considerable weight.

What is mental cruelty?

Any act which injures or threatens to injure the mental health of the complainant.

146

Is it mental cruelty for the husband to refuse medical attention to the wife?

Yes, in those states where mental cruelty is a ground for an absolute divorce.

A husband falsely accuses his wife of being an adulteress. Is this such cruelty as to entitle the wife to a divorce on the ground of mental cruelty?

Yes, provided she can back up her story by the corroboration of some witness.

A husband compels his wife to submit to an abortion. Shortly afterward, she files a divorce action against him. Will she succeed?

Yes, provided she can prove her case by the corroboration of some witness.

Is a relative a sufficient witness?

Yes, if the court believes in the witness's credibility. A mother, father, brother, sister, cousin, or any other relative of the complainant may testify on his or her behalf. The same applies to the defendant. After hearing all the evidence it is then up to the court to either grant the divorce decree, or reject the complainant's petition.

A woman has children by a former husband. The man is so eager to marry her that he agrees to let the woman bring her children into his home after the marriage. After the ceremony, the husband compels his wife to get rid of the children, informing her that if she doesn't he will leave. The wife refuses and the husband does leave. The wife sues for divorce. Will she succeed?

Yes, assuming she can prove her case. The wife may obtain a divorce either on the ground of mental cruelty in those states where mental cruelty is a ground for an absolute divorce, or on the ground of desertion.

147

A husband fails to talk to his wife, refuses to accompany her anywhere and, instead, spends his evenings with his friends. The wife files suit for divorce, charging mental cruelty. Will she succeed?

Yes, if she lives in a state where mental cruelty is a cause for divorce.

Without just cause, a husband persists in making constant insulting remarks about his wife's relatives. Is this sufficient to warrant a divorce on the ground of mental cruelty?

Yes, if that is a cause of divorce in her state.

A husband complained because his wife did not speak to him for days at a time. When she did speak it was only to abuse him for the meals he had prepared for the family. Would the husband be entitled to a divorce on the ground of mental cruelty?

Yes, in those states which allow an absolute divorce on this ground. In general, any conduct, by either spouse, which causes the other mental suffering, such as constant, abusive, and humiliating treatment of one spouse by another is mental cruelty.

Is it mental cruelty for the husband to handle the funds in a dictatorial manner, coupled with threats made to the wife?

No.

A wife refused to join her husband in a conveyance of real estate which resulted in a great financial loss to him. Does this constitute mental cruelty?

No.

A wife obtained all her husband's property by threatening to break off all sexual relations unless he turned over his property to her. After the husband conveyed his property, the wife drove her husband out of the house, where he was compelled to support himself. Could the husband get a divorce on the ground of mental cruelty?

Yes.

Shortly after the marriage, the husband offered money to his wife if she would return to her parents because her health became impaired. The husband complained that he didn't want nor could he afford to remain married to a "doctor's bill." Could the wife obtain a divorce on the ground of mental cruelty?

Yes, if that is a ground for an absolute divorce in her state.

A husband used coarse, offensive language to his wife, usually winding up the conversation with a stream of curses. Does this constitute mental cruelty?

Much depends on the degree of cultivation of the wife. What would amount to cruelty to a sensitive woman would not be cruelty to a brawling fishwife. If it were shown in the above example that the wife was unaccustomed to obscene, abusive language the chances are she could procure a divorce on the ground of mental cruelty, if that were a cause for divorce in her state.

A husband allowed his mother to interfere in his marriage, much to the anguish of his wife. In fact the mother-in-law constantly criticized the wife's housekeeping and rearing of the children. Is this mental cruelty?

Yes. In this case, the mental cruelty was performed indirectly, by the husband remaining passive when he should have defended his wife.

A husband inflicts unnecessarily severe physical punishment on one of his children with resulting impairment of health. Does this constitute mental cruelty?

Yes.

A husband refuses, without just cause, to allow the stepchildren to visit their mother in the home. Can the wife sue for divorce on the ground of mental cruelty?

Yes.

A husband or wife threatens to commit adultery. Would such a threat entitle the other spouse to sue for a divorce on the ground of mental cruelty?

Yes, in those states where mental cruelty is a ground for divorce.

While rummaging through the clothes closet, the wife discovers a number of love letters from other women, all addressed to her husband. The letters were written after the marriage. Would this be sufficient mental cruelty so as to entitle the wife to a divorce on the ground of mental cruelty?

Yes.

At a cocktail party the husband flirts outrageously with a number of women. Does this constitute mental cruelty?

No. Most courts view mere "flirting" with indulgence.

Is nagging by either husband or wife a basis for divorce on the ground of mental cruelty?

Yes.

Does it matter that the nagging was inspired by good motives?

Motives are irrelevant. It is the nagging itself that impairs mental health, not the purity of the motives.

A husband grew so fond of his dog that he had the animal sleep with him in his bed to which the wife violently objected. Is this mental cruelty so as to entitle the wife to an absolute divorce?

Yes, in those states where mental cruelty is a ground for divorce.

A husband insists that his wife perform certain "unnatural" sex practices to which his wife objects. Would the wife's refusal constitute mental cruelty so as to entitle the husband to a divorce?

Not if the wife is so revolted by the suggestion as to make further cohabitation impossible.

Much to the annoyance and disgust of his wife, the husband practices masturbation in her presence. Would the wife be entitled to a divorce on the ground of mental cruelty?

No.

Against the wife's objections, the husband insists on having sexual intercourse four times a week. Is this mental cruelty?

Only if such frequency impairs the wife's health or puts her in fear that such frequency will impair her health. To prove her case she would normally have to have a physician or psychiatrist testify on her behalf. Of course, the husband could rebut the testimony by equally competent witnesses that no impairment of health was involved.

A husband insists on having sexual relations with his wife while the latter is in the late stages of pregnancy. Is this mental cruelty?

Yes, if the obstetrician testifies that intercourse under such conditions would impair the health of the wife.

A husband insists on having sexual relations during his wife's menstrual period. Does this constitute mental cruelty?

Only if such an act were likely to impair the wife's mental health.

Is a single act of cruelty, either mental or physical, sufficient to entitle the other spouse to a divorce?

Not if the act were in a state which makes "extreme cruelty" a ground for divorce. In those states, there must be several or repeated acts of physical cruelty. In those states where "cruelty" alone is listed as a ground, one act of physical cruelty is usually sufficient.

How about mental cruelty? Is one act sufficient to introduce divorce proceedings successfully?

Usually, no. The courts generally insist that the mental cruelty be continuous and repeated.

What is meant by "extreme" cruelty?

Extreme cruelty is aggravated cruelty. It is a condition of extreme discomfort and wretchedness incapacitating or seriously endangering health. What constitutes "extreme" cruelty in one case may not be extreme cruelty or even cruelty in another case. In determining what constitutes cruelty, courts take into consideration the individual's culture, education, emotions, nervous reaction, and moral sense.

Is it cruelty entitling a spouse to a divorce where there are sharp political differences between husband and wife?

No.

Does the fact that a husband and wife are incompatible constitute cruelty?

No. To constitute cruelty the conduct of one of the parties must be such as to render cohabitation intolerable to the other.

Under what circumstances will a single act of cruelty entitle the aggrieved party to a divorce?

Actual physical violence inflicted by one spouse on the other would normally be sufficient to constitute cruelty.

As a result of brain surgery the husband's personality becomes altered and he treats his wife in a cruel and inhuman manner. Does

the husband's behavior entitle the wife to a divorce on the ground of cruelty?

No. The cruelty complained of must be willful and intentional. Since the husband's behavior was the result of brain surgery—assuming this could be corroborated by the surgeon—his "cruelty" would not be willful and intentional thus entitling the wife to a divorce.

A wife aids her children in their cruelty toward her husband. Would the husband be entitled to a divorce on this ground?

Yes.

May a wife obtain a divorce on the ground of cruelty if she can prove that her husband slapped her once or twice?

Not as a rule. The act must be of such violence as to place the wife in fear of her life.

A husband discovers that his wife has had a clandestine meeting with another man whereupon the husband becomes violent, insulting, and abusive. May the wife obtain a divorce because of the husband's cruelty?

Not if no blows were struck and the wife was not threatened with bodily harm.

Is it cruelty if the husband uses contraceptives to prevent his wife from becoming pregnant?

No.

Is it legal cruelty where a wife makes her husband's living with her unbearable by constant nagging, scolding, or fits of rage?

Yes, if they continue over a long period of time.

Is it cruelty entitling a husband to divorce where the wife refuses to attend to her household duties such as preparing dinner, or neglects the children?

Yes.

To prevent the wife from having children the husband compels her to submit to abortions. Does this constitute cruelty within the meaning of the law?

Yes.

Is it cruelty for the wife to refuse to enter into the social life desired by the husband?

No. Nor do disavowals of love, expressions of hate, and the like constitute mental cruelty.

A wife interferes with the husband's attempt to chastise their child. In the process the husband strikes the wife with his fist. Would the wife be entitled to a divorce on the ground of the husband's cruelty?

No. A husband may use force to protect himself from unreasonable interference by the wife in the proper chastisement of their child. On the other hand, if he mistreats the child solely to give the mother pain, and as a result her health becomes impaired, it is legal cruelty.

Does corporal punishment administered by a wife to her stepchild constitute cruelty to the husband, the father of the child?

Not unless the act is intended for the sole purpose of giving the father grief and to affect his health.

Is it cruelty entitling the husband to a divorce where the wife has him followed by detectives?

Not if she is induced to do so by the immoral conduct of her husband. It would be cruelty if her suspicions were without foundation.

154

Is it legal cruelty if the husband upbraids his wife for having crying spells?

No.

Can a wife obtain a divorce on the ground of cruelty if her husband threatens to leave her and go to another country?

No, the mere threat is insufficient.

Is it mental cruelty if a husband refuses to allow his wife to keep her brother's child?

No.

A wife falsely accuses her husband of adultery. Would this entitle the husband to a divorce on the ground of cruelty?

Yes. Even where such charges may not of themselves justify a divorce, they may have that effect if made in connection with offensive language or acts of violence or conduct creating a reasonable apprehension of violence.

Do false charges by a husband that his wife was unchaste before her marriage entitle her to a divorce on the ground of cruelty?

Yes.

Does the fact that a husband confesses to his wife that he has committed crimes against third persons entitle her to a divorce on the ground of cruel and inhuman treatment?

No.

Is it cruelty toward a husband for his wife to repeatedly leave his home for several days without excuse and consort with other men?

Yes.

Is it cruelty if the husband refuses or is unable to provide a home commensurate with the ideas of comfort and luxury entertained by the wife?

No.

Is it cruelty for the husband to insist that his wife account for all the money he has turned over to her?

No.

Does a wife's extravagance and dishonesty in money matters involving the husband in financial difficulties entitle him to a divorce?

No.

DESERTION

What is desertion?

Desertion, also known as abandonment, is the voluntary separation of one spouse from the other without the intention of returning. The desertion must be the deliberate act of the party complained against.

A husband is forced to leave his wife's home because of the nagging interference of his mother-in-law who lives with them. After waiting the time required by law in his particular state, the husband files a divorce action against the wife, alleging that he was forced to leave because of the behavior of his mother-in-law. Is he entitled to a divorce?

Probably. A husband has the right to determine whether or not he wants his in-laws to live with him. If he refuses to live with his in-laws, and his wife refuses to live with her husband because of this, the husband may secure a divorce against the wife on the ground that she forced him to leave her.

For business reasons, a husband wishes to move from one state to another. The wife refuses because her elderly parents are dependent on her. Would the husband be entitled to a divorce on the ground of desertion?

Yes, in those states where desertion is a ground for divorce. Generally speaking, it is the husband who has the right to establish the residence. The wife's refusal to follow her husband into another state constitutes desertion on her part, unless the refusal is justified by the fact that the wife's health or that of the children would be seriously affected or impaired.

A husband and wife agree to separate by mutual consent. Later, the wife in good faith, seeks a reconciliation, but the husband refuses to return. May the wife obtain a divorce on the ground of desertion?

Yes. In seeking to return in good faith, the wife offers to resume the marriage. The husband's refusal to return makes him the deserting spouse, entitling the wife to a divorce.

Without just cause a wife leaves her husband. Regretting her action shortly thereafter, the wife offers in good faith to return to her husband. The husband now refuses to accept her and files for a divorce. Will he succeed?

No. The husband is now guilty of "constructive desertion" because of his refusal to accept his wife's offer made in good faith. Constructive desertion exists when one spouse is compelled, by the wrongful conduct of the other spouse, to leave the matrimonial domicile. The party guilty of constructive desertion is the spouse forcing the other party to leave the home. The general rule is that the person at fault in the original separation, who desires to resume the marriage, must make a good-faith, unconditional offer to return. When such an offer is made and refused, the fault of desertion is thrown on the refusing spouse.

Is a wife legally justified in refusing to follow her husband to a foreign country?

No, she is not, unless she can prove that going to such a foreign country will seriously impair her health. Evidence from a competent physician is usually required to support such an allegation.

A husband deserts his wife. After six months the husband visits the wife at her apartment and persuades her to have sexual relations with him. The state law requires that the parties be separate and apart for 18 months in order to lay a foundation for an absolute divorce. Under these facts would the wife still be able to obtain a divorce on the ground of desertion?

Not in most states. If the husband could prove that he had sexual intercourse with his wife, the desertion period would have to start afresh, wiping out the six months the couple lived separate and apart. In short, the separation has to be a continuous one without sex relations between the couple.

What are Enoch Arden laws?

Such laws provide that where one spouse has been absent and unheard of for a certain period of time (usually seven years) and an unsuccessful attempt has been made to locate him, the marriage will be judicially declared to be at an end.

A husband is absent from his home for more than seven years and is unheard of by the wife who has made a genuine effort to locate him. The wife remarries and has children by her second husband. Five years after her second marriage her first husband shows up and insists on resuming the marriage. What are the first husband's rights?

The first spouse is still legally the husband of the wife. Had the wife retained counsel after the seven-year period and had the husband judicially declared dead by a court, she could have remarried whomever she pleased. The fact that she didn't, plus the fact that there was no judicial determination of the matter would make the second marriage invalid. The proper remedy for the wife, actually, would have been to have filed for a divorce on the ground of desertion after the statutory period for desertion had elapsed; in most states the period varies from 18 months to 5 years.

Is it necessary for the husband to have the wife's approval in changing or establishing the matrimonial domicile?

No.

A wife establishes a new home in which the husband lives with her. Later he leaves without requesting his wife to accompany him. Who has deserted whom?

The husband has deserted the wife. Had he requested the wife to accompany him and had the wife refused, she would have been guilty of desertion instead of the husband.

What is meant by "constructive desertion"?

Constructive desertion takes place when the spouse by his or her misconduct brings the cohabitation to an end, regardless of which spouse left the home.

A wife refuses to remove from her home to that owned by her husband. Her defense is that she would have to live apart from her adult children by a former husband. Is the wife guilty of desertion?

Yes. The law recognizes that the husband, as the wage earner, has the right to establish or change the domicile, and that he has the right to refuse to have outsiders live with him in his home.

Is it desertion for a husband to fail or refuse to provide a domicile at any place other than his parents' home?

Yes. A wife has a right to an independent home even if it be one small room.

A husband maintains his parents in his home, even though the parents are distasteful to the wife. He is financially unable to provide

159

and maintain a separate residence for his parents. The wife leaves. Is she guilty of desertion?

Yes. Had the husband been financially able to maintain the parents in a separate residence, and refused to do so, the law would consider him the deserter rather than the wife.

Is the refusal to have sexual relations for the statutory period a ground for desertion?

Yes, especially if such refusal is coupled with a substantial abandonment of other matrimonial duties, such as neglect of children, failure to provide a tidy home, or to prepare and serve food.

Can one spouse be guilty of desertion even if the couple reside in the same house or apartment?

Yes. It is the fact that the couple do not live as man and wife and do not have sexual relations that is important, not that they occupy separate rooms or twin beds within the same room.

Does separation by mutual consent constitute desertion entitling either party to a divorce?

No. To constitute desertion there must have been a willful abandonment without any intent to return. However, separation by mutual consent is in itself a cause for divorce. (*See* Chapter 6.)

Is a deserting wife or husband under any duty to seek a reconciliation?

Yes, and the offer to reconcile must be made in good faith, if the complainant has been guilty of misconduct.

A wife wrongfully deserts her husband. As a condition for her return the wife demands that they be married by a priest of the Catholic Church, a condition which the husband rejects. Who is the deserting party?

The wife, by imposing conditions she has no right to impose.

Under what circumstances is desertion legally terminated?

Desertion is ended by a sufficient and timely offer of a reconciliation. If before the required statutory period has elapsed, a spouse otherwise guilty of desertion makes a sufficient and timely offer in good faith to resume the marriage, the continuity of the period of desertion is interrupted and there can be no divorce.

Is a request on the part of the deserting spouse to talk matters over with the innocent spouse an offer of reconciliation?

No. The offer of reconciliation must be made in good faith, and not merely to lay a foundation for or to defeat an action for divorce.

Acting under the advice of her counsel, a deserting wife offers to return to her husband, an offer which is rejected. Is the wife still chargeable with desertion?

Yes. The offer of reconciliation must be made freely and sincerely and not as a legal trap. An offer of reconciliation, furthermore, must be free from improper conditions or qualifications. In addition, the guilty spouse must reform his or her habits and must be supported by reasonable assurances that the offer can be accepted with due regard to health, safety, and comfort. The offer must also be conciliatory, and backed by a willingness to furnish a suitable home. Finally, the person to whom the offer is made must be given a reasonable opportunity to consider the offer.

NONSUPPORT

What constitutes nonsupport?

Nonsupport is the failure of the husband to provide the wife and children with financial support consistent with his means. In twenty-seven states the husband's willful failure to support his family is a ground for an absolute divorce. It may also give rise to a divorce action based on desertion.

Are wives ever liable for the support of their husbands?

Yes, in a few states. A few courts now recognize that a wife may have a reciprocal obligation to support her husband, especially where the husband is ill, incapable of working, impoverished, or otherwise incapacitated, and where the wife has substantial means or earnings of her own.

Can a wife procure a divorce on the ground of nonsupport if the husband is unemployed through no fault of his own?

No. The nonsupport by the husband must be willful.

A husband earns $100 a week as a salesman. The wife believes the husband could earn more money as an automobile mechanic in which he has had a great deal of experience. Does the refusal of the husband to seek more profitable employment entitle the wife to a divorce on the ground of nonsupport?

No.

A wife works in order to help support the family. If she were to quit the husband would have difficulty meeting his bills. The wife does quit her job. Is she entitled to a divorce on the ground of nonsupport?

No, since the wife knew or should have known the economic circumstances of her husband at the time she married him. The husband's obligation is to do the best he can. He cannot be forced to switch jobs under pressure from his wife.

A wealthy widow and a man who earns only a fair salary agree to marry. Becoming dissatisfied, the wife now sues for divorce on the ground of nonsupport charging that her husband doesn't earn enough money to support her in her accustomed style. Will she succeed?

Probably not. Here the court would take into account the sharp discrepancy between the husband's and wife's income, and the fact that the wife knew at the time of the marriage that the husband could not possibly support her in the style to which she had become accustomed, and that to compel him to do so would be unreasonable.

A husband who earns $50,000 a year, tells his wife he makes only $15,000 annually and the couple live accordingly. The husband refuses to allow the wife to buy an automobile, a fur coat, or to have a servant to take care of three small children. May the wife obtain a divorce on the ground of nonsupport?

Yes, if she could prove that the husband willfully withheld a large proportion of his income from her. However, the husband could rebut the charge by pointing out that he was using the withheld money to invest for the future. The evidence, however, would have to be persuasive on his part that he was not supporting his family in a manner consistent with his means.

A woman married a millionaire. The husband supplied her with a beautiful home, servants, a car, and unlimited charge accounts. The only thing he failed to give her was cash. Would such failure entitle the wife to a divorce on the ground of nonsupport?

No, not as long as the husband maintained a relatively high standard of living. The fact that he did not give her a weekly allowance has been held immaterial.

Can the wife insist that the husband provide her with a weekly allowance, if he only earns a fair salary?

No. A wife cannot insist that a husband give her such an allowance as long as the husband provides her with the necessaries of life, such as food, clothing, shelter, and medical and dental care.

A husband is unable to support his wife because of his heavy gambling. Would this entitle the wife to a divorce on the ground of nonsupport?

Only if the wife can prove to the satisfaction of the court that she and her children have been deprived of the necessities of life.

163

HABITUAL DRUNKENNESS

What is habitual drunkenness, alcoholism, or habitual intemperance so as to entitle one to a divorce?

Constant indulgence in stimulants such as wine, brandy, beer, and whiskey, whereby intoxication is produced. The intoxication must be more than ordinary and the use more than occasional. It must be habitual and the habit must be actual and confirmed.

A woman marries an alcoholic with the hope of reforming him. After a few years of marriage the wife learns that the husband is still an alcoholic. Can she obtain a divorce on the ground of her husband's habitual drunkenness?

No. The fact that the wife knew of her husband's alcoholism prior to the marriage would bar her from obtaining a divorce on this ground.

Suppose the wife married the man on his express promise to reform. Would this alter the situation?

No.

Suppose the wife was unaware that her husband was an alcoholic before marriage? Would this affect the situation?

Yes, it would. The wife would then be entitled to a divorce. She might also be entitled to an annulment if she took prompt action after discovering that her husband was a habitual drunkard.

An alcoholic husband defends a divorce action on the ground that his wife also drinks. Is this a valid defense?

No. The fact that the wife drinks occasionally does not make her a habitual drunkard and would not prevent her from obtaining a divorce on this ground in those states where it is a legal cause for divorce.

164

A husband is admittedly an alcoholic but the wife makes no attempt to either reform or "cure" him. Must she attempt to reform him before she can obtain a divorce on this ground?

No. The mere fact that the husband is an alcoholic is sufficient. The fact that the wife did or did not attempt to reform her husband is irrelevant and immaterial.

DRUG ADDICTION

What constitutes drug addiction as a ground for divorce?

Habitual and excessive addiction to narcotics.

A wife is a drug addict and the husband files a bill for divorce. However, by the time the case is heard in court the wife produces medical testimony that she has been cured of the habit. Is the husband still entitled to the divorce?

No. To obtain the divorce the spouse must have been addicted up to and including the time the divorce is heard.

GROSS NEGLECT OF DUTY

What constitutes "gross neglect of duty" as a ground for divorce?

"Gross neglect of duty" is such glaring, shameful, or monstrous neglect of marital duties as to be legally inexcusable.

During her pregnancy and even at the birth of the child the husband roundly abused his wife. In addition, he had failed to provide any sort of social life. Would this constitute such gross neglect as to entitle the wife to a divorce?

Yes. Gross neglect may consist of a single grave offense. Simple neglect, however, is insufficient. There must not only be a failure

165

to perform a marital duty but the act complained of must be attended by circumstances of indignities or aggravation.

Because his wife is a hypochondriac, the husband refuses to call in a physician when she complains of some imaginary illness. Is the husband guilty of gross neglect?

No.

Can a husband obtain a divorce on this ground if the wife so neglects the children as to cause a scandal in the neighborhood?

Yes, here the indignities would not only reflect on the children, but on the father as well.

A wife refuses to cook for her husband, insisting that the couple go out each evening for dinner. Would this constitute gross neglect?

Probably, if such conduct persisted over a period of months or years.

A husband, able to do so, fails to provide his wife with the necessaries of life. Would this be gross neglect?

Yes, if such conduct persisted over a period of time.

PERSONAL INDIGNITIES

What is meant by "personal indignities" in those states which allow this as a ground for divorce?

Personal indignities usually consist of a course of conduct calculated to make the life of the complaining party intolerable. They consist of acts of rudeness, vulgarity, unmerited reproach, haughtiness, studied neglect, humiliating insults, intentional incivility, obvious disdain, abusive language, malignant ridicule, and every other sign of settled hate and estrangement.

How do personal indignities differ from acts of mental cruelty?

In mental cruelty the act complained of is dangerous to the health or life of the spouse. In personal indignities all that is necessary is to prove that the acts of one spouse make the other's life unbearable.

A husband repeatedly insists, over his wife's objections, that the latter perform all sorts of unconventional sex practices, frequently labeled perversions. Could the wife obtain a divorce on the ground of "personal indignities"?

Yes.

Is a single act of personal indignity sufficient to obtain a divorce on this ground?

No. Neither are trivial acts of misconduct.

Is it essential that there be physical violence or conduct creating fear of bodily harm or death?

No.

Is it necessary that the personal indignities force the other spouse out of the house?

No. However, the fact that the complaining spouse remains in the home is usually taken into consideration in determining the degree of severity of the alleged indignities.

Do false charges of infidelity or crime constitute personal indignities?

Yes. However, the charge must not only be false but must have been made with the intent to wound or hurt.

167

May drunkenness and the use of drugs constitute indignities?

Yes. But here again a single act of drunkenness is not an indignity to the person of the other. On the other hand, excessive drinking by one spouse, together with other acts of misconduct making the life of the other spouse intolerable, does furnish ground for divorce in those states where personal indignities are a cause for divorce.

Does lewd conduct or the communication of a loathsome disease constitute personal indignities?

Yes. A spouse who consorts openly and notoriously with disreputable members of the other sex may be held guilty of this offense.

Does compelling a wife to submit to excessive sexual relations constitute an indignity?

Yes. However, the mere refusal of a spouse to engage in sexual relations is generally not an indignity. If, however, the refusal lasts for the statutory period of desertion in the particular state such refusal may give rise to a divorce on the ground of desertion.

Does unkindness of a husband to the wife's children by a former marriage constitute indignities?

No.

Does the use of profane and vulgar language applied by a husband to his wife constitute a personal indignity?

Yes.

Both in private and in public, the wife constantly degrades and humiliates her husband by belittling practically everything he says. Would such behavior on the part of the wife entitle the husband to a divorce?

Yes, in those states where "personal indignities" is a ground for divorce. To obtain a divorce the husband would have to prove that the abuse heaped upon him was not an isolated act, but a constant course of conduct.

IMPOTENCY

What is meant by impotency?

Impotency in the male is the inability to achieve an erection for normal sexual intercourse with the wife. The impotency must have existed at the time of the marriage. The female equivalent of impotency is frigidity. Legally, impotency exists when either the husband or wife is unable to have "ordinary and normal" sexual relations with the other.

What is meant by "ordinary and normal" intercourse?

The insertion of the male penis into the female vagina, with a view toward having an orgasm.

Are fellatio and cunnilingus legally considered "ordinary and normal" intercourse?

No. Both these forms of sexual deviation derive pleasure from the application of the mouth to the sexual organs. When the wife does it to the husband it is known as fellatio. When the husband does it to the wife it is called cunnilingus.

A wife refuses to indulge her husband in an occasional fellatio. Can the wife obtain a divorce on the ground that her husband is impotent?

No. To obtain a divorce because of impotence it must be established that the husband—or wife for that matter—is unable to have normal intercourse, and that such inability existed at the time of the marriage. The question of impotency or frigidity is often a medical or psychiatric one. The husband's insistence on having

169

fellatio or the wife's insistence on having cunnilingus may also entitle either one to a divorce on the ground of cruelty.

The only way a husband can achieve an erection is to have his wife beat him with a strap. Is the husband's masochism a sufficient cause for divorce?

Probably. If it can be shown that the husband's masochism is the only way he can have an erection after which he inserts the penis into his wife's vagina (a practice which the wife finds repugnant) relief would probably be granted the wife by way of divorce either on the ground of the husband's impotence or because the repeated sexual deviation was a threat to the wife's mental health and so constituted mental cruelty.

After some brain surgery, the husband finds for the first time that he is impotent. After three months of such impotence the wife files for divorce. Will she succeed?

Not unless she can prove by competent medical testimony that the husband's impotency is permanent and incurable.

A husband finds that after marriage his wife is cold and unresponsive sexually, refusing to allow him ingress into her vagina. Does this constitute frigidity so as to entitle the husband to a divorce?

Yes, if it is determined that the frigidity is permanent and incurable.

A wife only allows her husband to have sexual intercourse with her once every month instead of once a week, as the husband wishes. Does this constitute frigidity so as to entitle the husband to a divorce?

No. The law has nothing to say about the frequency of sexual relations between the parties.

170

A husband and wife have not engaged in sexual relations with each other for more than 18 months, though they had had intercourse regularly prior to that time. Would either party be entitled to a divorce on the ground of impotency?

Not unless it could be shown that the husband or wife was actually impotent or frigid, and that such impotency or frigidity was permanent and incurable. However, the unjustified refusal to have sexual intercourse for the statutory period may give rise to a divorce on the ground of desertion.

Three years after a wife discovers that her husband is permanently or incurably impotent, she institutes divorce proceedings. Will she succeed?

No. To obtain relief, the divorce must be filed promptly after the impotency or frigidity is discovered.

While on the honeymoon, the wife discovers that she has a gross distaste for performing the sexual act, and that the act itself causes her a great deal of pain. Finding that the sex act is repulsive to his wife and that she refuses medical treatment, the husband sues for a divorce on the ground that his wife is frigid. Will he succeed?

Yes, if the husband can prove that performing the sexual act on the part of the wife is incurably abhorrent and painful. Alternatively, the husband could probably secure an annulment.

A few months after marriage the husband becomes impotent. Does this entitle the wife to a divorce?

No. The impotency must have existed at the time of the marriage.

Is premature ejaculation on the part of the husband a form of impotency?

Yes. Premature ejaculation is ejaculation that occurs too soon for satisfactory expression of the mutual love of husband and wife. Premature ejaculation often occurs prior to entrance into the vagina. If it does it may be considered a legal form of impotency. If the premature ejaculation occurs within a few seconds after entrance into the vagina it probably would not be considered such impotency as to entitle the wife to a divorce.

Can impotency be cured?

Yes, in many cases.

What is the treatment for impotency or frigidity?

Medical authorities agree that each case of impotency or frigidity is different and must be treated on an individual basis. Impotency is due to either physical or mental causes. Organically, impotency is associated with various physical deficiencies such an anemia, fatigue, exhaustion, and hypothyroidism. The cure lies in correcting the physical condition causing the impotency. In some cases physicians recommend sedation, including bromides, barbiturates, and alcohol, but never barbiturates and alcohol together. Impotency, however, is primarily psychological in character, being rooted in fear. The husband may unconsciously fear castration on the part of the wife. He may not wish to make his wife pregnant. He may not be able to have an erection because of a profound and unconscious distaste for women in general, and for his wife in particular. Accompanying the fears are usually residual feelings of guilt. Where the impotency is due to psychological or emotional reasons the patient should be treated by a competent psychiatrist, but only after physical causes have been excluded or treated.

INCOMPATIBILITY

What is incompatibility?

In those states where incompatibility is a ground for divorce a decree will be granted where it is conclusively shown that the married couple is incapable of existing together in peace and harmony. The incompatibility may be sexual, intellectual, financial, religious, or temperamental.

9 *The Easy Divorce States*

Which are the so-called easy divorce states?

Arkansas, Idaho, and Nevada.

Why are they known as liberal divorce states?

Because they require little actual residence (Arkansas, 60 days, Idaho and Nevada, 6 weeks) and because those states liberally interpret the grounds of divorce so that dissolving a marriage becomes a relatively painless affair.

Are divorces obtained in those states recognized as binding in other states?

For the most part yes, especially if the divorce is uncontested and both parties are represented by legal counsel.

What does the plaintiff have to testify to in a Nevada divorce case?

The plaintiff's testimony is brief, simple, and direct. The testimony takes no more than ten or fifteen minutes, after which the judge hearing the case signs the divorce decree. The plaintiff may remarry minutes afterward, if he so desires. Here is a typical transcript of the plaintiff's testimony:

173

Q. What is your name?

A. Jane Doe.

Q. What is your address?

A. 2000 Fremont Street, Las Vegas, Nevada.

Q. On what date did you come to Nevada to make it your home?

A. September 1, 1962.

Q. Have you been physically present in Nevada every day from that date up to the present time?

A. Yes.

Q. Do you intend to remain in Nevada permanently—or at least for an indefinite period of time?

A. Yes.

Q. Is everything in your complaint for divorce true?

A. Yes.

Q. Why do you want a divorce? How was your husband cruel to you?

A. He was cold and indifferent, showed me no love or affection.

Q. Was any of your husband's conduct your fault?

A. No.

Q. How did this conduct affect your health?

A. It made me nervous and upset.

Q. Do you believe your health would be further harmed if you were to return to your husband?

A. Yes.

Q. Is there, in your opinion, any possibility of a reconciliation between you and your husband?

A. No.

What other witnesses will have to testify?

Only one, the landlord or landlady housing the client, as to residence.

What questions are asked of the residence witness?

Q. What is your home address?

A. 2000 Fremont Street, Las Vegas, Nevada.

Q. How long have you lived in Nevada?
A. Two years.
Q. Are you acquainted with Jane Doe, the plaintiff in this action?
A. Yes.
Q. Have you seen Jane Doe in Nevada each and every day from September 1, 1962, up to and including the present date?
A. Yes.

Can the plaintiff remarry immediately after a divorce in Nevada or Arkansas?

Yes.

What is the procedure in a Nevada divorce where the defendant does not file an answer?

If defendant does not file an answer to a divorce bill it takes approximately 10 weeks before obtaining a decree. Plaintiff, as in consent cases, must establish 6 weeks residence, after which summons and bill are served personally on defendant. Twenty-two days after such service, divorce can be obtained immediately, provided defendant has not filed an answer or moved against complaint, in conformity with Nevada law. Where the plaintiff is a woman, default can almost invariably be counted upon. If defendant contests the Nevada proceeding, he is subject to an order for counsel fees and alimony pending the outcome of the litigation.

How long does it take to obtain a Nevada divorce if the whereabouts of the defendant is unknown?

101 days.

What is the prospect for employment in Reno or Las Vegas pending the six-weeks residence?

Clients who desire to work while in Las Vegas can usually count on securing a job. There is usually a demand for waitresses, bus boys, cashiers, etc., and other work in the hotels and casinos.

A husband remarries on the strength of a Reno divorce to which his wife consented through representation by legal counsel. Later, the husband dies, the second wife claiming a share of the estate. A child of the first marriage attacks the validity of the Nevada decree in order that he may claim a share of the property. Who will win?

The second wife. In an identical case decided by the United States Supreme Court, it was held that the Nevada divorce was valid since both husband and wife, through respective counsel, had submitted to the jurisdiction of the Nevada court. The child of the first marriage was therefore barred from receiving his share of the property, the bulk of the estate going to the second wife.

How are questions of alimony, custody of children, etc., determined in such liberal divorce states?

Usually by agreement of counsel for both husband and wife who draw up what are known as "stipulations" which are incorporated in the divorce decree.

Are such out-of-state divorces expensive?

Much depends on the standard of living of the party coming to Nevada, Idaho, or Arkansas for a divorce. The average estimate for a Reno divorce, including the six-weeks stay, runs to about $1500.

What legal fees will have to be paid?

There is first of all the legal fee to be paid to the attorney in the home state. This fee may vary from $250 to $10,000 or more, depending on the wealth of the clients and the complexity of the case. Then there is the fee to be paid to the attorney handling the out-of-state case, whether it be Nevada, Idaho, or Arkansas. The usual practice is for the local attorney to charge one fee which will include the out-of-state attorney's fee. The client should get a definite statement from his local counsel, preferably in writing, as to exactly what the fee will be and what it will include.

What does it cost to stay in Reno or Las Vegas for the necessary six-week period?

According to the Chamber of Commerce of Reno, a minimum of $132 will pay for board and lodging to establish the necessary residence. This is at the bare subsistence level and does not include recreation, transportation, or legal fees. For $50 to $55 a week fairly decent board and lodgings can be had. Apartments on a still higher level, often with linens, dishes, etc., can be had for $75 to $150 a month. Many prospective divorcees stay at dude ranches where the rate runs to about $100 a week. The rates in Idaho and Arkansas are somewhat lower.

Are both parties to a divorce represented by local counsel?

Yes. Both husband and wife, through their respective local attorneys, appoint attorneys in either of the three states who file and sign the necessary papers and take whatever testimony is necessary.

Is it necessary for the plaintiff or complaining party to actually testify in court?

Yes. But the testimony is very brief, rarely taking more than ten or fifteen minutes.

Are any witnesses necessary?

Only one who testifies that the complainant has been a resident of the state for the required period, either 6 weeks as in Nevada or 2 months as in Arkansas or Idaho.

Who arranges for the witness?

The attorney for the complainant who makes the arrangements for the complainant's lodging before arrival. The proprietor of the boarding house, motel, or dude ranch testifies that the complainant has resided therein for the required length of time.

177

How long does it take before the decree is actually signed?

The decree is usually signed a few minutes after testimony is taken.

Aside from the difference in residence, is there any advantage in obtaining a divorce in one of the liberal states rather than in another?

No. The client saves two weeks by going to Las Vegas or Reno, but because of the gambling attraction in both these towns a stay in either of them is likely to be more expensive than a comparable stay in Arkansas or Idaho.

On what ground are divorces usually obtained in the three "easy divorce" states?

Mental cruelty which the courts of those states interpret rather liberally.

What about Alabama? Isn't that an easy divorce state?

It was, but it isn't any longer. To obtain a divorce in Alabama it is necessary for the plaintiff or complainant to be a resident for one year.

A husband goes to Las Vegas to obtain a divorce, against the wishes of his wife. The husband obtains the decree. What can the wife do about it?

She can, through her attorney, contest the divorce in her own state on the ground that the husband's domicile in Nevada was fictitious and that he went to Las Vegas for the sole purpose of obtaining a divorce.

Does this mean that the Nevada decree will be set aside?

Not necessarily. The husband may have had actual legal grounds for the divorce which the wife's state would recognize in any event. Moreover, unless the public policy of the home state is offended, it will generally give "full faith and credit" to the divorce decrees of sister states. The home state is more likely to upset a contested Nevada divorce if the fraud was flagrant. If, for example, a husband in New York who has committed adultery goes to Nevada and obtains a divorce from an objecting spouse on the ground of "mental cruelty" there is a strong likelihood that New York would not recognize the out-of-state divorce but, on proper application by the wife, would grant her the divorce on the ground of adultery.

10 *Proving the Case*

A husband in Maryland files suit for divorce on the ground that his wife deserted him more than 18 months ago, taking the children with her. The wife now resides in Kentucky with her parents. Can the husband obtain a divorce?

Yes, provided he has the necessary corroborating witness to prove his case. Where the defendant resides inside the complainant's state, process is had by personal service, that is, the sheriff hands the defendant the divorce papers and/or summons. Personal service usually means just that, although a few states specify that it shall include leaving a copy of the summons, or summons and bill of complaint at the defendant's residence in his absence, or mailing him copies of the papers. Where the defendant resides out of the state "constructive" service is had by an order of publication, published in the local paper for a specified number of weeks. Constructive service by means of publication is also applicable when the defendant is absent from the state or cannot, after a diligent search, be located in the state.

Is an Order of Publication expensive?

The costs vary from state to state, but are usually less than $50.

Suppose the husband or wife does not know where the other spouse resides. Would this prevent one of the parties from obtaining a divorce?

No. Where the defendant's present address is unknown, the law requires that the complainant make a diligent search for the whereabouts of the defendant, so as to obtain either his or her present address or last known address.

What constitutes a diligent search?

The same amount of zeal that the plaintiff would exercise if the defendant owed him a large sum of money. Merely saying that the complainant tried to locate the defendant is insufficient. He must show to the satisfaction of the court that diligent efforts were made to locate the defendant. He may do this by making inquiries of the defendant's friends and relatives, or by producing copies of letters sent to the defendant's last known address. The attorney must be satisfied that a real effort has been made in order to satisfy the court that no unfair advantage has been taken of the defendant. Unless such diligence has been shown, a divorce decree will not be granted. The purpose, of course, is to notify the defendant of the divorce suit and so provide him or her with an opportunity to defend it.

In a divorce suit on the ground of adultery is it necessary to name the corespondent in the bill of complaint?

No. All that is necessary at the outset is to allege that the defendant committed adultery with a person or persons whose name or names will be mentioned at the hearing when testimony is taken. Of course, when testimony is taken the complainant will have to give a detailed account of the defendant's alleged adulterous behavior.

What proof must the complainant furnish at the divorce hearing?

He must prove each of the allegations contained in the bill of complainant or divorce bill. If the complainant alleges adultery he must prove adultery. If he alleges cruelty he must prove cruelty. If he alleges desertion he must prove desertion. He must also prove residence for the specified period.

What degree of proof is required?

In a contested divorce case there must be "a clear preponderance of evidence." In an uncontested case the evidence must be clear and convincing. Both adultery and cruelty may be established not only by direct evidence but also by indirect or circumstantial evidence, or by circumstantial evidence alone.

What evidence is necessary to prove adultery?

Both the opportunity and the disposition of the defendant to commit the act are in combination the indispensable ingredients in proving adultery by circumstantial evidence.

In an action for divorce on the ground of adultery, the wife introduces love letters from the husband's girl friend. Is this sufficient to obtain a divorce?

No, not if the letters omitted reference to a tryst or affair, or otherwise indicated that the woman was actually the paramour of the husband.

A suspicious wife hires a private investigator who discovers and reports to the wife that the husband has had lunch with a certain woman on at least three occasions. Would this be sufficient evidence for the wife to obtain a divorce?

Not by itself. The luncheons could have been innocent. Unless they were tied in with much more relevant facts the divorce bill would be dismissed.

A wife is seen in her nightgown at the door of a hotel room talking with a man not her husband. The man, apparently, was just leaving

her. At the hearing it was proved that the woman had been previously seen in the company of this man and that they had corresponded. Is this sufficient evidence on which the husband could obtain a divorce?

Yes. Here the circumstances add up to the reasonable suspicion that the wife had both the opportunity and disposition to commit adultery.

At a divorce hearing it was established that a wife allowed undue familiarity to be taken by a man not her husband and that she had long private interviews with him at night from which she came with her hair disarranged. It was also proved that the wife had expressed great admiration for the man and intense hatred for the husband. Is this sufficient evidence of adultery?

Yes. This is the kind of circumstantial evidence that would warrant the reasonable inference that the wife had both the disposition and opportunity to commit adultery.

A suspicious wife follows her husband's automobile after he has picked up a woman in a residential neighborhood at night. Is this sufficient evidence to maintain an action for adultery?

No, not standing by itself, especially since the wife had only her unsupported word that the husband had picked up the other woman. If the wife had someone else in her car who could also testify and corroborate what the wife had seen, the unexplained presence of the other woman in the automobile might give rise to the suspicion that the behavior of the couple was adulterous.

Is it permissible for the complainant to have as his corroborating witness a relative such as a brother, sister, child, father, or mother?

Yes, any corroborating witness may testify. It is then up to the court or jury to determine the credibility and objectivity of the witness.

What about private investigators or detectives?

There is no fixed rule or public policy forbidding their testimony, but their evidence, because it has been paid for by the complainant, is scrutinized with great care.

Is it permissible for the paramour—that is, the other man or woman —to testify?

Yes. Although admissible, such testimony is viewed with grave suspicion and acted on with extreme caution. The reason is that such testimony may represent collusion between complainant and defendant for the express purpose of obtaining a divorce.

In a divorce suit the defendant by his answer to the bill of complaint filed on his behalf by his attorney admits all of the allegations, including the charge of desertion. Does this mean that the complainant will not need a corroborating witness when testimony is heard?

No. Even when the defendant admits all the allegations it will still be necessary in most states for the complainant to prove the chief allegations by means of a witness.

What happens to a divorce action when either the plaintiff or defendant dies before a decree is issued?

The divorce action comes to an end, or to use legal jargon, the divorce is "abated."

Does this principle also apply to suits for separation and separate maintenance?

Yes. However, where the consequences of the divorce affect property rights of the parties to the suit, the heirs or personal representatives may have such an interest in the litigation that the divorce action will survive the death of the party, not for the purpose of continuing the divorce, but to determine the property rights of the survivors of the deceased.

A wife fears that her husband will flee the state and remove a considerable amount of property with him, as well as avoid alimony payments. Is there anything she can do to restrain him?

Yes. She can, through her attorney, attempt to persuade the court to issue a writ of *ne exeat,* which literally means "let him not go out." The writ is issued to restrain the defendant from leaving the state. Many courts, however, are reluctant to issue such a writ unless there is a clear and present danger that the defendant will flee the jurisdiction of the court.

Under what circumstances will such a writ be denied?

Where it appears that the divorce was not instituted in good faith but merely to collect money from the husband, or where the claim is for temporary alimony which has not been passed upon.

How does the husband defend himself against such a writ being issued?

By convincing the court that he has no intention of leaving the state.

What happens if the court is not convinced?

The court may require that the husband give security against his leaving the state or removing his property. In other cases the court may require the husband held under such a writ to give bond payable to the wife securing payment of alimony and performance of the court's orders concerning custody and maintenance of the children, before he will be permitted to leave the jurisdiction.

A wife suspects that her husband, against whom she has filed divorce proceedings, plans to remove the funds held in a joint checking account, sell a large quantity of common stocks, and convert other personal property to his own use. What can the wife do to protect her interests?

She can, through legal counsel, obtain an injunction to prevent the husband from disposing of his property pending the litigation. An injunction is a restraining order or writ issued by a court preventing a person from committing or doing an act which appears to be against equity or conscience.

May a wife procure an injunction preventing the husband from molesting her?

Yes, if she can persuade the court that such molestation has not only occurred in the past but is likely to occur in the future.

A husband suspects that his wife plans to leave his state and file a divorce action in Nevada. Can he obtain an injunction against his wife if he can support his allegations?

Yes.

Pending divorce proceedings can a wife obtain an injunction or restraining order preventing her husband from seeing or living with the "other woman"?

No.

A husband and wife jointly own their home. After filing a bill for divorce the wife now seeks to prevent her husband from visiting or living in the house. Can she obtain an injunction to this effect?

No. Pending the outcome of the divorce, both parties have equal rights to access to the home. Unless the wife can clearly show that the husband has been guilty of inflicting or threatening physical injury to her, the injunction will be denied.

Can a wife prevent her husband from returning, visiting, or living in the home owned exclusively by the wife?

No, at least not until the truth of her charges is determined, unless the grounds of her divorce are cruelty and habitual intoxication.

In an application for an injunction are both parties heard before a decision is reached?

Yes.

What is a decree nisi?

It is a divorce decree which is neither final nor absolute. It is used to denote that a rule, decree, or order shall take effect at a given time unless before that time it is modified or avoided by cause shown, or further proceedings, or by the fulfillment of some condition therein named.

What is an interlocutory decree?

An interlocutory decree is the court's judgment that a party is entitled to a divorce at some future time. It is in effect a preliminary or intermediate decree which directs some further proceedings before a final divorce can be had. Its purpose is to avoid fraud or collusion and to allow the couple a chance of reconciling their marital differences before the final decree is issued. In a decree nisi or an interlocutory decree remarriage is not permitted since the marriage has not been completely dissolved legally.

How may the right to a final decree of divorce be defeated after the interlocutory decree?

A final decree may be defeated

1. Because of the death of either party.
2. Where the plaintiff remarries under the mistaken notion that an interlocutory decree entitles him to an absolute divorce.
3. Because the plaintiff commits adultery.
4. Because the plaintiff condoned, reconciled, cohabited, or had sexual relations with the defendant.

Once having been obtained, can a divorce decree be set aside?

Yes. Even after a divorce decree has been signed by the court it may be set aside if the defendant can prove that the plaintiff ob-

187

tained the decree by either fraud or duress. The fraud may consist of perjured testimony given in favor of the plaintiff, such as a witness testifying falsely as to an alleged adultery. A husband who by threats of bodily harm forces a wife not to defend a divorce suit may have his divorce decree vacated. A divorce decree may also be set aside if the ex-husband and ex-wife give their consent or effect a reconciliation.

Is the failure to apply promptly after the discovery of fraud a bar to having a divorce decree set aside?

Yes. A decree will not be set aside for a party who has been guilty of unreasonable delay in applying for relief, especially when one or both parties have remarried.

Does the wife have to have the court's permission, in a divorce decree, to resume her maiden name?

No.

What remedy does a person have who loses a divorce case?

He can, through counsel, move to vacate the decree because of fraud or duress, or he can take an appeal to the state's highest appellate court, a rather costly procedure.

Who arranges for and obtains the necessary witnesses?

At the first or second conference between the complainant and his attorney the question of evidence and witnesses will arise. The attorney will ask the complainant what evidence he has to support his allegations that the defendant committed adultery, desertion, or whatever he is charged with. It is then up to the complainant to supply his attorney with the names and addresses of necessary witnesses so that they can be interviewed by counsel prior to the hearing to determine whether or not the complainant has sufficient evidence to make out a case. Either the complainant and/or his attorney will then try to persuade the witnesses to come into the lawyer's office prior to the hearing for a preview of their testimony.

Will the attorney tell the witnesses what to say?

Not if he doesn't wish to risk disbarment. No honest attorney will put words into a client's mouth; nor will he supply grounds for divorce where none actually exist or pretend that the client has complied with residence requirements when in fact he has not.

Does this mean that the attorney will not go over the client's or witness' story?

It does not. Before undertaking to file an annulment or divorce bill, an experienced, ethical attorney will make certain that the client and necessary witnesses are able to meet the statutory requirements of the state in which the divorce bill is filed. If they are not, he will refuse to undertake the case. An attorney has the right, however, to prepare his client and witnesses by going over the proposed testimony in the most rigorous manner possible and to even advise them on how to behave in court or in private chambers when testimony is taken.

A husband, through his attorney, files an annulment action alleging fraud. The fraud is based on the allegation that the wife promised, before the marriage, to enter into a religious ceremony to be performed by a Roman Catholic priest. The bill for annulment further alleges that the wife failed to keep her promise and that the husband has been injured thereby, and that moreover he would not have entered into the marriage had he known that the woman would not have kept her promise. What evidence will be necessary to sustain the allegations and procure the annulment?

In New York where annulments are as frequent as divorce and where the vast majority of annulments—like divorces—are uncontested, the usual practice is for the plaintiff or complainant to testify as to the time, date, and place of the alleged conversation and in whose presence the conversation took place. This provides the foundation for the corroborating witness. The husband may testify that his brother, sister, relative, or friend overheard the conversation. The corroborating witness testifies next. Her evidence is usually to the effect that she knew both parties prior to the marriage; that on a certain date she was present at the prospective bride's or groom's home or wherever the event is alleged to have taken place; that in the course of a conversation between the two parties she heard the prospective bride promise that she would go through a religious ceremony of her husband's faith; and that to the best of her knowledge and belief the couple have not gone through such a religious ceremony; that the failure to do so is entirely due to the woman; and that when the husband discovered the fraud or realized that the wife was not going through with the religious ceremony, he left the wife, and has not cohabited with her since the discovery of the alleged fraud.

What testimony is required where the annulment is based on the defendant's refusal to have children?

The usual testimony in liberal annulment states is for the plaintiff to testify that the husband (or wife) refused to have children; that he or she refused to have normal sexual relations or that he or she was only willing to have sexual intercourse with contraceptives. A witness testifies that the husband or wife, as the case may be, told her or him of the spouse's refusal to have children which in such liberal states as New York or California is usually sufficient to dissolve the marriage.

What proof is required in a divorce suit?

As with the annulments, the plaintiff or complainant must first file certain legal papers variously called the bill of complaint, petition for divorce, etc. A typical bill of complaint recites the names and addresses of the parties; that the plaintiff resided the minimal amount of time in the state in which the bill was filed; that the marriage took place at a time and place specified; that on or about a certain specified time and place the defendant willfully and without just cause deserted the plaintiff; that there is no reasonable possibility or expectation of a reconciliation; and that the parties have not cohabited or lived together as man and wife since the said desertion; that the plaintiff asks for an absolute divorce, alimony *pendente lite* (pending litigation), permanent alimony, custody of the children, and a reasonable counsel fee. The evidence must support each and every allegation made by the plaintiff.

What specific questions are asked of the plaintiff in an uncontested divorce action?

What is your name?

Where do you live?

How long have you resided in this state?

Where did you live before your present address?

When were you married to the defendant?

By whom were you married? (Note: Maryland is the only state requiring that a marriage be solemnized by a religious service.)

Were any children born of the said marriage?

Give their names and ages?

State in your own words what happened on or about the day you allege your husband (or wife) deserted you.

Did you give your husband just cause or reason for the said desertion?

Have you lived with your spouse since the said desertion?

Do you desire alimony for yourself and support for the minor children?

What is it you wish the court to grant you in this case? (The usual response is "I wish the court to grant me an absolute divorce.")

Are there states which do not require a corroborating witness?

In Connecticut divorces will not ordinarily be granted on uncorroborated evidence of parties in uncontested divorce cases, but they may be granted on the uncorroborated testimony of a party in a contested case. In Pennsylvania a divorce decree may be granted on the unsupported testimony of the complainant, but if plaintiff's testimony is contradicted and shaken by defendant, the divorce may not be granted.

11 Defending a Divorce Suit

How is a divorce action defended?

By making a general denial of the allegations contained in the plaintiff's bill of complaint.

Is it always advisable to defend a divorce action even if the defendant also desires the divorce?

Yes, if there are such questions to be settled as alimony, support, custody of the children, and division of the property.

What is the effect when the defendant, through counsel, files an answer to the divorce suit?

It places the case at issue and on the trial docket or calendar.

Does this mean that once an answer has been filed the case must be tried?

No. It can be, if both sides agree, or even if one side does not agree. If there is an agreement, one of the parties obtains the divorce, depending on which party has the legal grounds.

When is it unnecessary to retain counsel after one has been served with divorce papers?

When the defendant has no desire, for one reason or another, to contest the divorce and where the wife does not wish support for herself or children, and where no property rights are involved.

What are the defenses to a divorce action?

1. General denial of the allegations contained in the bill of complaint
2. Condonation and forgiveness
3. Connivance and procurement
4. Collusion
5. Recrimination
6. Agreement for separation
7. Invalidity of marriage
8. Antenuptial knowledge of cause
9. Want of capacity to commit offense

In what way is a general denial a defense to a divorce action?

Because it contradicts the plaintiff's assertion as to the existence of a fact. A husband asserts that his wife committed adultery at a certain time and place and with a certain man. The wife denies the charge by claiming that she never had sexual relations with the corespondent, and that she neither had the inclination nor the opportunity to commit adultery.

In what way is condonation a defense?

Condonation is the conditional forgiveness of a matrimonial offense on condition that it will not be repeated. To be an effective defense there must be knowledge on the part of the spouse of all the facts on which the divorce action is based. Second, a genuine reconciliation must have been accomplished. Third, the offending spouse must have been restored to all his marriage rights.

What are meant by marital rights?

Marital rights, as distinguished from marital relations or sexual intercourse, includes enjoyment or association, sympathy, confidence, domestic happiness, common dwelling, eating together, profiting by joint property rights, and intimacies of domestic relations.

Does a mere promise to forgive or an unaccepted offer to resume cohabitation constitute condonation?

No. The forgiveness must be actual and must be accompanied by an intention to forgive.

A husband commits adultery. The wife, with full knowledge of the facts, forgives the husband and resumes living with him as man and wife. A few months later the husband again commits adultery. To the divorce bill filed by the wife the husband pleads condonation. Will he succeed?

No. To be effective the condonation must be based on the condition that the offense will not be repeated. Since the husband again committed adultery the original forgiveness is revoked and the wife may obtain her divorce.

Is the defense of condonation applicable to other matrimonial offenses?

Yes. The policy of the law favors forgiveness in order to keep the family together. The defense of condonation can be claimed when the ground for the divorce is cruelty, habitual drunkenness, desertion, or nonsupport.

Does a spouse waive her rights when, after the husband has deserted her, she resumes cohabitation with him?

Yes. Once forgiven, past misdeeds cannot be made the basis of a divorce action.

How many acts of forgiveness does it take to nullify a lifetime of marital grievance?

Just one. A single, voluntary act of sexual intercourse by the innocent spouse, after separation because of cruelty, desertion, habitual drunkenness, or nonsupport, serves to condone the matrimonial offense and defeat the rights of the husband or wife.

Is it condonation if, after adultery has been committed, the husband forces the wife to have sexual relations with him?

No, the act must be free and voluntary, and not induced by fear, intimidation, trick, or fraud.

Is it condonation for a wife to continue living with her husband when she suspects but has no real proof that he has been unfaithful?

No. The forgiveness must be based on fact, not on mere suspicion. If the wife were later to confirm her suspicions, she could leave her husband and file for a divorce on adultery. However, should the wife continue to live with her husband knowing that he had committed adultery, her suit would be defeated.

Is it condonation for a wife to continue living with her husband after he has committed a matrimonial offense where the wife lacks sufficient means to take herself and the children elsewhere?

No. The law recognizes the existence of hardship cases. In situations where the husband or wife cannot afford to leave the apartment or home—but do not have sexual relations with each other— no defense of forgiveness is considered to have taken place.

After the husband's adultery the wife forgives and resumes sexual relations with him for two days, after which they quarrel, the quarrel being caused by the husband. The wife files suit on the ground of adultery, to which the husband's counsel pleads condonation, that is, that the wife forgave the husband and had sexual intimacies with him. Will the wife succeed in her suit?

No. From a legal point of view the wife condoned her husband's adultery by forgiving and having sexual intimacies with him. The fact that a few days later the wife changed her mind is both irrelevant and immaterial.

A husband forgives his wife's adultery. Later he discovers that the wife has lunches with her paramour, but there is no actual evidence of renewed adultery. Can the husband still obtain a divorce on this ground?

Yes. The fact that the wife continued to associate with her paramour, even though she did not have actual intimacies with him would enable the husband to revive the original adultery as a ground for divorce. The wife could not plead condonation.

Pending divorce proceedings the husband persuades the wife to have dinner with him after which they adjourn to his apartment where they engage in sexual relations. What is likely to happen to the divorce suit?

It will be defeated because the act of sexual intercourse constitutes a forgiveness of the original matrimonial offense.

Is it absolutely essential that there be sexual relations before there can be condonation?

In such states as Florida, Maine, and New Jersey it has been held that actual sexual intercourse between the husband and wife is necessary before there can be a condonation. In other states such as Georgia and Arkansas it has been held that such relations are not essential to constitute condonation.

After a husband physically assaults his wife the latter forgives him and continues to live with him as man and wife. A few weeks later the wife changes her mind and files for divorce. Will she succeed?

No. The fact that the wife continued to live with her husband after the act of cruelty constitutes legal condonation or forgiveness which bars the wife's right to a divorce.

A husband and wife occupy the same bed and room for more than two years. The wife files for a divorce, claiming that although she occupied the same bed with her husband she did not have sexual intercourse with him, a claim which is vigorously denied by the husband. Is the wife entitled to a divorce on this evidence?

No. The general presumption is that a husband and wife living in the same house have sexual relations. This is a presumption which can be rebutted, however. An even stronger presumption exists where the husband and wife occupy the same bed, so that any matrimonial offense such as adultery or cruelty will be considered forgiven or condoned through the couple's occupying the same bed. This strong presumption may also be rebutted though it is much more difficult from a practical point of view.

After a wife commits adultery she becomes repentant and tells her husband that she will behave properly in the future. The husband refuses to heed the pleas of his wife and files suit for divorce. Will he succeed?

Yes. The right of condonation or forgiveness lies with the innocent spouse, not with the guilty one.

A wife forgives her husband's adultery, and the couple effect a reconciliation. Shortly thereafter, in the course of a quarrel, the husband strikes the wife. The wife leaves the residence and, through her counsel, files a bill for divorce on the ground of adultery. The husband's attorney pleads that the wife condoned the husband's behavior. Is the latter contention correct?

No. Condonation is conditional on the spouse's subsequent good behavior. In the above example the husband's cruelty revived the original matrimonial offense of adultery. The same result would occur had the husband been guilty of habitual drunkenness, non-support, or desertion.

What is connivance?

Connivance is the corrupt consent of one spouse to the conduct of the other of which subsequently a complaint is made. In essence, connivance is the theory that the defendant in a divorce matter has been framed by the plaintiff and that therefore the latter is not entitled to a divorce. Connivance is the legal doctrine which declares that one seeking relief must come into court "with clean hands," that is, must himself be blameless.

A husband hires an attractive young man to seduce his wife in order to obtain a divorce on the ground of adultery. The wife is seduced, and the husband files his bill. Will he succeed?

No. Though the wife actually did commit adultery when she was seduced, the courts take the position that the adultery was contrived by the husband, and that she would not have succumbed had she not been tempted.

Is a husband guilty of connivance who observes acts of undue familiarity between his wife and her paramour and makes opportunities for them to be together?

Yes, since the husband is, in effect, aiding and abetting in the commission of the adultery.

What is collusion?

Collusion is an agreement between husband and wife whereby one of them for the purpose of enabling the other to obtain the divorce commits a matrimonial offense or fabricates or suppresses evidence. Divorces based on collusion are void, if discovered.

Is it collusion for a husband or wife to abstain from making a defense in a divorce action?

No.

Is it collusion for one of the spouses to agree to pay for the divorce?

No.

How is proof of collusion brought to the court's attention?

Usually by a third party who has knowledge of the facts.

May either party to a divorce use collusion as a defense, even though he or she participated in the agreement?

Yes.

Is it collusion for one side in a divorce case to present the other side with evidence without which a divorce would not be granted?

Yes.

Will a divorce fail because of collusion even if the two principal parties did not participate in the agreement?

Yes. It has been held that any third party who attempts to frame a divorce case—and succeeds—is guilty of such a collusive act as will bar the principals from obtaining the divorce, even though the latter are completely innocent.

Is it collusive for the husband and wife to agree to obtain a divorce?

Not necessarily. The agreement becomes collusive when the court suspects that a divorce has been filed not warranted by the true facts, or where the court rightly suspects that an attempt has been made to deceive it.

Is it collusion if the parties agree to apply for divorce on the ground of adultery which one of the parties has forgiven?

Yes.

Is it collusion for one spouse to furnish proof of acts of adultery already committed so as to enable the other spouse to obtain a divorce?

Yes.

Is it collusion for a couple to withhold evidence which weakens the complainant's case or to suppress facts constituting a good defense?

Yes.

Can a divorce be set aside when, a few years later, it is discovered that the adultery was by prearrangement of the parties?

Yes.

What is recrimination as a defense to a divorce action?

Recrimination is the doctrine that where both husband and wife are equally at fault a divorce will not be granted. Stated in another way, if both husband and wife have a right to a divorce neither of the parties has. Recrimination rests on the maxim that he who comes into equity must do so with clean hands, that is, must himself be free of guilt. It is based on the doctrine that one who seeks redress for the violation of a contract must himself have performed the obligations on his part. Thus where both husband and wife have committed adultery or cruelty neither can procure a divorce.

To successfully defend a divorce action must the complainant be guilty of the same offense as the defendant?

No. The general rule is that the offense pleaded in recrimination need not be of the same nature as the offense which defendant has committed. If, for example, the wife in her divorce suit charges that the husband committed adultery, it is a valid defense to defeat the divorce if the husband can sustain a charge that the wife committed legal cruelty or was guilty of desertion.

Both husband and wife have been guilty of various acts of physical cruelty. Would this prevent either party from getting a divorce on that ground?

Yes.

Is recrimination a valid defense if the wife is guilty of adultery and the husband guilty of physical cruelty?

Yes. The general rule is that where the plaintiff has himself violated one of the statutory grounds for divorce in his state he will not be able to procure a divorce, no matter how strong his evidence is against the defendant.

Is the doctrine of recrimination valid in all states?

No. California, Kansas, and Oklahoma take a considerably more tolerant view toward the doctrine of recrimination. In these states courts have the power to disregard the doctrine and can award a divorce to either party who has the necessary grounds. In Nevada "in any action for divorce when it shall appear to the court that both husband and wife have been guilty of a wrong or wrongs, which may constitute grounds for divorce, the court shall not for that reason deny a divorce, but in its discretion may grant a divorce to the party least in fault."

What is a countersuit?

A countersuit occurs where the defendant, having been served with divorce papers charging him with a matrimonial offense, denies the said charges in his own suit in which he charges the plaintiff with a matrimonial offense. For example, the wife charges the husband with adultery. Believing himself wrongly accused, the husband, through his counsel, files a countersuit denying the charges and bringing charges of cruelty against the wife. The case will then be heard on its merits with the court determining which party, if any, is entitled to the divorce.

Is it important whether the wife or husband files for the divorce?

It all depends. Generally speaking, a wife has considerable advantage if she files first. In the first place she is more likely to enlist the sympathy of the court. In the second place, if she can show need, she is entitled to alimony, pending litigation, support for herself, and a reasonable counsel fee. Since the overwhelming majority of divorce cases are uncontested and privately arranged, what is even more important is that the client be the innocent party to the divorce proceedings. For one thing the innocent party generally wins a more favorable settlement. If a woman, she will get alimony for herself and the children, as well as the custody of the children. In addition, she will by court order receive a counsel fee which the husband will have to pay. If the husband is the innocent party he will be relieved of alimony for the wife, though he will still have to support the children.

Finally, there is the question of stigma. The guilty party may have to explain to his children or to a prospective second wife or husband that he was guilty of wrongdoing in the legal sense of the term. He may have to explain to his children, for example, that he committed adultery or that he was guilty of cruelty toward their mother. He may also have to explain these things away to a prospective second wife. The innocent party to a divorce has, naturally, much less explaining to do, even though it may have been the wife's nagging or frigidity which drove the husband into adultery or compelled him, in self-defense, to resort to acts of mental cruelty.

A man and woman lived together for ten years as common law husband and wife. The wife now wishes to file suit for divorce? Can she?

Yes. In states where a common law marriage is recognized an action to a divorce will be sustained to the same extent as though the marriage were solemnized in strict accord with the law. The husband could not defend on the ground that the couple never went through a marriage ceremony.

Is drunkenness an excuse for marital misconduct?

Not unless the complainant induced or consented to the intoxication.

Does excessive drinking of a husband justify a wife's desertion when she knew about her husband's drinking habits before the marriage?

No. The fact that the wife married the man with knowledge of his drinking habits constitutes a waiver which the husband can set up as a valid defense to a divorce action.

12 *Alimony and Support*

What is alimony?

Alimony is the allowance a husband is compelled to pay, by order of court, for his wife's maintenance while she is living apart from him, or after they are divorced. It includes money for her living expenses and is allowed where absolute or partial divorces are granted.

What is temporary alimony?

Temporary alimony, also known as alimony *pendente lite,* is an allowance to the wife made by the court during the pendency of a suit for legal separation or divorce. The award is more or less routinely made if the wife is without separate means and the husband is able to support her.

Will temporary alimony be awarded the wife regardless of whether she is the plaintiff or defendant in a divorce action?

Yes, and it is awarded without regard to the merits of the case.

What do courts usually award wives as temporary alimony?

Generally, about a third of the husband's net income.

May the court award a wife temporary alimony out of the husband's real estate so as to deprive him of title to it?

No. Alimony is generally restricted to money awards exclusively.

If the wife has some income of her own though not sufficient to completely support herself will she still be granted temporary alimony?

Yes. In such a case the court will compel the husband to make up the difference.

Will a wife be awarded temporary alimony if she owns real estate but has no actual income?

Yes. A court will not usually ask a wife to resort to the corpus of her estate before calling on that of her husband.

Will a wife be awarded temporary alimony if she earns a sufficient income of her own?

Not as a rule.

In awarding temporary alimony do courts consider the wife's ability to earn her own living in the future?

Yes. But this will not defeat a wife's right to temporary alimony if she is not actually earning an income.

Will a wife be awarded temporary alimony where the husband and wife have been living apart for years and the wife has supported herself and appears capable of continuing to do so?

Usually a request for temporary alimony under such circumstances will be denied.

Is the allowance to a wife of temporary alimony based purely on the husband's earnings?

No. The allowance may be based on the husband's total earning capacity, even though he lacks both money and property.

Is the poverty of a husband a valid defense to a wife's claim to temporary alimony?

No, since courts consider that the husband should not have instituted the divorce action if he cannot furnish the wife with means to make her defense. However, the husband's poverty may be pleaded where the wife initiates the divorce action.

Will a husband be excused from paying temporary alimony because his income is less than the interest on his debt?

No.

Is a wife guilty of marital misconduct entitled to temporary alimony?

No. If a wife admits, through counsel, or does not deny charges of misconduct which are sufficient to entitle the husband to a divorce, her right to temporary alimony is barred. However, mere indiscretions of a trivial character will not justify refusing the wife temporary alimony. As many husbands have reason to remember to their sorrow, the wife is almost everywhere regarded as the favored suitor in a divorce case which places her husband at a serious disadvantage. Many unscrupulous, predatory wives use this advantage for everything it's worth.

Under what circumstances will an order for temporary alimony be terminated?

Temporary alimony terminates upon the death of either party. It also ceases upon a reconciliation of the husband and wife. Finally, it ends upon the termination of the suit.

May an unscrupulous wife delay the prosecution of a divorce case in order to continue receiving temporary alimony payments?

Yes. Many wives do so. However, if the court suspects the wife's real motive for the postponement of her case the allowance may be discontinued. This rarely happens.

Is the amount of temporary alimony likely to be more or less than the amount of permanent alimony?

Less. The usual basis on which temporary alimony is awarded, where no exceptional features are presented, is one-third of the husband's income and, where the wife's earnings during a certain period are below that amount, she is entitled to the difference.

May a husband recover the amount of temporary alimony because the wife's divorce suit fails or is dismissed by the court?

No.

For how long a period does temporary alimony last?

It ends with the final decree of divorce or with dismissal of the suit.

May the order for temporary alimony be modified?

Yes, though it rarely is. It may be modified when it is shown that to continue the original order would be a hardship on one or the other parties to the suit.

Is it advantageous for the wife to have temporary alimony continued as long as possible?

Yes. The longer the case is drawn out, the longer the period of temporary alimony. Since temporary alimony lasts until the final decree or dismissal of the case, it is wise for counsel for the husband to see that the case is heard on its merits as soon as possible.

Do courts go into the merits of the case before granting temporary alimony?

Not ordinarily. A court will grant temporary alimony if it is satisfied that the wife has a valid cause of action and that suit was brought in good faith.

Is temporary alimony granted as a matter of course to all wives?

No. The granting of temporary alimony is a matter of discretion for each court, depending on circumstances, though most courts grant such alimony almost routinely.

Will temporary alimony be granted a wife even though she is receiving support as a result of a criminal proceeding?

Yes. Temporary alimony is a civil process; the other is a criminal proceeding. There is no conflict between the two, though the judge hearing the divorce suit will take into consideration the fact that the husband is supporting his wife through criminal proceedings.

Is it possible to modify an order for temporary alimony, even if the husband is in arrears in his payments?

Yes, though courts do not view with sympathy husbands who are in default on their payments unless they can come up with a valid explanation.

What can a husband do if the wife deliberately delays bringing the case to an issue in order to prolong alimony payments?

The husband can, through his counsel, explain the facts to the court. If the court is convinced that the wife is using delaying tactics, it may end all temporary alimony payments.

Will a court award temporary alimony even though the husband is paying all his wife's bills?

Yes. An order for temporary alimony places the husband under the court's jurisdiction. The husband's payment of the wife's bills does not.

Is a husband discharged from the payment of temporary alimony when he is committed to jail for nonpayment or being in arrears?

No. The obligation to make the payments is a continuing and accumulative one.

Will the wife be refused temporary alimony if it is shown that she has the capacity to earn money but refuses to do so?

Courts, in awarding temporary alimony, will not go into the question whether the wife should or should not work. It is sufficient if it is shown that the wife does not work and lacks the means to support herself.

In addition to temporary alimony for herself and support for her children, what else is a wife entitled to?

She is entitled, usually, to a sum to defray the expenses of the suit and counsel fees. Everything else being equal, a wife will be more favorably treated if she is a defendant in a divorce action rather than the one who institutes the suit. The matter, however, is one entirely within the discretion of the court.

In determining the wife's counsel fee what does the court take into consideration?

The wife's necessity and the husband's ability.

If a wife has sufficient means to enable her properly to prosecute or defend a divorce action will she be awarded a counsel fee?

No.

Will an allowance for counsel be denied merely because the wife has independent means of her own but which does not produce substantial income?

It is the income that is important rather than the fact that the wife has independent means.

In a divorce action will a wife be awarded a sum to meet expenses in connection with the pending divorce case?

This is a matter within the court's discretion. It has been held that a wife is entitled to meet expenses incurred in investigating and acquiring information as to her husband's adulterous behavior; that she is entitled to an allowance to prove the grounds of divorce; expenses incurred in investigating the character of nonresident witnesses for plaintiff; the expense in taking depositions; expenses in taking a transcript of testimony; and the cost of printing the wife's record on appeal.

In determining the wife's counsel fee what factors are taken into consideration?

1. The nature of the services to be performed
2. The practice of the court
3. The finances of the parties
4. The wife's needs
5. The husband's ability
6. The relative responsibility or fault of the respective parties
7. The ages of the parties
8. The assistance, if any, of the wife in the accumulation of the husband's estate

What is permanent alimony?

This is money allowed the wife to take effect *after* the divorce is granted, and usually lasts during the joint lives of both parties. In Connecticut, Montana, New York, and Louisiana alimony ceases upon the remarriage of the wife.

Is a woman entitled to alimony under all circumstances?

In one form or another, alimony is granted in all of the states except North Carolina, Delaware, and Texas, when the woman secures the divorce, or where she is the innocent party in a suit brought against her.

Are husbands ever entitled to alimony?

Yes, in Illinois, West Virginia, and California.

Is a husband wholly relieved of his obligation to support his wife where she has means or income of her own?

No, but the wife's income and means will be taken into account in fixing the amount of alimony.

Are husbands as successful as wives in obtaining modification of alimony awards?

Wives are generally more successful, with the "little woman" still being regarded as the favored suitor.

Under what circumstances is a husband under no obligation to support his wife?

A husband is relieved of such support when:
1. The wife refuses to have sexual relations with him without just cause
2. Where she has unjustifiably left the husband's home and insists on living apart
3. Where the wife has left her husband for some sound legal cause such as cruelty or drunkenness, but lives in open adultery with another man
4. Where the husband wishes in good faith to move to another city, but the wife refuses to accompany him
5. Where the husband and wife live separate and apart as a result of a separation agreement and the husband is fulfilling his obligations
6. Where it has been judicially determined that neither the husband nor the wife is entitled to either an absolute or partial divorce and the wife refuses the husband's bona fide invitation to return to the home
7. Where the separation is by agreement and the fault is as much the wife's as the husband's

Is a wife entitled to support if she leaves her husband without just cause but later offers in good faith to return?

Yes.

Is a wife entitled to support where the husband agrees to the separation and later declines to discuss reconciliation?

Yes.

Can a wife obtain reimbursement where she uses her own money to pay household expenses?

No.

May a wife whose husband has abandoned her sue his estate to recover money she spent on her support from her own earnings?

Yes, since the husband is under an obligation to support the wife, especially if he wrongfully abandoned her. If the husband later comes into money before his death and subsequently dies, the wife may have a claim against his estate.

In New York may spouses contract to relieve the husband of his obligation to support his wife?

No. It has been held in New York that such an agreement is void and the wife is not even required to bring a court action to have the agreement set aside.

Is a husband under an obligation to support his wife in New York if the divorce decree itself is silent as to this point?

Yes. In such cases New York courts have the power to amend the divorce decree and allow support to the wife.

What is the basis for determining the amount of alimony a husband pays?

1. The husband's age, education, professional training, income, means, and prospects
2. The state of his physical and mental health
3. The wife's reasonable needs in relation to the husband's capacity to work

4. The wife's own means and income
5. The wife's age, ability to work, and potential earning capacity
6. The parties' station in life
7. The husband's reasonable needs
8. The length of the marriage
9. Whether it is a first, second, or third marriage
10. The conduct of each party during the marriage
11. Which party actually caused the collapse of the marriage
12. The number and ages of the children
13. The effect of income taxes on both parties

If the wife procures the divorce will the husband have to pay alimony to maintain the wife's former standard of living?

No, since many couples not only live up to all their income but often exceed it. If, after the divorce, a husband had to maintain the wife in her former exalted station, the chances are he would have little or no income for himself.

Is there a definite mathematical formula as to how much alimony husbands have to pay?

No. It is sometimes said that the husband will have to pay one-third or one-half of his income for the support and maintenance of his wife and children. Actually, the amount will vary with each individual case, depending on the factors listed above. A second wife in a marriage of brief duration will generally get less than a first wife who has been married fifteen or twenty years. A wife without children will usually get less than a wife with three small children.

Is a wife entitled to a certain portion of the husband's income as such?

No. She is merely entitled to support for herself and those children who have not yet attained their majority. Though the wife is still generally favored in the courts, when it comes to alimony, the financial severity usually imposed on husbands has been somewhat eased. In making an award for alimony, courts look to the total situation and seek to arrive at an equitable decision that recognizes the conflicting needs of all parties.

How long must the husband pay alimony where the wife procures the divorce?

A husband no longer has to support his wife when either he or she dies, when the wife leaves the husband without just cause, or because of the wife's misconduct, or on the wife's remarriage.

Are there any states where a valid divorce decree ends the husband's duty to support the wife?

Yes. In Pennsylvania and Vermont the husband does not have to pay alimony after the divorce has been procured, even if the wife obtained the divorce.

Is the husband's estate bound if the husband agrees to maintain the wife as long as she lives?

Yes, since this is not an agreement to pay alimony.

May a wife institute contempt proceedings against her husband if he fails to live up to one of the terms of said agreement?

No. Her only remedy is to go into court to have the agreement enforced. She can do this by suing for a separation or divorce and apply for alimony and counsel fees. She cannot have the husband jailed for contempt.

What determines the amount of permanent alimony?

The size of the husband's estate or the amount of his property are important factors in the determination of the question of alimony, especially when the husband's income is insufficient to furnish an adequate allowance.

What other factors are taken into consideration by the court in fixing the amount of permanent alimony?

Courts will consider the husband's age and health, his own needs, his obligations and debts, and whether or not the husband has dependents, such as children or other relatives, who have claims on him for sustenance or education.

What acts on the part of the wife are considered in determining the amount of alimony?

Her conduct, for one thing. For example, a wife's misconduct may warrant refusal of alimony, or the granting of a smaller sum than she would normally receive.

Does the wife's conduct or promiscuity prior to the marriage have any bearing on the amount of alimony to be awarded?

No.

What other factors help determine the amount of alimony a wife will receive?

1. Her age and health. If because of age or illness a wife is unable to contribute to her own support, courts will usually provide her with a more generous allowance. If the wife is young, vigorous, and in good health, she is likely to receive less.
2. Number of dependents. A wife with children, especially if their custody has been entrusted to her, will receive more alimony than a childless wife.
3. Her station in life. A wife who moves in the higher social circles will generally receive a greater allowance than a wife who moves in a lower one.
4. Her property, income, and earnings. A wife's property, income, and earnings are generally taken into consideration in determining the amount of alimony a husband must pay. This doesn't mean, however, that merely because the wife has property, income, or earnings of her own that she will be denied alimony.

215

Are wives ever allowed one-half of the husband's earnings, income, or property?

Yes, but only under unusual circumstances. Such an unusual circumstance exists where the wife contributed materially to the accumulation of the husband's property.

What is the usual amount of alimony awarded a wife?

Though there is no inflexible rule, the usual amount awarded is roughly one-third of the husband's net worth. If a man earns $100 a week his wife will not generally be awarded more than $35, perhaps even less. If the wife has two or three children, she may be awarded up to one-half of the husband's earnings. Each case is decided on its own merits, depending upon the state and the individual judge.

What are some typical alimony awards throughout the country?

In Arkansas $200 a month was allowed to the wife, where the husband earned $5,200 a year and he owned about $9,500 worth of residence and farm property.

In Georgia a husband earned $200 a month; the wife, who was in poor health was awarded $60 a month.

In Kentucky where the husband had an estate of $125,000 and an income of $30,000 the wife was awarded $250 a month.

In Maryland a $250 counsel fee was awarded plus a $200 per month temporary alimony where the husband was worth $30,000 and had an actual income of $11,302.

In New York a $200 a week temporary alimony was granted to a wife and three children where the husband was worth at least $1,000,000 and had practically confessed his guilt of adultery.

In Colorado an award was made to the wife of $20,000 where the husband owned property worth $50,000.

In Oklahoma a wife was awarded $300,000 where the husband was worth in excess of $1,000,000.

In Michigan a wife was awarded $150,000 where defendant's wealth was over $600,000, and plaintiff had done all that was required of her as wife and mother, and no justification existed for the husband's cruelty which had impaired the wife's health.

In Connecticut a wife was awarded $7,500, slightly more than one-fourth of the husband's estate.

In Indiana a wife was awarded $100,000 where the husband had accumulated $400,000 and had income from $35,000 to $82,500 annually.

Is alimony and support for the children usually reduced when the children come of age?

Yes.

Does the remarriage of the wife automatically reduce or eliminate the husband's alimony payments?

Not automatically, but upon application most courts on remarriage of the wife will vacate the order for further continuance of alimony payments.

Can alimony payments be reduced where the income of the wife and minor children exceed that of the husband?

Yes.

Is a husband entitled to a reduction where one of the children attains his majority but the reduced expense is offset by the increased cost of another child's maintenance?

No.

Does the remarriage of the husband entitle him to a reduction of alimony payments?

Upon proper application to the court, the husband's remarriage is certainly a fact which will be considered in order to enable him to fulfill his obligation to support his second wife and any children

217

he may have with her. However, the mere fact of remarriage does not of itself entitle a husband to a reduction.

Does the sexual misconduct of a wife, after divorce, entitle the husband to have alimony payments reduced?

No.

What are the advantages of a lump sum settlement as against periodic payments, or a trust or annuity for the wife?

There may be special advantages if the wife is young, has no children, the marriage has been of short duration, or where she already plans a second marriage. A lump sum agreement writes the end to a marriage. There is no need for further communication as to money matters, and the wife is completely on her own. She does not have to worry whether in the future the husband's income will be reduced or his estate dissipated.

What are the disadvantages of a wife receiving a lump sum settlement instead of periodic payments?

The biggest disadvantage is that she may so dissipate the lump sum that she will be left without visible means of support, leaving herself and her children stranded.

What are the advantages for the husband giving his wife a lump sum settlement?

He may get rid of his financial obligation to his wife in one fell swoop. By giving her a lump sum he will not have to increase payments in case his income increases or he falls heir to a windfall in the future.

What are the disadvantages to the husband of allowing a lump sum settlement to the wife?

He cannot deduct the lump sum for income tax purposes as he can with ordinary alimony payments. Besides, a lump sum settlement may be set aside and defeat the intentions of both parties by having the sum declared a gift subject to tax by the United States Government, if there is no divorce within two years. Finally, not all states recognize the validity of a lump sum settlement agreement. In those states which do not, the wife, after spending the lump sum, may make an application to the court for periodic payments, especially if children are involved and cannot be supported by the wife.

Is there any ideal solution to the lump sum settlement problem?

As good a method as any is to provide for an irrevocable trust for the wife and children. Under such an agreement a certain sum of money is set aside for the trust agreement, of which the wife receives only the interest. Under such an agreement she can never dissipate the principal sum and will never be in want. Such an arrangement is only practical, it must be pointed out, in the cases of extremely wealthy clients.

Can a lump sum settlement be paid in installments?

Yes. A husband who agrees to pay his wife $50,000 as a lump sum in lieu of all other claims she may have may, with his wife's approval, pay out the sum in five equal installments or whatever other arrangement is mutually agreed upon.

What happens if the wife dies after entering into a lump sum settlement with periodic payments, a number of payments of which are still due?

The wife's estate may recover the balance.

Must a husband continue to support a wife who is incurably insane after he obtains the divorce?

Yes, as a matter of public policy.

Do some states set limits as to the amount of alimony a wife can obtain?

Yes. Minnesota forbids the award of alimony in excess of half the husband's future earnings. Arkansas, on the other hand, allows the plaintiff one-third of all her husband's personal property and a life interest in one-third of his real property. This is the *minimum* a wife can be awarded. In Louisiana a wife cannot be awarded more than one-third of her husband's income, and in many cases she is awarded considerably less.

Can husbands collect alimony from their wives?

Yes. In Oklahoma, Ohio, California, Illinois, Massachusetts, Oregon, and North Dakota.

Under what circumstances will husbands be awarded alimony?

In those cases where it is shown that the husband is unable to work and has no income of his own, and where his wife does have earnings, income, or property.

Can alimony payments be revised?

Yes, by showing that a change of circumstances now exists between the former husband and wife which did not exist at the time the alimony was awarded.

What constitutes a "change of condition" to warrant a modification of the alimony award?

The husband may now be earning more than he did at the time of the divorce, or he may be earning considerably less. His health may have been affected. He may have come into a large inheritance, or his investments may have turned sour. For her part, the wife's circumstances may also have been altered. She may now be working and able to support herself. Or she may be ill and require medical or surgical attention.

Is it easy to collect alimony once it is awarded by the courts?

Not always. Some resentful husbands use all sorts of delaying tactics to forestall the checks from reaching the ex-wives on time. Some ex-husbands will send the checks a few days or weeks later. They may even misdirect the checks. Some wait until their ex-wives actually threaten them with jail before sending in the monthly payment.

What are a woman's remedies in case the ex-spouse is a reluctant alimony payer?

She can, through her counsel, attach her husband's salary, if he earns above a certain sum a week, or his property, if he has any. The court may also cite the ex-spouse for contempt and send him to jail for nonpayment. Unhappily, sending a husband to jail for nonpayment makes it even more difficult for the wife to support herself, and many wives are reluctant to take this step.

What can the wife do about alimony if the ex-spouse lives in a different state?

She has several possible remedies: she can follow the ex-husband to the new state and attempt to have the alimony order enforced there, or she can hire an attorney in the state where the ex-husband presently resides.

Can a husband be extradited if he moves to another state where he refuses to continue with alimony payments?

No, since the nonpayment of alimony is a civil offense, not a criminal one. The ex-husband who refuses to support his children can be extradited since such refusal constitutes a crime.

To whom is permanent alimony awarded where a divorce is granted to both parties?

It may be awarded to either, in the discretion of the court.

221

To what extent are alimony payments affected by the "guilt" or "innocence" of parties to a divorce?

They are affected to a very great extent. Actually, the whole theory of divorce is predicated on the guilt or alleged innocence of either or both parties. It is assumed that the party granted the divorce is innocent and that the party against whom the divorce is granted is guilty. This is usually an incredibly naïve assumption. For it often happens that a husband charged with adultery was driven into another woman's arms by the neglect or indifference of his wife. Since, in divorce actions, courts are not usually interested in the real causes of divorce as distinguished from the legal grounds, it will hold that the husband was guilty of adultery as charged, with the consequent illogical conclusion that the wife was "innocent" and is entitled to a divorce with alimony, counsel fees, and custody of the children.

Do alimony payments cease with the entry of the husband into military service?

No. They are merely suspended for the duration of the military service.

Can a husband and wife agree as to the amount of alimony payments?

Yes, but the agreement is still subject to the approval of the court. If the court determines that the amount of alimony is inadequate for the wife it will not hesitate to make the necessary changes.

Do courts take into consideration inflation or the rise in the cost of living in modifying alimony awards?

If, as a result of a sharp rise in the cost of living, the plaintiff's real income is reduced this will be considered by the court, along with other factors, in the plaintiff's request for a reduction in alimony payments.

In determining the question of alimony will the court consider that the husband has property in another state?

Yes. Courts take into consideration the net worth of the husband no matter where the property is located.

In determining the question of alimony will the court consider that the husband may have children from a prior marriage?

Yes.

In addition to jailing a husband for nonpayment of alimony, what else can the court do?

It can fine the husband or refuse to go ahead with the case until the arrears are made up, if the husband filed the original divorce action.

Is the ex-husband's estate liable for alimony arrearages?

Yes.

In anticipation of a divorce on the part of his wife, the husband fraudulently conveys away his property. Does this constitute contempt of court?

No. The proper remedy is to inform the court of the transactions involved which it will take into consideration in determining the amount of alimony.

May a wife attach her husband's automobile if he fails to pay his alimony installments on time?

Yes.

May a court compel a husband to put up security for alimony payments?

Yes, when it suspects that the husband may attempt to escape the jurisdiction of the court.

223

What can the wife do if she knows that her ex-husband has concealed his assets, refusing to pay alimony on the ground of poverty?

Upon being convinced of the above facts, the court could order the confiscation and sale of whatever assets can be found, and apply the proceeds to the payment of alimony.

What can a wife do if she suspects that the husband will attempt to avoid alimony payments by fleeing the jurisdiction?

She can obtain an injunction compelling the husband to remain within the jurisdiction of the court, insist that he put up a bond as security for payment, urge the court to confiscate whatever assets are available, suggest that a receiver be appointed for the husband's property, or suggest any other remedy that might be available.

What is the usual basis for computing the amount of alimony?

Courts generally take into consideration the previous year's income and estate, rather than an average of years.

What deductions are generally allowed the husband?

Deductions normally allowed include the husband's living expenses, debts, and expenses for ordinary current repairs to real estate, but not for permanent improvements.

Is a husband entitled, for alimony purposes, to deduct premiums for life insurance?

No.

13 *What About the Children?*

Does the mother or father have an absolute right to the custody of children?

No. Both parents are the joint natural guardians of the children, with the interests and welfare of the children the controlling consideration.

Is an agreement as to custody between parents binding on the courts?

No, even if the agreement itself is incorporated in the divorce decree. The court may set aside the agreement if, in the court's view, it is not in the best interests of the children. Of course, the court will not interpose its own judgment if the agreement does not violate the interests of the children involved.

What must be proved to deprive one of the parents of custody of the child?

It must be shown that the parent has neglected the child or had previously abandoned it, that the mother is incapable of raising the child, that she is a moral delinquent, is unstable emotionally, or is unable to furnish the child with adequate care.

What will a court do if it finds both mother and father unfit to have custody of the child?

It may award the child to a third party.

All things being equal, who will generally be awarded the custody of a child of tender years?

The mother, but again it must be reiterated that the rule in her favor is not absolute, but must yield to the paramount consideration of the child's welfare.

What is meant by a child of "tender years"?

A child under the age of six.

Is there any yardstick by which the mother's fitness to have custody of the children is measured?

Courts usually hold that the test is whether the mother's conduct is so depraved, immoral, and wicked that to allow the child to remain in the mother's custody would be harmful to its best interests.

Is it true that a wife who has committed adultery will be deprived of the custody of her child?

Not necessarily. Her conduct is often overlooked where the mother has not been grossly immoral or promiscuous, or where she marries the man with whom she committed adultery.

Will a mother be refused custody of her legitimate children if it can be proved that she previously had illegitimate ones?

Not necessarily. The court, in determining questions of custody, will take into consideration the total picture, past, present, and probable future.

226

Will a mother be deprived of custody if she is unable to provide a home for the child?

Yes.

Will a mother be denied custody of her children if she has been found drunk many times in their presence?

Yes.

Will a mother be denied custody where she has repeatedly taken the children to taverns?

Yes.

Will a mother be denied custody if it is proved that she is emotionally disturbed?

Yes, if the disturbance is serious enough.

To what extent are the wishes of the child taken into consideration?

If the child is sufficiently mature to have intelligent views and desires as to which parent he prefers to live with, his wishes will be consulted by the court, though they may not necessarily control the court's decision.

What does the court consider before making up its mind on the question of custody?

1. The fitness of the parents as revealed by their past records
2. Which parent was at fault in breaking up the home
3. Whether the wife, if awarded custody, would remove the children from the state
4. Whether there have been any violations of the court's orders, such as payment of alimony, for example
5. The financial position of the parties
6. Their love for the children

227

7. The religion of the parents
8. The preference of the children

What kinds of custody does the law provide?

Joint custody, divided custody, and split custody.

What is joint custody?

This type of custody provides that although the child (or children) lives most of the year with one parent, both father and mother have joint control of its care, upbringing, and education, and equal voice in decisions pertaining to its health, religious training, vacations, schools, trips, and summer camps.

What is divided custody?

This type of custody allows one parent to have the child for a part of the year, the other parent for the remainder of the year. Each spouse has reciprocal visitation privileges, with each parent controlling the child during the period of its care.

What is split custody?

This type of custody divides the children among the two parents.

Which type of custody does the law favor?

Joint custody. The law looks with disfavor on both divided and split custody though under the proper circumstances it will make such awards.

Will a court allow custody of a child to be taken from both parents?

Yes, but only under exceptional circumstances. This may occur where it is proved that both parents are morally unfit or uninterested in retaining custody.

Do courts ever award custody of a child to the stepmother as against the natural mother?

Yes, where the general welfare of the child so indicates.

What can a father do where, under a court order, the mother seriously interferes with the father's rights of visitation?

Many courts hold that under these facts the father will be relieved of supporting the child; other courts hold that the father should not be relieved of his support obligation, on the theory that the sins of the mother should not be visited on the children.

Is a husband relieved of his obligation to support his ex-wife, under a separation agreement, if the ex-wife denies her former husband reasonable visitation privileges to the children?

Yes. However, the ex-husband is not relieved of his obligation of support for all time. The separation agreement is merely suspended during the period the visitation privileges are violated.

May a father relieve himself of his obligation to support his child if he relinquishes his visitation privileges?

No. The obligation to support one's child is a continuing one and is independent of the wishes or desires of the father.

May a parent remove a child from one state in order to deprive the court of that state of jurisdiction to deal with that child?

No.

Under what circumstances will a court allow a parent to remove a child from one state to another?

Removal is most likely to be granted where the spouse remarries and her new husband lives outside the state. Under such circum-

229

stances the court may disregard the clause in a separation agreement forbidding the removal of a child to another state.

Does this mean that the father loses his visitation privileges if his ex-wife remarries and moves to another state?

No. The father still has such rights. He may, upon proper application to the court, require the wife to furnish bond in order to guarantee such visitation privileges.

For what other reasons will a court allow a parent to remove a child from the state?

The two other most important reasons are health and business. In each case, however, the court will scrupulously go into all the facts in order to determine the validity of the applicant's claim.

May a father relieve himself of his obligation to support his child?

No. A mother who agrees to support the children may at any time, even if the agreement is in writing, change her mind and require the father to support the child.

Under what circumstances may a custody order be changed?

1. Where the custodial parent alienates the child's affections from the other parent
2. Where there is a serious interference with the other spouse's visitation rights
3. Where the custodial parent is unable to keep the child in school
4. Where the custodial parent unlawfully removes the child from the state
5. Where the custodial parent has become mentally ill

May a divorced wife, upon remarriage, change the child's name to that of the stepfather?

Not unless she obtains the real father's consent.

Is a mother bound to obey a separation agreement in which she agrees to raise the child in the husband's religion?

No. Most courts believe that a child's religious training should be left to the child, if old enough, or, if it is not, then the religious training should be controlled by both parents, instead of by one.

Do courts attempt to keep brothers and sisters together when making custody awards?

Yes. The controlling question is: what is in the best interest of all the children? Most courts find that it is usually in their best interests to award all the youngsters to one parent, usually the mother.

Why are children so often awarded to the mother?

There are practical reasons for this. If the children are very young they obviously will require a mother's care and attention. Moreover, since virtually all husbands work they are unable to take care of their children, even if they wanted to, and not all husbands want to. Fathers are also less likely to contest the mother's claim to custody, since it allows men greater freedom to come and go. Conversely, custody for the mother imposes great problems and burdens for her, especially if she wishes to remarry.

What is the effect if a mother, granted custody by the court, removes the child to another state without the knowledge or approval of either the court or the father?

The mother may be guilty of kidnaping. She may also forfeit whatever rights she may have to support, even if such support is contained in a divorce decree or separation agreement.

May a child refuse to see a visiting parent?

Yes, especially if the child had some basis in fact for such refusal.

231

Will a court compel a child to allow the parent to visit him?

Yes, especially if the child's behavior is arbitrary or has been influenced by the custodial parent. Many mothers, having custody of their children, often subtly poison their minds against the father. For that matter fathers who have custody often attempt to influence the child against the mother. It is in order to prevent such hostility from continuing that courts will often intervene.

What happens upon the death of the parent awarded custody?

Usually, the child is awarded to the surviving parent, unless there are grave reasons for not doing so. In some cases where the surviving parent is obviously unfit to take care of the child, the court may award custody to the grandparents or other relatives, or if this isn't feasible the child may be referred to a foster home or community agency.

Who gets the child if the custodial parent becomes insane?

The surviving parent, or if this isn't in the best interests of the child, any other relative or third party.

Upon the death of the child which parent has the right to determine its burial place?

The parent awarded custody. Such a parent has also the right to determine the religious service, if any, to be performed.

Does a father's obligation to support his child cease with his wife's remarriage?

No. The father is obligated by law to support his child until he or she attains his or her majority, no matter how many times the mother remarries.

Is a father obliged to support his child even though the child is abusive and insulting to the father's second wife?

Yes.

How do courts determine the amount of money awarded to a parent for the custody of the child?

The amount is determined by the father's income, the mother's income, the age and needs of the child, and the station in life of the parents.

Should the alimony awarded the wife, and support money awarded children, be lumped together in a divorce decree?

No. They should be listed separately, since the wife's alimony is fixed while that of the children is not. If lumped together the wife cannot usually obtain an increase. Listed separately she can apply, if necessary, for an increase in the support for the children.

Will the court uphold a written agreement, incorporated in the divorce decree, as to the amount to be paid for the child's support?

Yes.

Will a court insist that a father send his son or daughter to college?

Yes, if the father has ample means and the child shows both an aptitude for college work as well as a desire to attend.

At what age does a father no longer have to support his minor children?

When the child attains his 21st birthday.

Is a father obliged to pay for emergency expenses for his child while under a divorce decree he is required to pay only a specific sum?

No. The sum specified in the divorce decree is the only one the father is compelled to pay. A better practice is to arrange for such emergencies through a separation agreement which can outline

233

what constitutes an emergency and the father's obligations thereunder.

May a father be compelled to switch jobs or occupations in order to meet support payments?

No.

May the ex-wife refuse to allow the father the right to visit the child, if the father refuses to make his regular payments?

Yes, she can, and the courts will back her up generally.

May the ex-wife refuse to allow the father visitation privileges if the latter is in arrears on his alimony payments?

No.

Who has control of the child's earnings?

The parent who has custody of the child, at least until the child is twenty-one.

Is a decree as to custody final?

No, it is always subject to modification by further order of the court.

Does the marriage of an 18-year-old daughter relieve the custodial parent of his obligation to support?

No, though as a practical matter the husband usually assumes such obligation after the marriage.

Will a mother be permitted to remove an asthmatic child to a better climate?

Yes, if she can prove that such removal is essential to the child's health.

Will a parent lose custody of a child if, in violation of a court order, the parent removes the child from the state?

Usually not. Instead the court allows the parent to retain custody of the child within the state, after fining the parent for contempt of court.

Does the court lose its jurisdiction over a child's custody after the child is taken out of the state?

No. The court's jurisdiction is an all-embracing one and follows the child no matter where it is taken, even if abroad.

What remedy has a wife who supplies a child's necessities for which she seeks reimbursement from the father?

Assuming the divorce court has not awarded support for the child, she can file suit in any other court for the money so spent.

If the mother who has been awarded custody of her child later abandons it would this entitle the father to custody?

Everything else being equal, the father, if he so desired, would be awarded custody.

Must the ex-husband continue to support his children if his ex-wife remarries and the second husband adopts the children into the family?

No. The first husband is relieved of his obligation, but only with the permission of the court. The proper procedure is for the first husband to file an application in court to have the support decree modified because of the new condition.

Can a support decree be modified as the children grow older and their economic needs increase?

Yes. Here again the correct procedure is to have the court modify the decree on proof that the children require more support than before. A child who reaches school age may require more financial support than an infant.

How can the father make certain that the money he contributes to his child's support is actually going to the child and not to the mother?

One way is to require that the mother post a bond or other security to see that she fulfills her obligations. Another method is to call the matter to the attention of the court for whatever action it deems advisable.

If the mother or father is refused the child's custody can an appeal to a higher court be taken?

Yes.

What allowances for support of children have been held reasonable by the courts?

In Indiana $200 per month was allowed for support of three children between the ages of nine and thirteen, one of whom required special care and attention.

In Louisiana $125 per month was allowed where the father had income of $12,000 per year, for the support of his thirteen-year-old daughter, custody of whom had been awarded the wife.

In Kansas $100 a month was allowed for a child's support where the father earned $5,000 a year.

In New York $95 per month was allowed for each child where the husband, who had remarried, received approximately $5,800 a year.

In Washington $60 a month was allowed for the support of a seven-year-old daughter of the husband who earned $270 a month.

14 *Dividing the Property*

Do courts have jurisdiction to settle property questions in divorce cases?

Strangely enough many courts lack such jurisdiction and cannot divide property even if they wanted to.

What is the most practical method of dividing such marital property?

By far the best method is for each party to employ counsel to work out a fair settlement and incorporate the agreement into legal form, as in a separation agreement. To allow the court to make a property division, even in those states where it is permitted, is a costly, time-consuming process, and often grossly unfair to one of the parties. Lawyers are far better equipped for the job, since they are more likely to be aware of the real causes for the divorce, rather than the purely legal grounds. Moreover, they are more apt to know what each party has actually contributed to the marriage financially.

In dividing the property, do some states penalize the so-called guilty party to a divorce action?

Yes. In the so-called community property states—Arizona, California, Idaho, Louisiana, Nevada, New Mexico, Texas, and Washington—the basic principle is that property acquired by a husband and wife after marriage is community property in which both the husband and wife have a half interest. However, the basic principle is often misapplied with manifest injustice to the "guilty" party.

In what way can there be an unfair distribution of the property in these community property states?

Where a person obtains a divorce on grounds of adultery or cruelty the court may divide the community property in the way it sees fit. This places a premium on the legal ground for divorce instead of on the real reason why the marriage broke up. A husband, for example, may have committed a single act of adultery when he was away from home yet have the bulk of his property which he had accumulated over a lifetime taken away from him; or take another example, a husband may have had sexual relations with another woman because his wife was a nag, or because she was untidy, or because she was sexually unresponsive. Here, too, the court may decree that the wife, the so-called "innocent" party be given the bulk of the husband's accumulated lifetime savings.

Are women who commit adultery affected in their property rights?

Yes, and not only in community property states. In Maine, for example, a husband is entitled to one-third of his wife's estate if she has sexual relations with another man, even though her husband's indifference or neglect drove her to adultery. Divorce is an adversary proceeding, with the court pinning a label of guilt or innocence on the husband or wife with often dire consequences attached thereto. If courts were really interested in discovering the basic psychological reasons for the marital breakup there would be much less injustice. In Illinois and Massachusetts if the wife obtains the divorce, the wife retains her dower interest in her husband's estate, usually one-third. In Arkansas the wife who is successful in divorce proceedings is entitled to a one-third interest in her husband's land for life.

Assuming the husband and wife are unable to agree on a division of the property, who is legally entitled to it?

Basically what has to be determined is who had legal title before the marital rift. Was the personal property bought by the husband with his money? Was it bought by the wife out of funds given her by her husband? Was the purchase made from her own funds, independent of that of her husband?

To whom does the jewelry and furs belong when purchased with the husband's own money?

The wife.

To whom does the TV set and the Hi-Fi equipment belong?

If the husband bought these items with his own funds and has receipts for them in his name they belong to him. If bought with the funds of both husband and wife they belong equally to both and should be divided if there is to be a separation or divorce, or if this is not feasible, an allowance should be made, depending upon who retains which item.

How about money in a checking or bank account?

The presumption is that the money is held as joint tenants which means that each person has an undivided interest in the entire account. Neither, therefore, can withdraw the money on deposit without the consent of the other. However this is merely a presumption which can be rebutted by showing that all the money in fact belonged to the husband. In a joint tenancy, there is no right of survivorship, as with tenants by the entireties. Upon the death of one of the joint tenants, the money goes to his heirs or legal representatives. Where funds are held as tenants by the entireties, the money goes directly to the surviving spouse. Where funds are held as tenants by the entireties, a spouse can legally withdraw all the funds and this is often done by an unscrupulous spouse during the time he or she contemplates a divorce.

239

To whom does household furniture belong?

Household goods and furniture are generally considered as belonging to both husband and wife. In practice, attorneys attempt to make some sort of equitable distribution, taking into consideration who actually paid for the furniture, and the needs of the husband, wife, and children. Here, too, a money allowance is often made the husband if he gives all, or a large portion of the furniture, to his wife.

What is the legal effect where the husband transfers personal property of his own to his wife and himself jointly?

The presumption, which can be rebutted, is that the husband merely intended that the wife have a right of survivorship only, that is, the property is to go to his wife only upon his death, and that during his lifetime he has the power to dispose of it as he wishes.

Upon the breakup of a marriage to whom do the wedding presents belong?

All gifts given in contemplation of marriage, unless specially earmarked for either the bride or groom, are the property of both and should be equally divided.

Does this also apply to money gifts given the married couple?

Yes.

Will the law compel a husband and wife to sell their home, before the divorce, and divide the proceeds?

No. The ownership of a house during marriage is technically known as a tenancy by the entireties. This means that the property is not subject to partition during the marriage. It also means that both spouses must join in the sale or conveyance. Upon the death of either spouse the entire property goes to the survivor.

What occurs with such property when the marriage ends in divorce?

The tenancy by the entirety is terminated and the ex-spouses become tenants in common, after which the court may decree partition and divide the proceeds.

What is the effect where the husband purchased a home with his money but took title jointly with his wife?

The law presumes that the husband made a gift of one-half of the home to the wife and that a tenancy by the entirety is created, entitling each to an equal interest in the property, the surviving spouse getting the entire property upon the death of the deceased spouse.

Can a court order an ex-husband to convey real estate to his former wife where the property was purchased with the wife's money, but placed in the husband's name?

Yes.

What about the case where the wife holds property in her own name but the property was acquired by funds belonging solely to the husband?

The husband may regain possession of such property unless the wife can prove by strong evidence that a gift to her was intended.

In a community property state is it possible for one party to waive his or her rights by a written agreement?

Yes.

Under what circumstances will a wife forfeit her rights to community property?

When she willfully and adulterously lives with another man.

241

When does community property begin?

With the onset of the marriage.

Does divorce dissolve community property?

Yes, if the divorce is final.

Is separate property owned by the man and woman prior to the marriage considered community property?

No.

What is the customary method of establishing community property rights after a separation?

The best method is for each spouse to employ counsel to enter into a written agreement providing for the division of the community property.

Will a court accept such a written agreement as binding on both parties?

Yes, if the agreement is reasonable on its face.

A wife moves from New York to Nevada in order to obtain a divorce, leaving her husband in New York. Since Nevada is a community property state would she be entitled to one-half of her husband's earnings?

No.

What

15

to Do

about Taxes

Does a husband living separate and apart from his wife have to pay income tax on his alimony payments?

Not if he meets certain basic requirements. To avoid paying taxes on such alimony the husband must show:

1. That a written separation agreement was completed after August 16, 1954
2. That payments are periodic
3. That they are required under the terms of a court decree of divorce or separation or a written agreement providing for such payments
4. That alimony payments are received after the divorce decree
5. That the payments are made in discharge of a legal obligation based on marriage

If the husband meets these requirements who pays the income tax on the alimony payments?

The wife, actually. Alimony payments made by the husband are considered part of the wife's gross income and taxable as such.

243

What is meant by periodic payments?

Periodic payments are those made at fixed intervals. Payments to a wife on a weekly, monthly, semi-monthly, bi-monthly, quarterly, semi-annually, or annual basis are all considered periodic payments.

Is money paid to a wife under an annulment deductible by the former husband?

No. Since an annulment renders a marriage null and void from the very beginning there is no valid marriage within the meaning of the Internal Revenue Act.

What about the wife who received the annulment? Does she have to pay a tax on the money she obtained from her ex-husband?

No. Since the court declared the marriage void she may retain any money she received without paying income taxes on it.

Does the wife have to pay income taxes on money received from the former husband for support of their children?

No. Such payments are not regarded as income so far as the wife is concerned. The husband must pay any tax money specifically intended for the support of the children.

Suppose the wife receives one sum of money monthly without its being specifically earmarked as to what amount is for the wife's support and what for the children's support. Is the entire sum taxable?

Yes. The entire sum is regarded as income to the wife and is taxable to her.

How can this be avoided?

The best way is to make certain that the attorney sets forth in the divorce decree or separation agreement exactly how much is to be paid to the wife by way of alimony, and how much is to be paid to the children by way of support.

Are lump sum settlements deductible for income tax purposes?

No.

Are temporary alimony payments deductible by the husband?

Yes.

May a husband deduct alimony payments for tax purposes where the agreement is a verbal one?

No. The agreement must be in writing.

Are attorneys' fees deductible in divorce and separation cases?

No, since they are not considered business expenses.

If the lump sum is paid in installments over a period of years would they be deductible by the husband and taxable to the wife?

The Internal Revenue Code provides that such installments are not necessarily periodic payments unless the fixed or principal sum must or may be paid over a period ending more than ten years from the date of the divorce decree or separation agreement. Under such an arrangement no more than ten per cent in any single taxable year can be deducted by the husband nor more than ten per cent can be claimed as income by the ex-wife.

From a tax point of view should a husband under an installment lump sum agreement attempt to pay off the entire obligation at one time?

No. If he does, he gains no tax benefits, since the Internal Revenue will only allow him to deduct ten per cent of the principal sum.

245

May a husband deduct alimony payments under an interlocutory decree?

Yes.

While living separate and apart or awaiting the divorce decree is it advisable for the husband and wife to file separate or joint income tax returns?

A joint return wherever possible. Such a return may save both husband and wife considerable money, since they can take advantage of the split income tax provision.

Does bankruptcy discharge a husband's obligation to support his wife and children?

No.

16 *After Divorce— What?*

What are some of the major problems divorcees face?

In the main they can be divided into emotional, sexual, economic, and social adjustments.

What emotional adjustments confront the divorced person?

These vary with the individual. A well-balanced, relatively mature person who has long been out of love with his wife will react one way. The neurotic husband still in love with his wife will react another way. The stable, independent wife in love with another man may look forward with eagerness to a divorce, while the helpless, dependent woman who has been rejected by her spouse may react in an altogether different fashion. In general, the divorced individual is usually in a highly disturbed emotional state, due both to the tensions and conflicts which preceded the divorce and the adjustments he will have to make after the divorce has been granted.

What are some of the immediate emotional reactions the average divorcee experiences?

He may completely reject the fact of divorce. He may be unusually calm or display wild manifestations of grief, or wallow in self-pity

247

or self-justification or react with nervous shock so as to require the services of a psychiatrist. Depending upon the innate strength of the individual and the residual attachment to his former spouse, the divorcee's reaction may take the form of loss of self-confidence and ambition, doubts, indecisions, sleepless nights, nightmares, despondency, and alcoholism.

What sexual adjustments will the divorcee have to make?

The case is different for the ex-husband and for the ex-wife; here again, how a spouse reacts will depend on the nature, depth, and quality of his or her sexual drive, the state of his or her conscience, and how emancipated or conventional the individual is. The spouse with a strong libido who in his marriage has pursued an active sexual life has a number of possible choices. His divorce may have so soured him on women in general that he may practice rigid celibacy for a while. Or he may attempt to channel his sexual energies into work or play. On the other hand, he may attempt with varying degrees of success to enter into a new love affair as quickly as possible, on the not implausible theory that one of the best ways to forget an old love is to take on a new one. The ex-wife, on the other hand, is confronted with the still-prevailing double standard of morality. If she yearns for sex she may acquire a reputation as a promiscuous woman and conceivably injure her chances for remarriage. Much depends on the social and intellectual circle in which she moves. A conservative social circle will be scandalized by an ex-wife who makes a habit of going to bed with another man; a bohemian or artistic circle will tend to accept such behavior with a great deal more tolerance. Basically, similar problems confront the divorcee with only an average or even below par libido, except that the sexual urge in such cases is apt to be under greater control and so cause much less mischief. In short, each individual has to work out his own salvation based on his personality, temperament, background, and the social climate in which he moves and breathes.

After divorce, is the ex-husband or the ex-wife apt to make the better sexual adjustment?

The ex-husband. Studies by Kinsey indicate that the divorced male resumes an active sexual life, with one or more partners, a short time after marriage. One major reason for this, of course, is that the male is the aggressor. After the divorce the average male can call up and date any one of a number of women or he can frequent bars where lonely, sex-deprived women are apt to congregate. It is much more difficult for a woman to do the same thing. For one thing, the sexual role of women is less aggressive than that of the man. For another, many women are less likely to have or enjoy sexual relations with men without the accompanying feelings of tenderness or affection. The result is that for many women—especially since there are not enough men to go around—sexual activity ceases almost completely after divorce.

What are some of the principal social adjustments a divorced person will have to make?

One of the most important is the need to make new friends. After divorce, formerly mutual friends often take the side of either the ex-husband or the ex-wife, depending in part on who was the "guilty" and who the "innocent" party in the divorce proceedings. The ex-wife often becomes the symbol of the "helpless little woman" in need of comfort and protection while the male is left to fend for himself as best he can. It is invariably the male who finds himself bereft of couples who formerly dined and wined at his home, and who has to make the greater social adjustments. Everyone, in a word, feels sorry for the little woman who simply had to get a divorce because her husband committed adultery, forgetting that more often than not it was the wife's shrewishness or frigidity or her gross and patent incompetence as a cook or housekeeper that finally drove the husband into the arms of another woman. The lamentable fact is that it is generally the ex-husband who has to seek new friends and who develops—at least during the first six months—feelings of loneliness, anxiety, and insecurity, while the ex-wife is consoled, comforted, and reassured.

249

What are the economic adjustments a divorcee will have to face?

These depend on the financial arrangements in the divorce decree. If the husband wishes to avoid unfavorable publicity as a result of an affair with another woman, he may be blackmailed by his wife to the point where he has little left to support himself. If, on the other hand, he is fortunate enough to find his wife neither vindictive nor venomous he may still have to provide her with alimony and support for the children which may leave little for himself or for any possible remarriage. Normally, of course, the earning capacity of the husband continues, whereas the financial status of the wife undergoes a marked change. Unless the wife is fortunate enough to have married a wealthy man in the first place, the chances are far from favorable that she will receive enough money to support herself in the style to which her husband formerly accustomed her. In fact, divorce often reduces the living standards of both ex-spouses.

What alternatives does the ex-wife have once divorce removes her former economic security?

The ex-wife can return to the home of her parents, if they are willing. She can find a job if she has had some previous training or experience. She can seek public or private relief. She can become the mistress of some man in the hope that he will support her indefinitely, a rather unlikely prospect considering that men tire of mistresses almost as readily as they tire of their wives. Or she can seek alimony.

Are most divorced wives awarded alimony?

No. Alimony is only awarded to about one-third of all divorced women. If the wife is childless and able-bodied, the court will not ordinarily award alimony unless the husband is wealthy and has been guilty of a grave marital offense such as adultery. Most divorced women are thus compelled to enter the labor market.

What is the most popular solution to the problems of the divorcee?

Remarriage. Just as divorce has become increasingly the solution to an unhappy marriage so remarriage continues to remain the panacea for divorce. As a solution remarriage has much to commend it. It provides companionship for the lonely, an outlet for the libido, as well as economic security for either the wife, husband, or both. Equally important, remarriage offers status to two people who were more or less rootless and emotionally dislocated. All the available evidence suggests, in fact, that more divorced people are remarrying than ever before. Actually, an estimated seventy-five to eighty per cent of all persons currently obtaining a divorce remarry within five years. In sharp and melancholy contrast about one-half of the men and three-fourths of the women who had lost their spouse by death in the previous five years do not remarry.

Is a divorcee better off severing all ties and moving to another part of town or even to another city?

Not unless the divorcee is involved in a major scandal that could prove ruinous to his career or the wife's reputation is so besmirched that she will find it impossible to remain in town. Of course, if the divorcee is so emotionally disturbed by the divorce and is still in love with her ex-spouse, she may want to move to either a new neighborhood or even to a different city. But the psychological fact is that you can't solve a problem by running away from it. During a stressful situation, however, it is often wise to get away for a few weeks or even months in order to build up strength with which to cope with problems that seem for the moment crushing and overwhelming. Seeing a psychiatrist is often helpful too.

Should a divorced man choose a small, furnished apartment until he decides where he will settle?

Yes. Unless the divorcee is sufficiently affluent to hire a suite in a first-class hotel he is probably better off in renting a small furnished apartment. For one thing he doesn't have to buy furniture; for another thing he usually doesn't have to sign an annual lease.

251

Finally he doesn't have to bother with linens, sheets, and pots and pans, all of which are supplied in most furnished apartments. After six months or a year the divorcee can then make up his mind about what he wants to do. He may decide, by that time, that he's had enough of bachelorhood and remarry. He may prefer to furnish his own apartment or he may wish to continue as he is.

Should the divorced woman without children try to keep up her house or sell it and rent an apartment?

Running a house, even with a husband around, is often difficult enough. Running it without a man is virtually impossible as well as wildly extravagant. Of course if the ex-wife was able to extract a handsome property settlement from her former husband so that she is amply supplied with funds, she may want to continue with the house, but she would be far better off, in general, in an apartment where she would have less work and more leisure. In addition, she can often judiciously invest the proceeds from the sale of the house either in sound common stocks, or in a savings bank or federally insured building and loan association.

Is the divorced woman with children better off in a house or apartment?

In a house, probably. Depending on the number of children, a house is better adapted to the needs of children than an apartment. Many apartment houses in fact, object to children, especially small ones. And the cost of a two- or three-bedroom apartment is likely to be even more expensive than a moderately priced house.

Is it difficult to adjust to a lower income away from old friends?

Much depends on the individual and the social set in which he moved. Obviously an ex-wife who has to work for a living will find it difficult to maintain membership in the country club or entertain in the manner in which she did previously. Since the wife usually retains most of the friends formerly shared by both her and her husband, she will have to play it more or less by ear. Old friends can be both comforting and understanding and often include the ex-wife in their social events. But sooner or later she will have to reciprocate. If her friends are really friends they won't expect her to be extravagant; if her "friends" do expect the ex-spouse to entertain them as royally as when she had ample funds, they will either gradually drop her or she should set about finding a new set of friends who are not quite so demanding.

Which jobs are best for divorcees with children?

Any job which pays reasonably well and does not involve neglect of the children. If the ex-wife can afford it, a part-time job is best of all since she should be home before the children return from school. Unfortunately, there aren't too many such jobs available. Typing in the home is one possible solution.

What is the best way to manage the first few months after divorce?

The first few months are the most difficult and trying. "To fill the hour," said Emerson, "that is happiness." Keeping busy is by all odds the best solution. Clubs, dating, bowling, social activities, movies—all these help one forget the past and prepare for the future. Some divorcees find the first few months after divorce exceedingly difficult. Some require psychiatric help until they get over the hump; others, probably better integrated personalities to begin with, take this transitional period in stride as they take life itself in stride.

To whom should a divorcee go for help in financial matters?

If there is difficulty in managing finances she should seek assistance from her accountant, her lawyer, or her banker. If she needs help with investments her best bet is either her banker or a reputable broker. Friends and relatives are also a good source of advice provided they themselves are successful.

Should a divorcee move in with parents during the period of adjustment following divorce?

No. One of the signs of a relatively mature individual is the ability to stand on his own feet and cope with problems as they arise. Moving in with parents, unless there is no other way out, presents more problems than it solves, both for the divorcee and for the parents.

Can one become accustomed to being the "extra" at dinners and parties?

Being an "extra" at a dinner or party isn't nearly as formidable as it sounds. The only difficulty is receiving enough invitations. Eligible men are nearly always welcome and so are divorced women.

How can a divorcee reciprocate during this trying period?

One way is to invite your friends to a cocktail party at your home. Another is to send them occasional gifts in appreciation of their aid and comfort.

How should you behave if you run into your ex-spouse at a party?

Unless the divorce was accompanied by an unusual amount of venom and bitterness, there's no reason why an ex-spouse shouldn't be treated with courtesy and respect. Ex-spouses often become good friends after divorce, especially since they see little of each other. If seeing an ex-spouse becomes emotionally disturbing, then the wisest course is to make your apologies to your host and leave as soon as possible.

Should you go into details about your divorce with your friends?

No. The less said about the real reasons for your divorce the better. A simple statement to the effect that you were incompatible should suffice. Any friend who attempts to probe more deeply is really doing a disservice.

Should you accept all blind dates merely to go out?

Getting out after a divorce is important, and if you have good judgment and a sense of humor you will know which dates to accept
and which to reject. If you lack these qualities, no amount of advice
is going to do much good.

How vulnerable are newly divorced people?

They are vulnerable in the extreme. With few exceptions, the
average divorcee is lonely, despondent, and insecure. He needs
companionship and equally important he needs someone to restore
faith in himself, to prop up his deflated ego, especially where the
other spouse obtained the divorce. Feeling rejected by his spouse
and separated from his children, a man naturally tends to be
drawn to anyone who expresses sympathy for his plight. His sexual
urge as well as his need for companionship contribute to his vulner-
ability. Thus the male divorcee, like the female, tends to marry on
the emotional rebound which is not conducive to a successful
second marriage.

Do divorcees tend to confuse the need for companionship with love?

Yes. Love is sex *plus* friendship. In love one person's psychological
needs are often complemented by the other's, and there is a blend-
ing of personalities so that the couple are stronger for having each
other. The craving for company to avoid the pangs of loneliness is
not necessarily love, though it may develop into it. Marriage based
on real love can bring years of happiness; to marry merely out of
loneliness is folly.

Are divorcees better off having an affair rather than in jumping into a hasty second marriage?

A hasty second marriage based on nothing more tangible than
sexual attraction can be disastrous, both emotionally and financially, especially for the male. It is very much like jumping from
the frying pan into the fire. For the woman, a second divorce can

be even more emotionally disturbing than the first divorce. For with each divorce feelings of guilt accumulate. In an affair, as in courtship, the tendency is to put one's best foot forward. There is the excitement and lure of the forbidden. Marriage is something else again. In marriage what is important are two relatively stable personalities or two neurotics who complement each other's emotional needs. Marriage requires a high degree of consistent cooperation as well as some basic interests in common between the man and wife. An affair, on the other hand, normally tends to be more or less exclusively sexual with a high degree of emotional excitability. For the woman, getting involved in an affair can be a serious disadvantage since it removes the need for marriage. Many potential husbands reason that if they can get what they want by means of an affair they would be foolish to undertake the lifetime support of that same woman through marriage. In an affair, a man has all the advantages with none of the disadvantages that go with wedlock.

How long should a divorcee wait before remarriage?

A minimum of six months to a year. After a decree, the divorcee is usually emotionally disturbed and vulnerable to the first sympathetic woman or man he or she meets. He thus needs time to regain his composure, to restore his sense of balance as well as humor, and to allow himself the opportunity to meet as many different women (or the women, men) as possible in order that he may choose more wisely the second time. All studies indicate that the longer the period of acquaintance between the man and woman the greater the chance of success of a first marriage, and what is true of a first marriage is even truer of a second.

How successful are second marriages?

Available evidence suggests that second marriages succeed far more often than is usually thought. The greater instability of second marriages has been commonly assumed by both marriage authorities and by psychiatrists. It was thought, for example, that those who divorced were by personality divorce prone, and that they would destroy a second marriage as they destroyed the first. In view of the fact that one-fourth of all marriages end in divorce and that of the remainder probably half of all couples remain unhappily wed for reasons of their own, first marriages turn out, on close inspection, to be considerably less stable than is popularly assumed. Moreover, there is the strong possibility that one of the partners to the marriage which ended in divorce is not a marriage destroyer at all, but that given another opportunity would make a success of the second marriage. In one study, eighty-seven per cent of the remarried divorced mothers maintained that their present married life was much better than their former, and eight per cent claimed that it was a little better. Some people do learn from experience!

What are the chances of a successful marriage when both parties have been married twice before?

Second marriages are on the whole less successful than first marriages and third marriages are usually less successful than second marriages. This is the broad statistical picture. However, divorced persons are something more than mere statistics and there are many exceptions to the general rule. If an individual is able to profit by his emotional experience, a second marriage is likely to be better than the first even in the case where two divorced people wed. Much depends on the individual. A divorce-prone person's remarriage is likely to end either unhappily or in the divorce courts. This is so largely because of the individual's temperament, personality, and background.

Do divorcees, when they remarry, have frequent arguments with their second husbands about their first husbands?

Not if they wish to preserve their second marriages. As a rule, divorcees refrain from arguments about the first spouse and, if they are wise, refrain from probing too deeply into the real reasons for the divorce.

257

Do people tend to remarry the same type of person they divorced?

To some extent, yes. However, those who are able to profit by their experience tend to make wiser choices. It is usually the neurotic type of individual who tends to repeat himself in the type of person he marries, with further disastrous results.

What are a divorcee's chances of remarriage when she has children?

With or without children, the divorcee has a much better chance of marriage than either the widowed or the single woman. The same holds true for the male. Even in the later ages the divorced individual has a much better chance for remarriage than either the widowed or single individual.

What are the possibilities of a successful marriage for a divorced woman with children to a man without children?

A great deal depends on the man's temperament, personality, and age, as well as that of the woman's. A widower or divorced male often marries a woman considerably younger than himself. It is not unusual, for example, for a man of fifty to marry a woman of thirty. In such a case the children are apt to be young. Whether the man can accept having youngsters around him without their getting on his nerves is something he will have to decide for himself. Many men can't, even though they may be fond of children. They find that it's one thing to have children around them for a half hour or so, but quite another thing to have them around the house for hours at a time. Moreover, there is always the consciousness that his wife's children are not his children. In addition, there is the complication of the real father's visitation privileges which may prove embarrassing to the new husband. All this and more may prove discouraging. Yet there are many men who make the transition with relative ease, and whose lives are enriched by the presence of children. No man's life is really complete unless he has been married. And no married man's life is complete unless he has been a father, whether natural or otherwise.

If the mother remarries what is the best arrangement for the father's visitation rights?

Having the real father visit the home of his ex-spouse whenever he wishes can be embarrassing both to the ex-wife and her new husband, as well as to the children. A good arrangement is to have the real father telephone well in advance of the time of his arrival, and if the new husband is at all sensitive, to have the latter out of the house when the father comes calling. Visitation privileges should be restricted to week ends or holidays. A sensible arrangement, if at all possible, is to have the father call for the children outside the home, instead of having him come into it.

Can a divorcee with children move out of town or out of the state?

Yes, if the separation agreement preceding the divorce so provides. Where there is no separation agreement or where the agreement is silent as to this point, the wife usually has to obtain the court's permission before she can remove the children. Courts will generally grant such permission, even against the opposition of the father, if the mother can prove that such a change is necessary for the health of the children or essential in terms of her own health. Courts will also approve the removal of children where the mother wishes to remarry someone living out of the state, provided there is a bona fide offer of marriage.

Does the mother have full responsibility for all decisions concerning the children's health, education, and welfare or must she have permission from their father?

If the mother was awarded sole custody of the children she has full responsibility and she need not consult or obtain her former husband's consent when making decisions. If the custody has been jointly awarded the mother and father the approval of both is needed. In case of any serious conflict the court will make the final decision. In many cases questions of custody and responsibility are disposed of in a formal separation agreement which becomes part of the divorce decree.

Can a divorced mother hold down a job and still give proper attention to the children?

Many mothers do, without neglecting their job or the children. Other mothers find handling two jobs impossible and overwhelming. Again, some mothers neglect their children even if they don't hold down a job, while a loving, competent mother can take practically anything in stride.

How do you explain the fact that you are "dating" to your children?

If the children are too young to understand what a divorce means, no explanation is necessary. If they are old enough to understand, a straightforward explanation should be given to the effect that a divorce became necessary simply because mother and daddy couldn't get along. As for the dating, older children should be told that mother is going out because she needs entertainment and diversion. Whenever possible the questions asked by children should be answered as truthfully as possible without going into lengthy or involved explanations.

How do you explain to children that you plan to remarry?

Simply by telling them you have fallen in love with someone and that someone is in love with you; that the prospective husband wants to take care of the children as well as of you.

What is the best way for children to get to know their prospective stepfather?

By having him over for dinner as often as possible so that he can get to know the youngsters and the youngsters him. Equally important, the prospective stepfather should try to share in the children's activities. Only if this is done for a minimum period of six months is it possible to determine whether the youngsters and the prospective stepfather will get along well together.

Do most children adjust to divorce?

Probably not. However, recent studies indicate that it is not the divorce which leaves emotional scars but the conflict and hostility between the parents which led up to the divorce. In short, it is the unhappy marriage itself that destroys the child. In ninety-nine cases out of a hundred it is the mother who obtains custody of the youngster. Yet the child needs the father, the absent parent, as an object of love, security, or identification. Sometimes, in fact, the child even uses the father as a figure against whom to rebel. Deprived of the steadying influence of a father, the child's personality is distorted and complicated by feelings of hostility and guilt. The hostility may be directed at both the mother and father, the former for having caused the separation from the latter, or against one parent. The feeling of guilt, on the other hand, may be based on the fact that the child's loyalty is now divided between the parents or is centered exclusively on one parent. The simple truth is that a child needs both parents, since both have different sets of skills and attitudes to give him. He needs both a father and mother to give him a feeling of emotional security—a sense of belonging and of being loved. Losing this sense of security through divorce, a child often becomes confused, rejected, and demoralized and goes through life an emotional cripple.

What can a parent do if the child is not adjusting to the divorce?

Perhaps the best solution, if finances permit, is to call in a child psychiatrist. Mental hygiene clinics attached to hospitals, and child guidance centers or clinics can also be helpful, especially to those with limited funds.

Are we influenced by our former mates in choosing a second mate?

Yes. In choosing a husband or wife we are influenced by both conscious and unconscious reasons. On a conscious level we all want mates who are physically attractive, are good companions, have character and integrity as well as all the other virtues one can think of. Unhappily, many men and women find these qualities

261

conspicuously lacking after marriage. This is one of the important reasons so many marriages end in divorce courts. But the choice of a mate is probably more often due to unconscious factors than to purely conscious ones. For example, many individuals desire to find in a mate a substitute for the loved parent. A girl will often seek a husband who resembles her father. A boy who has known a mother's love will look for a wife who represents a modified parent substitute. Actually, finding a parent substitute in a mate is probably the most normal and dependable form of love choice.

What other unconscious elements take place in the choice of a mate?

1. The need for dependency, based on the early parent-child relationship. Instead of allowing youngsters to grow into mature, independent, and self-reliant individuals, many parents attempt to make their children dependent on them. The child is thus unable to stand on his own two feet, cannot make decisions, and looks constantly to his parents for guidance, help, and support. When eventually the child grows up he carries over these habits into adolescence and adulthood with crippling effect. Many husbands—because of long years of dependency on their parents—are simply unable to make decisions once they are married. As they were dependent on their mothers, so they are now dependent on their wives. Many such husbands (and wives) cannot accept responsibility at all.

2. The concept of the ideal mate. All of us, when we come to choose a mate draw upon our past experiences and present values. Our concept of the ideal mate changes as the individual matures, and is composed of our parents, relatives, friends, heroes, and motion picture stars. In finally choosing a husband or wife we compromise between our idealized image of the person we want and what is available.

3. The fulfillment of personality needs. Ideally people should fall in love with those whom they need to complete themselves emotionally. If a man who feels inadequate and insecure falls in love and marries a woman who constantly bolsters up his ego and restores his self-confidence, such a marriage may be successful, pro-

vided the wife, in the process, is fulfilling her own emotional needs, whatever they may be. In short, marriages are apt to be most rewarding when the husband and wife complement and supplement each other's basic conscious and unconscious desires. In such a marriage both husband and wife find themselves emotionally enriched. Being mutually dependent on each other, the couple are welded into a firm, permanent union which is likely to grow stronger with the years.

Do divorcees tend to go to opposite extremes in looking for a new mate?

Yes, consciously. A woman who has married an alcoholic may the next time marry a teetotaler. Unconsciously, however, she tends to marry the same type of *total* personality she married before even if, superficially, she goes to opposite extremes in looking for a new mate. In general, relatively normal people tend to marry other relatively normal people. Neurotics are attracted to other neurotics. Exceptionally, the normal person marries a neurotic. If the unconscious needs of *both* parties are met there is no reason why the marriage can't be successful, even in the case where neurotics marry each other. The best chance for marital success exists, everything else being equal, when two well-balanced individuals have at least one major interest in common, as well as feelings of tenderness and sexual attraction for each other. The marriage of two neurotic individuals is much more hazardous since neither knows what he or she really wants and both are likely to be too self-centered for each other's good. The exception, as already mentioned, is when the neurotic husband finds in his spouse the fulfillment of deep-seated emotional needs. Finally, the marriage of a normal or conventional individual to a neurotic is not likely to be successful since there is likely to be a great deal of misunderstanding and frustration. In remarriages, however, it is this latter group from which are likely to come reasonably successful marriages. The normal person, with a reshuffling of the marital cards, may meet and wed another normal individual. The neurotic may either remain single permanently and so remove himself from the mar-

263

riage market or be attracted to another neurotic who in some way will satisfy powerful emotional needs of which he himself is unaware.

Is it wise to avoid all chance of social contact with the ex-mate?

Yes, if the divorce has left nothing but bitterness and hostility in its wake. To go some place knowing that the ex-spouse will be there is to revive old sores. The only reason for maintaining social contact with the ex-spouse is that you still care for him and hope to remarry him. This sometimes happens, but not often and when such remarriages do ocurr they are not apt to be too successful.

Should a divorcee get involved with a married man?

Not if she's really smart, since such an affair can be ruinous to all parties concerned. For a man, an affair can mean the breakup of a reasonably satisfactory marriage, divorce, alimony, and the loss of children to whom he may be devoted. It may even result in a scandal that can destroy his business or professional career. In addition, there is the emotional strain of leading a double life which takes its toll both physically and mentally. For the woman, an affair is equally hazardous. In the first place, the affair may wind up by merely remaining an affair, or it may be terminated abruptly. In the second place, the woman may become so emotionally involved as to insist on marriage and when divorce is not forthcoming, for one reason or another, may succumb to alcoholism or even mental illness as a way out of her difficulties. Thirdly, a woman who carries on an affair with a married man frequently runs the risk of tarnishing her reputation which may make her less eligible for subsequent marriage.

Are second marriages successful when for financial reasons both husband and wife must work?

Yes, if both parties are reasonably mature and are willing to make sacrifices. Marriage is a partnership requiring the utmost co-operation. This is especially true when both husband and wife are compelled to hold down jobs. The husband, for example, should do everything he can to ease the wife's burden by helping out as much as he can around the house. The wife must refrain from belittling her husband's inability to support her on his own income. That each spouse is willing to work to support the common household is in itself an encouraging sign. It is even more encouraging when both husband and wife appreciate what the other is trying to do and each provides the emotional support without which no marriage can be a success.

How can a wealthy person protect himself financially in a second marriage?

By entering into an antenuptial agreement with his or her prospective spouse. Such an agreement may take the form of a settlement deed in which one of the prospective spouses conveys real property before the marriage, or it can take the form of reciprocal settlement deeds if both parties are persons of means. An antenuptial settlement may also take the form of a deed or deeds of gift of personal property. Both parties by contract may agree to transfer real or personal property after the marriage, or only one party may agree to do so. The contract may take the form of an agreement in which one or both parties agree to make payment after the marriage. Finally, either or both parties may agree to waive rights to the property or estate of the other, or to each other.

Aren't such agreements rather cold-blooded and calculating?

Not necessarily. Actually, antenuptial agreements are becoming increasingly common, especially in the case of second or third marriages. In fact, they are a practical way of settling financial problems before marriage. A wealthy widow may not—because of her children or grandchildren—want to turn over even a part of her fortune to her second husband, at least until he has proved his mettle. A sound method of avoiding such problems is to enter into an antenuptial agreement in which both agree to waive respective rights in each other's property or estate. If, on the other hand, one or both parties wish to make some financial arrangements to take place either before or after the marriage, the antenuptial agreement is the instrument by which this intention can be carried out. For the wealthy man entering his second or third marriage such a contract can save him an enormous amount of money in terms of alimony and property settlement in case the second marriage also ends in divorce. And what is true of the man is almost equally true of the woman.

Are such agreements enforceable?

Yes, providing both parties are represented by different legal counsel.

Directory
of Lawyers'
Referral Services

ALABAMA

Mobile
  Lawyers' Referral Service, Mobile Bar
  Association, 121 S. Royal Street

Montgomery
  Lawyers' Referral Service, Montgomery County Bar Association, 19 Adams
  Avenue

ARIZONA

Phoenix
  Lawyers' Reference Service, Maricopa
  County Bar Association, Title and
  Trust Building

Tucson
  Lawyers' Reference Service, Pima
  County Bar Association, 82 S. Stone
  Avenue

ARKANSAS

Little Rock
  Lawyers' Referral Service, Pulaski
  County Bar Association, 733 Pyramid
  Life Building

CALIFORNIA

Bakersfield
  Lawyers' Reference Service, Kern
  County Bar Association, Kern County
  Law Library, 1672 K Street

Compton
  Lawyers' Reference Service, Compton
  Judicial District Bar Association, 215
  South Acacia Street

Fresno
  Lawyers' Reference Service, Fresno
  County Bar Association, 505 Mason
  Building

Glendale
  Lawyers' Reference Service, Glendale
  Bar Association, 500 North Brand Blvd.

Long Beach
  Lawyers' Reference Service, Long
  Beach Bar Association, Suite 420, 115
  Pine Avenue Building

Los Angeles
  Lawyers' Reference Service, Los Angeles Bar Association, 510 S. Spring
  Street
  Lawyers' Reference Service, Southwest
  Los Angeles Bar Association, 1707
  West 49th Street

Montebello
  Lawyers' Reference Service, Whittier
  Bar Association, 1403 Whittier Blvd.

Oakland
  Lawyers' Reference Service, Alameda
  County Bar Association, 1419 Broadway

267

Palo Alto
Lawyers' Reference Service, Palo Alto Bar Association, 537 Middlefield Road

Pasadena
Lawyers' Reference Service, Pasadena Bar Association, 97 East Colorado Street

Pomona
Lawyers' Reference Service, Pomona Valley Bar Association, 230 Investment Building

Redwood City
Lawyers' Reference Service, San Mateo County Bar Association, Hall of Justice and Records

Richmond
Lawyers' Reference Service, Richmond Bar Association, 340 11th Street

Riverside
Lawyers' Reference Service, Riverside County Bar Association, 3972 Main Street

Salinas
Lawyers' Reference Service, Monterey County Bar Association, 243 Salinas Street

San Bernardino
Legal Aid and Lawyers' Reference Service, San Bernardino County Bar Association, Winstead Building, 308 D Street

San Diego
Lawyers' Reference Service, San Diego County Bar Association, Room 820, Bank of America Building

San Francisco
Lawyers' Reference Service, Bar Association of San Francisco, 220 Bush Street
Lawyers' Reference Service, Lawyers' Club of San Francisco, 461 Market Street, Room 413

San Jose
Lawyers' Reference Service, Santa Clara County Bar Association, 303 Commercial Building, 28 North 1st Street

Santa Ana
Lawyers' Reference Service, Orange County Bar Association, Room 18, Hopkins Building, 114½ West Fourth Street

Santa Barbara
Lawyers' Reference Service, Santa Barbara County Bar Association, 21 East Cañon Perdido Street

Santa Cruz
Lawyers' Reference Service, Santa Cruz County Bar Association, 204 Church Street

Vallejo
Lawyers' Reference Service, Solano County Bar Association, Fisch-Higgins Building, Room 410, 327 Georgia Street

Van Nuys
Lawyers' Reference Service, San Fernando Valley Bar Association, 6356½ Van Nuys Boulevard

Willows
Lawyers' Referral Service, Glenn County Bar Association, Bank of America Building

CANADA

Vancouver, B.C.
Lawyers' Referral Committee, Vancouver Bar Association, Standard Building, 510 W. Hastings Street

COLORADO

Boulder
Lawyers' Referral Service, Boulder County Bar Association, National State Bank Building

Colorado Springs
Lawyers' Referral Service, El Paso County Bar Association, Independence Building

Denver
Lawyers' Referral Service, Denver Bar Association, 525 Mile High Center, 1700 Broadway

Pueblo
Lawyers' Referral Service, Pueblo County Bar Association, 303 Bon Durant Building

CONNECTICUT

Bridgeport
Lawyers' Referral Service, Bridgeport Bar Association, Fairfield County Law Library, County Courthouse

Lawyers' Referral Service, State Bar Association of Connecticut, 1115 Main Street

Hartford
Hartford County Lawyers' Referral Service, 95 Washington Street

New Haven
Lawyers' Referral Service, New Haven County Bar Association, 169 Church Street

New London
Legal Aid and Lawyers' Reference Service, New London County Bar Association, County Courthouse

Norwich
Legal Aid and Lawyers' Reference Service, New London County Bar Association, 10 Shetucket Street

Waterbury
Waterbury Legal Aid and Reference Service, Inc., Waterbury Bar Association, 35 Field Street

DELAWARE

Wilmington
Lawyers' Reference Service, Delaware State Bar Association, Room 153, Public Building, 10th and King Streets

DISTRICT OF COLUMBIA

Washington
Lawyers' Referral Service, District of Columbia Bar Association, 1044 Washington Building

FLORIDA

Clearwater
Lawyers' Referral Service, Clearwater Bar Association, Law Library, County Courthouse

Gainesville
Lawyers' Referral Service, Eighth Judicial Circuit Bar Association, 241 West University Avenue

Jacksonville
Lawyers' Reference Service, Jacksonville Bar Association, 501 Florida National Bank Building

Miami
Lawyers' Referral Service, Dade County Bar Association, 514 Metropolitan Bank Building

Miami Beach
Lawyers' Referral Service, Miami Beach Bar Association, 706 1st Street

Naples
Lawyers' Referral Service, Collier County Bar Association, 878 Fifth Avenue South

Orlando
Lawyers' Referral Service, Orange County Bar Association, 160 East Washington Street

Tampa
Legal Aid Bureau, Bar Association of Tampa and Hillsborough County, County Courthouse

GEORGIA

Atlanta
Lawyers' Reference Service, Atlanta Bar Association, Fulton County Courthouse

Macon
Lawyers' Referral Service, Macon Bar Association, Southern United Building

Savannah
Lawyers' Referral Service, Savannah Bar Association, County Courthouse

HAWAII

Honolulu
Lawyers' Referral Service, Bar Association of Hawaii, 813 Alakea Street

IDAHO

Boise
Lawyers' Referral Service, Third District Bar Association, First National Bank Building

Idaho Falls
Lawyers' Referral Service, Ninth Judicial District Bar Association, Courthouse Building (c/o Probate Judge)

Pocatello
Lawyers' Referral Service, The Book Arcade, Bannock Hotel

ILLINOIS

Champaign
Lawyers' Referral Service, Champaign County Bar Association, 44 Main Street

Chicago
Lawyers' Reference Plan, The Chicago Bar Association, Suite 1140, 29 S. LaSalle Street

Lansing
Lawyers' Referral Service, Harvey-Calumet Bar Association, 3450 Ridge Road

Sterling
Legal Aid and Lawyers' Referral Service, Whiteside County Bar Association, City Court Room, City Hall

INDIANA

Fort Wayne
Lawyers' Referral Service, Allen County Bar Association, 104 West Berry

Indianapolis
Lawyers' Referral Service, Indianapolis Bar Association, 615 N. Alabama Street

South Bend
Lawyers' Referral Service, St. Joseph County Bar Association, Courthouse

IOWA

Davenport
Lawyers' Referral Service, Scott County Bar Association, Union Arcade

Des Moines
Committee on Legal Aid and Lawyers' Reference, Polk County Bar Association, 1000 Fleming Building

Douds
Lawyers' Referral Service, Van Buren County Bar Association, P.O. Box 236

Ottumwa
Lawyers' Referral Service, Second Judicial Bar Association, Law Library, Courthouse Building

Storm Lake
Lawyers' Referral Service, Buena Vista County Bar Association, Pendleton Building, 5th and Cayuga Street

Waterloo
Lawyers' Referral Service, Black Hawk County Bar Association, 602 Waterloo Building

KANSAS

Emporia
Lawyers' Referral Service, Bar Association of the State of Kansas, Citizens National Bank Building

Kansas City
Lawyers' Referral Service, Kansas City Bar Association, Bennett Building

KENTUCKY

Covington
Lawyers' Referral Service, Kenton County Bar Association, Covington Courthouse

Louisville
Lawyers' Reference Service, Louisville Bar Association, 400 Courthouse

LOUISIANA

Baton Rouge
Lawyers' Referral Service, Baton Rouge Bar Association, 101 Old State Capitol Building

New Orleans
Lawyers' Referral Service, New Orleans Bar Association, 908 International Building

Shreveport
Legal Aid and Lawyers' Referral Service, Shreveport Bar Association, 608 Courthouse

MAINE

Portland
Lawyers' Referral Service, Cumberland Bar Association, 97-A Exchange Street

MARYLAND

Baltimore
Lawyers' Referral Service, Bar Association of Baltimore City, 617 Mercantile Trust Building

MASSACHUSETTS

Boston
Lawyers' Reference Service, Boston Bar Association, 35 Court Street

MICHIGAN

Detroit
Lawyers' Reference Service, Detroit Bar Association, 577 Penobscot Building

Flint
Lawyers' Referral Service, Genesee County Bar Association, 404 Dryden Building

Grand Rapids
Lawyers' Reference Service, Grand Rapids Bar Association, 1060 Michigan Trust Building

Hamtramck
Lawyers' Reference Service, Hamtramck Bar Association, 9544 Joseph Campau Avenue

Kalamazoo
Lawyers' Reference Service, Kalamazoo Bar Association, 212 Commerce Building

Mount Clemens
Lawyers' Referral Service, Macomb County Bar Association, 22 N. Broadway

Muskegon
Lawyers' Reference Service, Muskegon County Bar Association, 408 W. Western Avenue

Pontiac
Lawyers' Reference Service, Oakland County Bar Association, 815 Pontiac State Bank Building

Port Huron
Lawyers' Referral Service, St. Clair County Bar Association, 510 Peoples Bank Building

Saginaw
Lawyers' Referral Service, Saginaw Bar Association, c/o Saginaw Community Chest, Eddy Building

MINNESOTA

Duluth
Lawyers' Referral Service, Legal Aid Service of Duluth, Inc., 222 Providence Building

Minneapolis
Hennepin County Bar Reference Committee, 1451 Northwestern Bank Building

St. Paul
Lawyers' Reference Service, Ramsey County Bar Association, Minnesota Building

MISSOURI

Clayton
Lawyers' Referral Service, St. Louis County Bar Association, Courthouse

Farmington
Lawyers' Referral Service, St. Francois County Bar Association, Columbia Street

Kansas City
Lawyers' Referral Service, Kansas City Bar Association, 626 Lathrop Building

St. Louis
Lawyers' Referral Service, The Bar Association of St. Louis, 418 Olive Street, Suite 1015

NEW JERSEY

Camden
Legal Aid Society, Camden City Hall

Morristown
Lawyers' Referral Service, Morris County Bar Association, Room 307, Courthouse

Newark
Lawyers' Reference Plan, Essex County Bar Association, 55 Commerce Street

Paterson
Lawyers' Referral Service, Passaic County Bar Association, 152 Market Street

Toms River
Lawyers' Referral Service, Ocean County Bar Association, 110 Hooper Avenue

NEW MEXICO

Albuquerque
Lawyers' Reference Service, Albuquerque Bar Association, First National Bank Building

271

NEW YORK

Albany
Albany Referral Service, Albany County Bar Association, Albany County Court

Bronx
Lawyers' Referral Service, Bronx County Bar Association, 851 Grand Concourse

Brooklyn
Lawyers' Reference Service, Brooklyn Bar Association, 123 Remsen Street

Buffalo
Lawyers' Reference Service, Erie County Bar Association, 77 West Eagle Street

Dansville
Lawyers' Referral Service, Livingston County Bar Association, Main Street

Jamaica
Lawyers'. Referral Service, Queens County Bar Association, 88-11 Sutphin Boulevard

Mineola
Lawyers' Referral Service, Bar Association of Nassau County, 120 Mineola Boulevard

New Rochelle
Lawyers' Referral Service, New Rochelle Bar Association, 271 North Avenue

New York City
Legal Referral Service of The Association of the Bar of the City of New York and The New York County Lawyers Association, 42 West 44th Street

Rochester
Lawyers' Reference Service, Rochester Bar Association, 209 Powers Building

Syracuse
Lawyers' Reference Service, Onondaga County Bar Association, 107 James Street

Utica
Lawyers' Referral Service, Oneida County Bar Association, Mayro Building

White Plains
Lawyers' Referral Service, White Plains Bar Association, 199 Main Street

Yonkers
Lawyers' Referral Service, Yonkers Lawyers Association, 20 South Broadway

NORTH CAROLINA

Charlotte
Lawyers' Referral Service, Twenty-Sixth Judicial District Bar Association, Law Building

Lumberton
Lawyers' Referral Service, Robeson County Bar Association, Scottish Bank Building

NORTH DAKOTA

Fargo
Lawyers' Referral Service, Cass County Bar Association, Cass County Courthouse

OHIO

Akron
Lawyers' Referral Service, Akron Bar Association, 305 Y.W.C.A. Building

Canton
Lawyers' Reference Service, Stark County Bar Association, Peoples-Merchants Building

Celina
Lawyers' Referral Service, Mercer County Bar Association, Wyckott Building

Cincinnati
Lawyers' Reference Service, Cincinnati Bar Association, 400 Hamilton County Courthouse

Cleveland
Lawyers' Referral Service, Cleveland Bar Association, Manger Hotel, East 13th and Chester Avenue

Cleveland
Lawyers' Referral Service, Cuyahoga County Bar Association, 838 National City Bank Building

Columbus
Lawyers' Reference Service, Columbus Bar Association, 40 South Third Street

Dayton
  Lawyers' Referral Service, Dayton Bar Association, 502 American Building
Springfield
  Lawyers' Referral Service, Springfield Bar and Law Library Association, Mitchell Building
Steubenville
  Lawyers' Referral Service, Jefferson County Bar Association, 102 North 3rd Street
Toledo
  Attorney Reference Service, Toledo Bar Association, 218 Huron Street
Van Wert
  Lawyers' Referral Service, Van Wert County Bar Association, Courthouse
Warren
  Lawyers' Referral Service, Trumbull County Bar Association, 130 Pine Ave.
Youngstown
  Lawyers' Referral Service, Mahoning County Bar Association, Mahoning County Courthouse

OKLAHOMA

Stillwater
  Lawyers' Referral Service, Payne County Bar Association, County Attorney's Office, Courthouse

OREGON

Eugene
  Lawyers' Referral Service, Lane County Bar Association, 858 Pearl Street, P. O. Box 1147

PENNSYLVANIA

Allentown
  Legal Service Office, Bar Association of Lehigh County, 527 Hamilton Street
Altoona
  Lawyers' Referral Service, 402 Penelec Building
Beaver
  Lawyers' Referral Service, Beaver County Bar Association, 325 Commerce Street
Easton
  Lawyers' Referral Service, Northampton County Bar Association, Northampton County Courthouse, County Solicitor's Office
Johnstown
  Lawyers' Referral Service, Cambria County Bar Association, 702 First National Bank Building
Media
  Lawyers' Referral Service, Delaware County Bar Association, Courthouse
Norristown
  Lawyers' Referral Service, Montgomery Bar Association, 100 W. Airy Street
Philadelphia
  Lawyers' Reference Service, Philadelphia Bar Association, Room 601, City Hall
Pittsburgh
  Lawyers' Referral Service, Allegheny County Bar Association, Ninth Floor, City-County Building
Uniontown
  Lawyers' Referral Service, Fayette County Bar Association, Blackstone Building, East Main Street
Washington
  Lawyers' Referral Service, Washington County Bar Association, Washington Trust Building
Wilkes-Barre
  Lawyers' Referral Service, Wilkes-Barre Law and Library Association, Luzerne County, Luzerne County Courthouse
Williamsport
  Lawyers' Referral Service, 331 Pine Street

RHODE ISLAND

Providence
  Lawyers' Referral Service, The Rhode Island Bar Association, 1114 Industrial Bank Building

SOUTH CAROLINA

Charleston
  Legal Aid Office, 33 Broad Street

TENNESSEE

Nashville
  Lawyers' Referral Service, Nashville Bar Association, Stahlman Building

273

TEXAS

Amarillo
Legal Aid Service, Amarillo Bar Association, Barfield Building

Austin
Legal Aid Clinic, Texas University Law School

Bryan
Lawyers' Referral Service, Brazos County Bar Association, 505 Varisco Building

Corpus Christi
Lawyers' Referral Service, Nueces County Bar Association, Courthouse

Dallas
Lawyers' Referral Service, Dallas Bar Association, Adolphus Hotel

El Paso
Lawyers' Referral Service, El Paso Bar Association, County Courthouse

San Antonio
Lawyers' Referral Service, San Antonio Bar Association, Bexar County Courthouse

Waco
Lawyers' Referral Service, Waco-McLennan County Bar Association, Liberty Building

VIRGINIA

Norfolk
Legal Reference Bureau, Norfolk and Portsmouth Bar Association, Bank of Commerce Building

WEST VIRGINIA

Charleston
Lawyers' Reference Service, Kanawha County Bar Association, Transit Building

WISCONSIN

Galesville
Lawyers' Referral Service, Tri-County Bar Association

Milwaukee
Lawyers' Referral Service, Milwaukee Bar Association, 324 East Wisconsin Avenue

Directory
of Legal
Aid Services

ALABAMA

Birmingham
  Legal Aid Society of Birmingham, 318 Jefferson County Courthouse

Florence
  Legal Aid Society of Lauderdale County

Mobile
  Committee on Legal Aid, Mobile Bar Association, Law Library, New Courthouse Building

Montgomery
  Legal Aid Office, 4th Floor, Courthouse

ARIZONA

Phoenix
  Maricopa County Legal Aid Society, 706 Security Building, 234 North Central

Tucson
  The Legal Aid Society of Pima County Bar Assn., Pima County Courthouse Annex, 112 West Pennington

Window Rock
  Navajo Legal Aid Service, The Navajo Tribe

ARKANSAS

Fort Smith
  Sebastian County Legal Aid Society, Welfare Building

Little Rock
  Pulaski County Legal Aid Bureau, 901 Pyramid Building

CALIFORNIA

Alhambra
  San Gabriel Legal Aid and Lawyers' Reference Service, Room 104, 924 East Main Street

Bakersfield
  Legal Aid Service, Kern County Bar Association, 300 Moronet Building, 1522 Eighteenth Street

Baldwin Park
  San Gabriel Valley Legal Aid Foundation, 14327 East Ramona Boulevard

Fresno
  Legal Aid Society of Fresno County, Fresno County Bar Association, 505 Mason Building, 1044 Fulton Street (21)

Hermosa Beach
  Legal Aid Program of the South Bay District Bar Association, P. O. Box 66, 421 Pier Avenue

Long Beach
Legal Aid Foundation, Suite 512, 115 Pine Avenue (2)

Los Angeles
Legal Aid Foundation, 444 Cotton Exchange Building, 106 West Third Street (13)

Modesto
Legal Aid Program, c/o A-1 Secretarial Service, 812 Fourteenth Street

Oakland
Legal Aid Society of Alameda County, Room 312, 1815 Telegraph Avenue (12)

Ontario
The West End Legal Aid Society, 208 Emmons Building, 309 North Euclid Avenue

Palo Alto
Legal Aid Program, Palo Alto Bar Association, Family Service Association, 375 Cambridge Avenue

Pasadena
Legal Aid Society of Pasadena, 97 East Colorado Street

Pomona
San Gabriel Valley Legal Foundation, 642 South Main St.

Redwood City
Legal Aid Society of San Mateo County, Hall of Justice

Richmond
Legal Aid Program, 202 County Building 100 37th Street

Riverside
Legal Aid Society of Riverside, 3637 5th Street

Sacramento
Legal Aid Society of Sacramento County, 235 Ochsner Building, 719 K Street (14)

Salinas
Monterey County Legal Aid Society, c/o Alisal Chamber of Commerce, 924 Sanborn Road

San Bernardino
Legal Aid Society of San Bernardino, 308 North D Street

San Diego
Legal Aid Society of San Diego, Inc., 102 Welfare Building, 645 A Street (1)

San Francisco
Legal Aid Society of San Francisco, 503-8 DeYoung Building, 690 Market Street

San Jose
Legal Aid Society of Santa Clara County, 601 Commercial Building, 28 North 1st Street (13)

San Rafael
Legal Aid Society of Marin County, 333 Albert Building, 1010 B Street

Santa Ana
Legal Aid Society of Orange County, 206 North Main Street

Santa Barbara
Legal Aid Foundation of Santa Barbara County Bar Association, 716 A Street

Santa Cruz
Legal Aid Program, 204 Church Street

Santa Monica
Legal Aid Society of Santa Monica, 315 Juniper Building, 309 Santa Monica Boulevard

Santa Rosa
Legal Aid Foundation of Sonoma County, P.O. Box 1644

Seaside
Monterey County Legal Aid Society, c/o Seaside Chamber of Commerce, 505 Broadway Avenue

Stockton
San Joaquin County Legal Aid Society, 504 Belding Building, 110 North San Joaquin Street (2)

Vallejo
Solano County Legal Aid Scoiety, 601 Georgia Street

Van Nuys
Legal Aid Association of the San Fernando Valley, Room 214, 6356½ Van Nuys Boulevard

Ventura
Ventura County Legal Aid Association, Room 227, County Courthouse, Patrick Loughran, Atty.

Walnut Creek
Central Contra Costa Legal Aid Program, P.O. Box 431

Watsonville
Legal Aid Program, 439 A Main Street, P.O. Box 166

COLORADO

Boulder
Legal Aid Clinic, University of Colorado Law School

Colorado Springs
Legal Aid Society of Colorado Springs, 461 Independence Building

Denver
Metropolitan Legal Aid Society of Denver, 314 14th Street (2)
Branch Offices:
Robert H. Sanheim, 7720 W. 57th Avenue, Arvada (Jefferson County)
Haydn Swearingen, 3503 S. Broadway, Englewood (Arapahoe County)
James R. Stitt, 3110 W. 72nd Avenue, Westminster (Adams County)

Pueblo
Legal Aid Society of Pueblo, Thatcher Building

CONNECTICUT

Bridgeport
Legal Aid Division, Department of Public Welfare, 835 Washington Avenue (4)

Hartford
Legal Aid Society of Hartford County, Inc., 550 Main Street

New Haven
Municipal Legal Aid Bureau, 169 Church Street

Norwich
Legal Aid and Lawyers' Reference Service, New London County Bar Association, 287 Main Street

Waterbury
Waterbury Legal Aid and Referral Service, Inc., 35 Field Street

DELAWARE

Wilmington
Legal Aid Society of Delaware, 412 North American Building, 10th and Market Streets

DISTRICT OF COLUMBIA

Washington
Legal Aid Society of the District of Columbia, Central Building, 805 G Street N.W. (1)
Bar Association Legal Assistance Office, 201 Civil Building, Municipal Court for the District of Columbia
Georgetown Legal Aid Society Georgetown Law Center
Howard University Law School Branch, Sixth Street and Howard Place, N.W.

FLORIDA

Jacksonville
Duval County Legal Aid Association, Inc., 212 O'Reilly Building, 237 West Forsyth Street (2)

Lakeland
Legal Aid Clinic of the Lakeland Bar Association, Broderick Building

Miami
Legal Aid Society of Dade County Bar Association, 911 Metropolitan Bank Building (32)

Miami Beach
Miami Beach Bar Association–Legal Aid Committee, 420 Lincoln Road (39)

Orlando
Legal Aid Office, Orange County Bar Association, County Courthouse

Pensacola
Escambia County Legal Aid Society, Box 1111, Escambia County Courthouse

St. Petersburg
Legal Aid Society of St. Petersburg, County Law Library, 300 County Building

Tampa
Legal Aid Society of Tampa and Hillsborough County, County Courthouse

West Palm Beach
Legal Aid Society of Palm Beach County, 506 Citizens Building

GEORGIA

Athens
Athens Legal Aid Society, 204 Clarke County Courthouse

277

Atlanta
Atlanta Legal Aid Society, Inc., 923 Fulton County Courthouse (3)

Augusta
Committee on Legal Aid, Augusta Bar Association, c/o County Welfare Department, Richmond County Courthouse

Columbus
Committee on Legal Aid, Columbus Lawyers' Club, c/o Travelers Aid—Family Service, Inc., 1425 3rd Avenue

Macon
Macon Legal Aid Society, Inc., Room 405, Grand Building

Marietta
Legal Aid Office, Juvenile Court Building

Savannah
Savannah Legal Aid Society, 4th Floor, Chatham County Courthouse

HAWAII

Honolulu
Legal Aid Society of Hawaii, 813 Alakea Street

ILLINOIS

Aurora
Legal Aid Bureau, c/o Family Service Association, 79 River Street

Champaign-Urbana
Legal Aid Committee of the Champaign Co. Bar Association, Courthouse, Urbana

Chicago
Legal Aid Bureau of the United Charities, 123 West Madison Street (2)

Legal Aid Department, Jewish Family and Community Service, 1 South Franklin Street (6)

Glen Ellyn
Legal Aid Society, 438 Main Street

Pekin
Legal Aid Society of Tazewell County, Civil Defense Room, City Hall

Peoria
Greater Peoria Legal Aid Society, 204 City Hall, 419 Fulton Street

Rockford
Legal Aid Society of the Winnebago County Bar Association, 1st Floor, Courthouse

Sterling
Legal Aid Society of Whiteside County, 212 3rd Avenue

INDIANA

Evansville
Legal Aid Society of Evansville, Inc., 303 Courthouse Annex

Fort Wayne
Legal Aid of Fort Wayne, Inc., Foellinger Community Center, 227 East Washington Street

Indianapolis
Indianapolis Legal Aid Society, Inc., Room 122, 615 North Alabama Street

South Bend
Legal Aid Society of St. Joseph County, Inc., 203 Lafayette Building (1)

IOWA

Des Moines
Legal Aid Society of Polk County, Hawley Welfare Building, 700 6th Avenue (9)

Waterloo
Black Hawk County Legal Aid Society, Inc., Community Services Building, 1028 Headford

KANSAS

Kansas City
Legal Aid Society of Wyandotte County, Courthouse

Topeka
Legal Aid Bureau, Topeka Bar Association, 401 Columbian Building

Wichita
Legal Aid Society of Wichita, Inc., Sedgwick County Courthouse

KENTUCKY

Louisville
Legal Aid Society of Louisville, 205 South 4th Street, Third Floor (2)

LOUISIANA

Baton Rouge
Legal Aid Society of Baton Rouge, 101 Old State Capitol, North Boulevard (1)

New Orleans
New Orleans Office, Legal Aid Bureau, Civil Division, 909 International Building (12)

Shreveport
Legal Aid Society of Caddo and Bossier Parishes, 608 Caddo Parish Courthouse

MAINE

Portland
Legal Aid Office Courthouse

MARYLAND

Baltimore
Legal Aid Bureau, Inc., People's Court Building, Fayette and Gay Streets (2)

MASSACHUSETTS

Boston
The Boston Legal Aid Society, 14 Somerset Street (8)

Cambridge
Harvard Legal Aid Bureau, Gannett House, Harvard Law School (38)

New Bedford
Legal Aid Society, 210 Bookstore Bldg., 222 Union Street

Springfield
The Legal Aid Society of Springfield, 145 State Street

Worcester
Legal Aid Society of Worcester, Room 300, 311 Main Street

MICHIGAN

Battle Creek
Calhoun County Legal Aid Society, 604 Post Building

Detroit
Legal Aid Bureau, 51 West Warren Avenue (1)

Flint
Genesee County Legal Aid Society, Inc., 404 Dryden Building (2)

Grand Rapids
Legal Aid Society of Grand Rapids and Kent County, 304 Association of Commerce Building

Jackson
Jackson County Legal Aid Society, 132 West Washington Street

Kalamazoo
Kalamazoo County Legal Aid Bureau, 415 County Building

Lansing
Legal Aid Bureau, 615 North Capitol Avenue

Pontiac
Oakland County Legal Aid Society, 221 National Building

MINNESOTA

Duluth
Legal Aid Service of Duluth, Inc., 304 Moore Memorial Building (2)

Minneapolis
The Legal Aid Society of Minneapolis, Inc., 234 Citizens Aid Building (4)

St. Paul
Legal Aid Department, Family Service of St. Paul, 104 Wilder Building (2)

Jackson
Legal Aid of Jackson, Public Welfare Building, 355 South Congress Street

MISSOURI

Kansas City
Legal Aid Bureau, City Hall (6)
Tenth and Forest Legal Aid Clinic, 1112 E. 10th Street (6)

St. Louis
Legal Aid Bureau, 3rd Floor, Municipal Courts Building, 14th and Market Streets (1)

Springfield
Legal Aid and Lawyers' Referral Service of the Green County Bar Association, 324 Woodruff Building

NEBRASKA

Lincoln
Lincoln Legal Aid Bureau, College of Law Building

Omaha
Omaha Legal Aid Clinic, Creighton University Law School, 26th and California Streets

NEVADA

Las Vegas
Clark County Legal Aid Society, 1622 S. Commerce Street

NEW JERSEY

Asbury Park
Legal Aid Society of Monmouth County, 709 Bangs Avenue

Atlantic City
Legal Aid Society of Atlantic City, 407–408 Schwehm Building

Bridgeton
Bridgeton Branch, Legal Aid Society of Cumberland County

Camden
Legal Aid Society of Camden County, 599½ Carman Street

Elizabeth
Legal Aid Society of Union County, Courthouse, Broad Street

Hackensack
Legal Aid Bureau of the Bergen County Bar Association, Inc., 1 Courthouse

Jersey City
Legal Aid Society, 15 Exchange Place

Lambertville
Legal Aid Society of Hunterdon County, 40 E. Delaware Avenue

Millville
Millville Branch, Legal Aid Society of Cumberland County

Morristown
Legal Aid Society of Morris County, 308 Courthouse

Mt. Holly
Legal Aid Society of Burlington County, Burlington County Courthouse, High Street

Newark
Essex County Legal Aid Association, 235 Hall of Records, Market and High Streets

Newton
Sussex County Legal Aid Society, Courthouse, Hall of Records, Courthouse

Paterson
Legal Aid Society of Passaic County, 152 Market Street

Phillipsburg
Warren County Legal Aid Society, 83 South Main Street

Salem
Salem County Legal Aid Society, 191 East Broadway

Somerville
Somerset County Legal Aid Society, Administration Building

Toms River
Ocean County Legal Aid Society, 212 Washington Street

Trenton
Legal Aid Society of Mercer County, 16 North Willow Street

Vineland
Vineland Branch, Legal Aid Society of Cumberland County

Wildwood
The Legal Aid Society of Cape May County, 3407 New Jersey Avenue

NEW MEXICO

Albuquerque
Legal Aid Society of Albuquerque, 46 County Courthouse

NEW YORK

Albany
Legal Aid Society of Albany, Inc., 82 State Street (7)

Batavia
Legal Aid Committee, Genesee County Bar Association, County Building

Bay Shore
Legal Aid Society of Suffolk County, 71 East Main Street

Binghamton
Legal Aid Committee, Broome County Bar Association, 2nd Floor, County Office Building

Buffalo
Legal Aid Bureau of Buffalo, Inc., Dun Building, Swan & Pearl Streets

Ithaca
Cornell Legal Aid Clinic, Myron Taylor Hall

Mineola
Legal Aid Society of Nassau County, 120 Mineola Boulevard

New York City
Family Location Service, 31 Union Square (3)

The Legal Aid Society, 11 Park Place (7)
Civil Branch Offices, Uptown Office, 290 Lenox Avenue (27)

Niagara Falls
Niagara Falls Legal Aid Society, Niagara County Building

Poughkeepsie
Dutchess County Legal Aid Society, Room 303, 234 Main Street

Rochester
Legal Aid Society, 25 Exchange Street (14)

Syracuse
Frank H. Hiscock Legal Aid Society, 610 Paramount Theater Building, 428 South Salina Street (2)

Utica
Legal Aid Society of Oneida County, Inc., Mayro Building

White Plains
Westchester County Legal Aid Society, 65 Court St.

Yonkers
Legal Aid Service, Family Service Society, 219 Palisade Avenue

NORTH CAROLINA

Charlotte
Legal Aid Office, Legal Aid Committee of the 26th Judicial District, Bar Association, Courthouse

Winston-Salem
Legal Aid Society of Forsyth County, O'Hanlon Building

OHIO

Akron
Summit County Legal Aid Society, 80 West Center Street

Canton
Stark County Legal Aid Society, 618 Second Street, N.W.

Cincinnati
Legal Aid Society of Cincinnati, 312 West Ninth Street (2)

Cleveland
Legal Aid Society of Cleveland, 603 Louisville Title Building, 118 St. Clair Avenue, N.E. (14)

Columbus
Legal Aid and Public Defender Association, City of Columbus, City Hall Annex

Dayton
Legal Aid Service, Dayton Bar Association, 502 American Building (2)

Hamilton
Butler County Legal Aid Society, Inc., 501 Rentschler Building

Springfield
Legal Aid Office, Springfield Bar and Law Library Association, 3rd Floor, Clark County Courthouse

Toledo
Toledo Legal Aid Society, 218 Huron Street

Warren
Legal Aid and Lawyers' Referral Committee, Trumbull County Bar Association, 130 Pine Street, S.E.

Wooster
Wayne County Legal Aid Society, Courthouse

Youngstown
Legal Aid Society of Youngstown, Courthouse Basement (3)

OKLAHOMA

Duncan
Stephens County Legal Aid Society, Courthouse

Oklahoma City
The Legal Aid Society of Oklahoma County, Inc., 622 County Courthouse

Tulsa
Tulsa County Legal Aid Society, Inc., 603 County Courthouse

OREGON

Eugene
Legal Aid Committee, Lane County Bar Association, Lane County Courthouse

Portland
Legal Aid Committee, Oregon State Bar, 826 County Courthouse

Salem
Salem Legal Aid Clinic, College of Law, Willamette University

281

PENNSYLVANIA

Allentown
Legal Service Office, Lehigh County Bar Association, 508 Hamilton Street

Doylestown
Legal Aid Office, c/o Bucks County Law Reporter, Bucks County Courthouse

Easton
Committee on Legal Aid, Northampton County Bar Association, Courthouse

Erie
Legal Aid Department of the Family & Child Service, 110 West 10th Street

Harrisburg
Legal Aid Committee, Dauphin County Bar Association, Blackstone Building

Jenkintown
Jenkintown Branch Office, Legal Aid Committee, Montgomery County Bar Association, York Road and Greenwood Avenue

Lancaster
Legal Aid Bureau, Lancaster Bar Association, 110 East King Street

Media
Legal Service Committee, Delaware County Bar Association, Courthouse

Norristown
Legal Aid Committee, Montgomery County Bar Association, 100 West Airy Street

Philadelphia
Legal Aid Society of Philadelphia, Social Service Building, 311 South Juniper Street (7)

Temple University Branch
Legal Aid Society of Philadelphia, 1715 North Broad Street (22)

Pittsburgh
Legal Aid Society, 200 Ross Street (19)

Pottstown
Pottstown Branch Office, Legal Aid Committee, Montgomery County Bar Association, 635 High Street

Reading
Legal Aid Committee, Berks County Bar Association, 522 Court Street

Wilkes-Barre
Legal Aid Society of Luzerne County, 66–68 North Main Street

Williamsport
Legal Service Office, Lycoming Law Association, 416 First National Bank Building

York
York County Legal Aid and Defender Office, York County Bar Association, 208 York County Courthouse

RHODE ISLAND

Providence
Legal Aid Society of Rhode Island, 100 North Main Street (3)

SOUTH CAROLINA

Charleston
Legal Aid Office of Charleston, 33 Broad Street

TENNESSEE

Chattanooga
Legal Aid–Lawyers' Referral Committee, Chattanooga Bar Association, Hamilton County Law Library, Professional Building, Georgia Avenue

Knoxville
Legal Aid Clinic, University of Tennessee, College of Law, Law Building, 1505 Cumberland Avenue (16)

Memphis
Legal Aid Office of Memphis and Shelby County, 409 Shelby County Office Building (3)

Nashville
Free Legal Clinic, Nashville Bar Association, 409 County Courthouse (3)

TEXAS

Abilene
Legal Aid Office, County Courthouse

Amarillo
Amarillo Legal Aid, Inc., Petroleum Building

Austin
Legal Aid Clinic, Texas University Law School

Beaumont
Jefferson County Legal Aid Association, Jefferson County Courthouse

Corpus Christi
Legal Aid Society of Nueces County, Courthouse Building

Dallas
Dallas Legal Aid Society, Inc., Room 428, Fidelity Building, 1000 Main Street

Legal Aid Bureau, City-County Department of Public Welfare 4917 Harry Hines Boulevard (35)

Legal Aid Clinic, Southern Methodist University School of Law, Hillcrest at Daniels

Fort Worth
Legal Aid Service of the Fort Worth Legal Foundation, Tarrant County Courthouse

Houston
Legal Aid Clinic, 216 Lawyers Building, 1029 Preston Avenue (2)

Legal Aid Clinic, School of Law, Texas Southern University, 3201 Wheeler Avenue

Midland
Midland Legal Aid Association, Box 670, County Courthouse

San Antonio
Bexar County Legal Aid Association, 2B Bexar County Courthouse

Tyler
Legal Aid Society, County Courthouse

Waco
Waco Legal Aid Clinic, 209 McClennan County Courthouse

Wichita Falls
Legal Aid Society, Courthouse

UTAH

Salt Lake City
Legal Aid Society, 509 Atlas Building (1)

VERMONT

Bennington
Bennington Legal Aid Service, 100 South Street

Burlington
Legal Aid Committee, Chittenden County Bar Association, 62 W. Allen Street, Winooski, Vermont

VIRGINIA

Arlington
Legal Aid Bureau, Courthouse Square

Richmond
Legal Aid Bureau, Family Service Society of Richmond, 221 Governor Street (19)

Roanoke
Legal Aid Receptionist, Roanoke Family Service Association, Inc., 442 King George Avenue, S.W.

WASHINGTON

Bellingham
Legal Aid Bureau of Whatcom County, Whatcom County Courthouse

Seattle
The Seattle–King County Legal Aid Bureau, 325 Lyon Building (4)

Spokane
Legal Aid Committee, Spokane County Bar, 2nd Floor, Courthouse Annex

Tacoma
Legal Aid Office, Tacoma and Pierce County Bar Association, 625 Perkins Building

WEST VIRGINIA

Charleston
Legal Aid Society of Charleston, 203 Berman Building, 612 Virginia Street E.

WISCONSIN

Beloit
Legal Aid Society of the Rock County Bar Association, Municipal Building, 220 West Grant Avenue

Janesville
Legal Aid Society of the Rock County Bar Association, Rock County Courthouse

Madison
Legal Aid Society, 2059 Atwood Avenue

Milwaukee
Legal Aid Society, 610 North Jackson Street (2)

283

Oshkosh
Legal Aid Service, Winnebago County Bar Association, 230 Courthouse

Racine
Racine County Legal Aid Society, Courthouse

CANADA

Toronto, Ontario
Ontario Legal Aid Plan, Law Society of Upper Canada, Osgoode Hall (1)

Montreal, Quebec
The Legal Aid Bureau of the Bar of Montreal, New Courthouse, 100 Notre Dame Street East

Montreal Legal Aid Bureau, Inc., 1040 Atwater Avenue (6)

PHILIPPINE ISLANDS

Manila
Free Legal Aid Clinic, Women Lawyers' Association of the Philippines, 389 San Rafael, at Legarda Street

PUERTO RICO

Rio Piedras
Legal Aid Clinic, College of Law, University of Puerto Rico

San Juan
Sociedad Para Asistencia Legal, Box 1528

A Dictionary
of Legal Terms

A

A mensa et thoro A partial divorce.

A vinculo matrimonii An absolute divorce.

Ab initio From the beginning.

Abet To encourage, set on, stir up, or excite to commit a crime.

Abortion The premature exclusion of the human fetus, after the period of quickening which, when procured or produced with a malicious design or for an unlawful purpose, is a criminal offense.

Abrogate To annul a law by an act of the same power which made it; to repeal.

Absolute conveyance A conveyance by which the right or property in a thing is transferred, free of any condition or qualification.

Absolute divorce *See* Divorce.

Absolute estate An estate in lands not subject to or defeasible upon any condition.

Absolute property Full and complete ownership of chattels in possession.

Action The formal means or method of pursuing and recovering one's rights in a court of justice. A formal proceeding (or series of proceedings) in a court of justice between plaintiff and defendant by which the recovery of some alleged right is claimed by the one and resisted by the other; also the means by which such claim is enforced or denied by the court.

Ad litem With reference to a term commonly applied to guardians.

Administer To manage; to take charge and dispose of the personal property of an intestate, or a testator having no executor, according to the law.

Administration The management and disposition of the estate of an intestate, or of a testator having no executor.

Administration cum testamento annexo Administration granted in cases where a testator makes a will, without naming any executors; or where the executors who are named in the will are incompetent to act, or refuse to act; or in case of the death of the executors, or their survivors.

Administration de bonis non or **de bonis non administratis** Administration granted for the purpose of administering such of the goods of a deceased person as were not administered by the former executor or administrator.

Administration durante in absentia Administration granted during the absence of an executor.

Administration durante minore aetate Administration granted during the minority of an executor.

Administration pendente lite Administration granted during the pendency of a suit touching the validity of a will.

Administrator A manager or conductor of affairs, especially the affairs of another, in his name or behalf.

Administratrix A female who administers, or to whom the right of administration has been granted.

Adoption A legal taking or choosing of another's child as one's own.

Adult A term applied to males after the age of fourteen, and to females after twelve, in the common law. One who is of full age, usually by statute, twenty-one for males, eighteen for females.

Adultery Unlawful sexual intercourse between a married person and one of the opposite sex, whether married or single.

Advocate One who is called upon to assist or defend another.

Affiant A person making an affidavit.

Affidavit An oath in writing, sworn before some judge, officer of a court, or other person legally authorized to administer it.

Affinity The relationship which marriage creates between the husband and the blood relations of the wife, and between the wife and the blood relations of the husband.

Age A period of life at which persons become legally competent to do certain acts or enter into certain contracts, which before they were incompetent to do or enter into.

Agreement A coming together of parties in opinion or determination; a mutual contract for a consideration, between two or more parties.

Alienation Transfer to another; the act of making a thing another's conveyance, particularly of real estate, comprising any method wherein estates are voluntarily resigned by one man and accepted by another.

Alimony An allowance made to a wife out of the husband's estate, for her maintenance, either during a matrimonial suit or at its termination, when she has proved herself entitled to a separate maintenance.

All fours A case is said to go upon all fours, when it is exactly similar in its circumstances to the case in support of which it is quoted; also when it is exactly in point.

Allegation Statement or pleading.

Ambiguity Doubtfulness, uncertainty, or obscurity of meaning. Ambiguity in written instruments is either patent, that is, open or apparent, or latent, that is, hidden or concealed.

Amend To free from error or deficiency; to correct an error; to supply a deficiency.

Amendment The correction of an error committed in any process, pleading, or proceeding at law or in equity; and which is done either of course or by the consent of parties or upon motion to the court in which the proceeding is pending.

Amicable action An action between friendly parties; an action commenced and carried on according to a mutual understanding and arrangement.

Ancestor One who has gone before in a family. One who has preceded another in a line of descent; one from whom a person is descended.

Anni nubiles The marriageable age of women, twelve years at common law.

Answer In a general sense, any pleading (except a demurrer by which the party claims that he is not bound to answer) framed to meet a previous pleading.

Ante Before.

Appeal The complaint to a superior court of an injustice done or error committed by an inferior one, whose judgment or decision the court above is called upon to correct or reverse. The removal of a cause, or of some proceeding in a cause, from an inferior to a superior court, for the purpose of re-examination or review.

Appearance The coming into court of either of the parties to an action, or of their attorneys.

Appellee The party against whom an appeal is made.

Arrest of judgment The act of staying a judgment, or refusing to render judgment in an action at law, after verdict, for some matter appearing on the face of the record which would render the judgment, if given, erroneous or reversible.

Assault An unlawful setting upon one's person. An intentional attempt, by violence, to do bodily injury to another.

Assent Agreement to, or approval of an act or thing done.

Assign To make or set over to another; to transfer; as to assign property, or some interest therein. To transfer by writing.

Assignee A person to whom some right or property is assigned, transferred or made over by another.

Assignment A transfer or making over by one person to another, of any property real or personal in possession or action or of any estate or right therein.

Assignor One who makes an assignment; one who assigns or transfers to another.

Attachment A taking or seizure of a person or property, by virtue of a legal process. A writ of process for the taking or seizure of persons or property.

Attest To witness or testify. To witness the execution of an instrument, and to subscribe the name in testimony of such fact.

Attorney at law One who is put in the place, stead, or turn of another to manage his matters of law.

Award The judgment or decision made and given by an arbitrator or arbitrators, or an umpire, respecting any matter in dispute submitted to them.

B

Bar The place in court which counselors or advocates occupy while addressing the court or jury, and where prisoners are brought for the purpose of being arraigned or sentenced; usually designated by a material enclosure of some kind, to which the name of a bar may with more or less propriety be given.

Barrister One who appears at the bar of a court in discharge of his duty, as an advocate; one called to the bar; a pleader at the bar, counselor, or advocate.

Bastard Of spurious origin; base or low born. An illegitimate child; one who is born of an illicit union. One that is not only begotten, but born out of lawful matrimony.

Bastardy A defect of birth, objected to one begotten out of wedlock. The state or condition of a bastard.

Battery The unlawful beating of another. Any unlawful touching of the person of another, either by the aggressor himself, or any other substance put in motion by him, provided it is willfully committed or proceeds from the want of due care.

Bench warrant A warrant issued by or from a bench, or court. A process for the arrest of a party against whom an indictment has been found.

Bequeath To give personal property by will.

Bequest A gift of personal property by will; a gift of a legacy.

Bigamy The crime of marrying a second time during the life of an existing valid marriage; or of having more wives or husbands than one at the same time.

Bill of divorce A formal written statement of complaint to a court of justice.

Bill of costs A statement in writing of the items composing the amount of the costs awarded a plaintiff or defendant in an action or other judicial proceeding.

Bill in equity or chancery A complaint in writing, under oath, in the nature and style of a petition, addressed to the chancellor or judge or judges of a court of equity, setting forth all the facts and circumstances upon which the complaint is founded, and praying for such equitable relief or for such decree as the party may conceive himself entitled to or the court may deem proper to grant.

Bill of particulars A written statement or specification of the particulars of the demand for which an action at law is brought, or of a defendant's setoff against such demand (including dates, sums, and items in detail), furnished by one of the parties to the other, either voluntarily or in compliance with a judge's order for that purpose.

Blackmail A rent or tribute formerly paid by the poorer inhabitants of some of the northern counties of England to some powerful Scottish border chieftain in order to be protected from the depredations of the border thieves. Now, money extorted from one by threats of exposure, ill treatment, etc.

Blood Kindred; relation by natural descent from a common ancestor; consanguinity. A person is said to be of the blood of another, when he is descended from, or collaterally related to him.

Bona fide In good faith; honestly; without fraud, collusion, or deceit; really, actually, without pretense; innocently, ignorantly, without knowledge or notice.

Bond A deed or instrument under seal, by which a person binds or obliges himself, his heirs, executors, and administrators to pay a certain sum of money to another. The party thus binding himself is called the obligor; the party to whom he is bound, the obligee; and the instrument itself a writing obligatory.

Breach The breaking or violating of a law, right, or duty, either by commission or omission.

Breach of covenant The nonperformance of any covenant agreed to be performed, or the doing of any act covenanted not to be done.

Brief An abridgment of a plaintiff's or defendant's case, prepared by his attorney, for the instruction of counsel on a trial at law. It generally consists of an abstract of the pleadings, a statement of the facts of the case as they will be proved, and a list of the names of the witnesses, with a statement of what each will prove. To these are sometimes added observations in the nature of suggestions to counsel.

Burden of proof The necessity or duty of proving a fact or facts in dispute on an issue raised between the parties in a cause.

C

Carnal knowledge Sexual intercourse or connection.

Caveat A formal notice or caution, given by a party interested, to a court, judge, or public officer, against the performance of certain judicial or ministerial acts. A process used in the courts in England, and in probate courts of similar jurisdiction in the United States, to prevent the proving of a will or the granting of administration; and in the English and United States courts, to prevent the granting of letters patent.

Caveat emptor The buyer must take care, or be on his guard; the purchaser must examine for himself the article offered to him for sale and exercise his own judgment respecting it. If he purchases without examination, after a hasty examination, or in mere reliance upon the seller, and the article turns out to be defective, it is his own fault. He has no remedy against the seller unless the latter expressly warranted the article, or made a fraudulent representation concerning it or, knowing it to be defective, used some art to disguise it. This is a leading maxim of the law relating to the contract of sale, and its application is not affected by the circumstances that the price is such as is usually given for a sound commodity.

Certiorari A writ, used generally for the purpose of removing causes before trial or judgment, from inferior to superior courts. It is issued out of the superior court (or in England, out of the court of chancery), and is directed to the judges or officers of the inferior court, reciting the will of the king or people to be certified of the proceeding and commanding the record to be sent or returned before them.

Cestui que trust Beneficiary. One entitled in equity to take the rents and profits of lands whereof the legal estate is vested in some other person who is called the trustee; or, in other words, he who is the real, substantial, and beneficial owner of lands which are held in trust, as distinguished from the trustee.

Chancellor The presiding judge in the court of chancery.

Chancery, or court of chancery A court of equity; the name given to a court in which equity is either exclusively or chiefly administered; the court of the chancellor. Sometimes used as a synonym of equity or proceedings in equity.

Charge A burden; an incumbrance or lien upon land; a duty or liability attached to, or obligation imposed upon, a person. An address by the presiding judge to a jury impaneled in a case, after the case has been closed on both sides, recapitulating and commenting upon the testimony adduced by the respective parties and instructing the jury in any matter of law arising upon it.

Circuit A civil division of a country, state, or kingdom for the more convenient administration of justice; courts being held in the different circuits at stated periods by the judges of the superior courts, who go around for that purpose.

Circumstantial evidence Evidence derived from circumstances, as distinguished from direct and positive proof. Evidence operating in the way of inference from circumstances.

Client A person who employs or retains an attorney, solicitor, proctor, or counselor to appear for him in court, to advise, assist, and defend him in legal proceedings and to act for him in any legal business.

Code A collection or compilation of laws by public authority. A code may be either a mere compilation of existing laws or a new system of laws founded on new fundamental principles.

Cohabit To live together as husband and wife.

Collusion A deceitful agreement or compact between two or more persons as in a divorce suit where the grounds for divorce are agreed upon so as to eliminate the possibility of a contest.

Common law The whole body of the law of England, as distinguished from the civil and canon laws. That branch of the law of England which does not owe its origin to parliamentary enactment. The common law is the common jurisprudence of the people of the United States. It was brought with them as colonists from England and established here, in so far as it was adaptable to our institutions and circumstances.

Competency Capability; admissibility. Applied to witnesses, it signifies legal ability to be received and examined on the trial of a cause.

Complainant One who complains of another by instituting legal proceedings against him.

Complaint An accusation or charge against a person as having committed an alleged injury or offense.

Conclusive evidence Evidence which, in its nature, does not admit of explanation or contradiction. Evidence which, of itself, whether contradicted or uncontradicted, explained or unexplained, is sufficient to determine the matter at issue.

Conclusive presumption A species of presumption of law, which cannot be disputed or rebutted.

Concubine A woman with whom a man cohabits without marriage as distinguished from a lawful wife.

Condition precedent A condition preceding an estate; a condition which must happen, or be performed, before the estate to which it is annexed can vest or be enlarged. A condition preceding the accruing of a right or liability.

An act essential to be performed by one party, prior to any obligation attaching upon another party, to do or perform another given act.

Condonation Forgiveness. The forgiveness by a husband or wife of a breach of marital duties on the part of the other, as of acts of adultery or cruelty.

Confidential communication *See* Privileged Communication.

Consanguinity Kindred or alliance in blood. Relation by blood, as affinity is relation by marriage.

Consideration The material cause of a contract, without which no contract is binding. The reason which moves the contracting party to enter into the contract. The thing given in exchange for the benefit which is to be derived from a contract; the compensation. The price or motive of the contract.

Construction A putting together of the words of an instrument; an arrangement or marshaling of words or clauses so as to extract, by a process of inference, the meaning or intent; exposition; interpretation.

Constructive notice Notice inferred by law, as distinguished from actual or formal notice; notice in law; that which is held by law to amount to notice. Actual notice to a party's attorney is constructive notice to the party himself.

Contempt Disobedience or disregard of authority. A disobedience to the rules, orders, or process of a court of justice, or a disturbance or interruption of its proceedings. Contempts are either direct, which openly insult or resist the powers of the court or the persons of the judges who preside there; or consequential, which, without such gross insolence or direct opposition, plainly tend to create a universal disregard of their authority. They may be divided into those that are committed in the face of the court, which are punishable by commitment and fine, and those committed out of court, which are punishable by attachment or imprisonment.

Contra A term constantly used in law reports to denote the opposition of counsel in a cause; the disallowance by the court of a point in argument; the opposition of cases cited as establishing opposite doctrines.

Contra bonos mores Against good morals.

Contract An agreement, upon sufficient consideration, to do or not to do a particular thing. The writing which contains the agreement of parties, with the terms and conditions, and which serves as a proof of the obligation.

Contumacy Disobedience to the rules or orders of a court, especially a refusal to appear in court when legally summoned.

Conversion An appropriation of property; one of the grounds of the actions of trover. "Conversion" and "carrying away" are not synonymous or convertible terms; there may be a conversion without any carrying away.

Convey To pass or transmit from one to another; to transfer property, or the title to property, by an instrument in writing. In a stricter sense, to transfer by deed or instrument under seal.

Conveyance An instrument in writing by which property or the title to property is transferred from one person to another.

Corespondent The person charged with adultery and made a party to a suit for divorce.

Costs The expenses which are incurred either in the prosecution or defense of an action, or in any other proceeding at law, or in equity; consisting of the fees of attorneys, solicitors, and other officers of court, and such disbursements as are allowed by law.

Counsel An advocate; a counselor or pleader, who assists his client with advice, and pleads for him in open court. This word has no plural, and is used to denote either one or more counsel.

Counselor, counselor at law A person whose occupation and office it is to give counsel or advice as to the management of suits and other legal business, to conduct the trial or argument of causes in court (in which sense the word is synonymous with advocate) and to do any other acts requiring a personal presence there.

Court of chancery *See* Chancery.

Court of record A court where the acts and judicial proceedings are enrolled in parchment (or paper) for a perpetual memorial and testimony, and which has power to fine and imprison for contempt of its authority.

Courts of assize and nisi prius Courts in England composed of two or more commissioners, called judges of assize, who are twice in every year sent by the queen's special commission, on circuits all around the kingdom to try, by a jury of the respective counties, the truth of such matters of fact as are then under dispute in the courts of Westminster Hall.

Covenant The agreement or consent of two or more by deed in writing, sealed and delivered, whereby either or one of the parties promises to the other that something is done, or shall be done.

Covenant in law A covenant implied by law from certain words in a deed which do not express it.

Coverture The condition of a woman during marriage.

Credibility Worthiness of belief; that quality in a witness which renders his evidence worthy of belief. After the competence of a witness is allowed, the consideration of his credibility arises, and not before.

Criminal conversation Unlawful intercourse with a married woman.

Criminate To expose a person to a criminal charge. A witness cannot be compelled to answer any question which has a tendency to incriminate him.

Cross bill A bill filed by a defendant, in a suit in equity, and frequently in bills of divorce, against the plaintiff or complainant in order to obtain some relief against him.

Cross-examination The examination of a witness by the party opposed to the party who has first examined him, in order to test the truth of such first or direct examination. Cross-examination is usually by the party who did not call the witness, but the courts frequently permit an adverse witness to be cross-examined by the party who calls him.

Cruelty Such conduct on the part of a husband toward his wife as affords a reasonable apprehension of bodily hurt. It is usually considered ground for divorce.

D

Deceit A subtle trick or device.

Declaration of trust A declaration by a party who has made a conveyance to another that the subject conveyed is to be held in trust. An admission by an individual that a property, the title of which he holds, is held by him as trustee for another.

Decree The judgment of a court of equity or admiralty, answering to the judgment of a court of common law. A decree in equity is a sentence or order of the court, pronounced on hearing and determining the rights of all the parties to the suit, according to equity and good conscience.

Decree pro confesso A decree entered when the defendant has defaulted in a divorce suit in the time prescribed by the rules of court. The effect of such a decree is that the facts set forth in the divorce bill are taken as true, and a decree made according to the equity of the case. After a decree pro confesso is taken, the plaintiff proceeds to prove his case and, if convincing to the court, a divorce will be granted. The process is known as an *ex parte* proceeding which means that only the plaintiff and his witnesses are heard instead of both plaintiff and defendant.

Deed A writing sealed and delivered by the parties. A writing under seal containing a conveyance, bargain, contract, covenants, or matters of agreement between two or more persons.

Defamation The offense of injuring a

291

person's character, fame, or reputation, either by writing or by words. Written defamation is otherwise termed libel, and oral defamation, slander.

Defendant The party against whom an action of law or in equity is brought; the party denying, opposing, resisting, or contesting the action.

Defense A denial, by the defendant in an action at law, of the truth or validity of the plaintiff's complaint.

Demurrer An allegation of a defendant which, admitting the matters of fact alleged by the bill to be true, shows that, as they are therein set forth, they are insufficient for the plaintiff to proceed upon, or to oblige the defendant to answer; or that, for some reason apparent on the face of the bill, or because of the omission of some matter which ought to be contained therein, or for want of some circumstance which ought to be attendant thereon, the defendant ought not to be compelled to answer. It therefore demands the judgment of the court, whether the defendant shall be compelled to make answer to the plaintiff's bill or to some certain part thereof.

Deponent One who deposes (that is, testifies or makes oath in writing) to the truth of certain facts; one who gives, under oath, testimony which is reduced to writing; one who makes oath to a written statement. The party making an affidavit is generally so called.

Depose To state or testify under oath, in writing; to make a statement or give testimony under oath, which is reduced to writing; to make a statement which is reduced to writing and sworn to. A word constantly used in affidavits, as "A. B. of—, being duly sworn, deposes and says that," etc.

Deposition The testimony of a witness under oath or affirmation taken down in writing, before a commissioner, examiner, or other judicial officer, in answer to interrogatories and cross interrogatories, and usually subscribed by the witness,

Desertion Abandonment; the act of leaving or forsaking a service, duty, or person. The act of forsaking, deserting, or abandoning a person with whom one is legally bound to live, or for whom one is legally bound to provide, as a wife or husband. It is a usual ground for at least a partial divorce and, after a certain period, for an absolute divorce.

Dictum A saying or remark; an opinion expressed by a judge in deciding a cause or question, either aside from the point to be decided (hence said to be extra-judicial) or obiter (by the way).

Disbar To expel a barrister from the bar, so as to forbid him from practicing law.

Discovery, bill of A bill for the discovery of facts resting in the knowledge of the defendant, or of deeds or writings or other things in his custody or power.

Dismiss To send away; to send out of court; to dispose of finally.

Distrain To take and keep the property of another as a pledge, in order to compel the performance of some duty; such as the payment of rent, the performance of services, or an appearance in court.

Divorce The separation of husband and wife by the sentence of the law.

Divorce a mensa et thoro A partial or qualified divorce, not affecting the marriage itself, by which the parties are separated but forbidden to live or cohabit together.

Divorce a vinculo matrimonii A total divorce of husband and wife, dissolving the marriage tie, and releasing the parties wholly from their matrimonial obligations.

Docket A brief or abstract in writing. An abridged entry of an instrument or proceeding in an action; a list or register of such abridged entries. The list or calendar of causes ready for hearing or trial, prepared by clerks for the use of courts, is, in some states, called a docket.

Domicile The place where a person has his home. A residence at a particular place, accompanied with positive or presumptive proof of an intention to remain there for an unlimited time.

Domicile of origin The home of the parents. That which arises from a man's birth and connections. The domicile of the parents at the time of birth, or what is termed the domicile of origin, constitutes the domicile of an infant and continues until abandoned, or until the acquisition of a new domicile in a different place.

Dot Dowry, or marriage portion.

Dower That portion (usually one-third) of a man's lands and tenements to which his widow is entitled, to have and hold for the term of her natural life.

Dower by the common law The ordinary kind of dower in English and American law, consisting of one-third of the lands of which the husband was seised in fee at any time during the coverture.

Dowry The portion or property which the wife brings her husband in marriage.

Duces tecum A term applied to certain writs, in which a party summoned to appear in court is required to bring with him some piece of evidence, or other thing requested by the court.

Due process of law Law, in its regular course of administration through courts of justice. Due process of law implies a judicial trial, and not a mere declaration of legislative will by the passing of a law.

Duress Constraint, compulsion. The state of compulsion or necessity in which a person is induced, by the restraint of his liberty or menace of bodily harm, to execute a deed, or do any other legal act or to commit a misdemeanor.

E

Equity In a general sense, natural right or justice as addressed to the conscience, independently of any express or positive rule or law. In a stricter sense, the application of the principles of natural right and reason in the actual administration of justice; either by supplying rules for cases not provided for by the positive law, by mitigating the rigor of the law itself by a liberal and rational interpretation of its rules, or by adapting its remedies more exactly to the exigencies of particular cases. An elaborate system of rules and process, administered in many cases by distinct tribunals (termed courts of chancery) with exclusive jurisdiction over certain subjects. Its doctrines are founded upon the basis of natural justice, but its action has become systematized and as carefully regulated by fixed rules and precedents as the law itself. It is also no longer a mere principle or even a system of interpretation, but a system of practical remedy, remarkably direct and thorough in its operation, from its close investigation of facts and its precise adaptation of remedies.

Escheat The reverting of lands to the state on the death of the owner without lawful heirs.

Escrow A scroll or writing. A deed (and the term includes a bond) delivered to a third person to hold or keep until some act is done or condition performed, and then to be delivered to the grantee or obligee, at which time it takes effect and becomes a deed to all intents and purposes.

Esquire A name or title of dignity in English law, above the rank of gentleman, and below knight. Also, a title of office given to sheriffs, sergeants, and barristers at law, justices of the peace, and others.

Estate The interest which any one has in lands, or in any other subject of property. The property itself, in which one has an interest; technically called the corpus. Thus lands are real estate; goods and chattels are personal estate.

Estate pour autre vie An estate in lands which a man holds for the life of another person.

Estate in common An estate in lands held by two or more persons, with interest accruing under different titles; or accruing under the same title, but at different periods; or conferred by words of limitation importing that the grantees are to take in distinct shares.

Estate in coparcenary An estate acquired by two or more persons (usually females), by descent from the same ancestor.

Estate by the curtesy A species of life estate to which a man is, by law, entitled to claim on the death of his wife.

Estate in dower A species of life estate which a woman is, by law, entitled to claim on the death of her husband.

Estate in fee simple An estate to a man and his heirs forever; the entire and absolute interest and property in land.

Estate in fee tail, or **estate tail** An estate of inheritance which a man has, to hold to him and the heirs of his body, or to him and particular heirs of his body.

Estate in joint tenancy An estate in lands or tenements granted to two or more persons, to hold in fee simple, fee tail, for life, for years, or at will.

Estate for life A freehold estate, not of inheritance, which a man has, to hold for the term of his own life, or for that of any other person.

Evidence That which tends to render evident or clear; the means by which the truth of a fact or point in issue is made clear or demonstrated. Proof, either written or unwritten, of facts in issue between parties. The terms evidence and proof are constantly used in practice as synonymous.

Ex post facto law A law which operates by after-enactments. A law which makes an act done before its passage, and which was innocent when done, criminal. A law which renders an act punishable in a manner in which it was not punishable when committed. Such acts are unconstitutional.

Examiner in chancery An officer of the court of chancery before whom witnesses are examined and their testimony reduced to writing, for the purpose of being read on the hearing of the cause.

F

Fee simple A pure fee; an absolute estate of inheritance; that which a person holds inheritable to him and his heirs forever.

Feme A woman; a wife.

Feme covert A married woman.

Feme sole A sole, single, or unmarried woman.

Fraud Any cunning, deception, or artifice, used to circumvent, cheat, or deceive another.

Fraudulent conveyance A conveyance, the object, tendency, or effect of which is to defraud another, or the intent of which is to avoid some debt or duty due by, or incumbent on, the party making it.

G

Gift A voluntary and gratuitous conveyance or transfer of lands or goods from one to another, not founded on the consideration of money or blood.

Guardian A keeper or protector; one who has the charge or custody of any person or thing. In a stricter sense, one who has or is entitled to the custody of the person or property of an infant.

H

Hearsay evidence Evidence of what others have been heard to say; testimony from the relation of third persons.

Heir One who, upon the death of another, acquires or succeeds to his estate by right of blood and by operation of law.

Heir apparent An heir whose right of inheritance is indefeasible, provided he outlive the ancestor.

Heir by devise One to whom lands are devised by will; a devise of lands.

Heir at law, or **heir general** He who, after his ancestor's death, has a right to all his lands, tenements, and hereditaments.

Heir presumptive The person who, if the ancestor should die immediately, would, in the present circumstance of things, be his heir.

Heirloom A personal chattel which goes by special custom to the heir, along with the inheritance, and not to the executor or administrator of the last proprietor.

I

In loco parentis In the place of a parent.

Incest Sexual intercourse between persons who, by reason of consanguinity or affinity, cannot lawfully be united.

Indirect evidence That kind of evidence which goes to prove a principal fact by establishing other or subordinate facts, from which the principal fact may be inferred or presumed.

Infant A person under the age of twenty-one years; a minor.

Injunction A prohibitory writ, granted by a court of equity and which may be obtained in a variety of cases, to restrain the adverse party in the suit from committing any acts in violation of the plaintiff's rights.

Interlocutory decree A preliminary or intermediate decree; a decree which does not determine the suit, but directs some further proceedings before a final decree can be had. A decree pronounced for the purpose of ascertaining matter of law or fact preparatory to a final decree.

J

Joint tenancy A joint holding; a union or conjunction of interest in land or other property.

Joint tenants Joint holders; persons who hold an estate or property jointly, or in that peculiar mode called joint tenancy.

L

Laches Slackness, negligence, or remissness. Neglect to make a claim within a reasonable time.

Leading question A question put or framed in such a form as to suggest the answer desired by the interrogator.

Lex domicilii The law of the domicile.

Limited divorce A divorce for a limited time; a separation from bed and board. *See* Divorce a mensa et thoro.

Lineal descent The descent of one person from another; as a son from a father, in the right or direct line.

M

Marriage settlement A settlement made by a husband out of his estate, before or after marriage, for the benefit of his wife, or of his wife and children.

Master in chancery In equity practice, an important officer of courts of equity, who acts as assistant to the chancellor or judge, and whose principal duty consists in inquiring into various matters referred to him for the purpose of reporting them to the court.

Misrepresentation A false or erroneous representation. A misrepresentation of a material fact, whether it be made through mistake or design.

Morganatic marriage A marriage between a man of superior and a woman of inferior rank, in which it is stipulated that the latter and her children shall not enjoy the rank or inherit the possessions of her husband.

N

Ne exeat regno or **ne exeat** A writ issuing out of chancery forbidding the person or persons to whom it is directed from leaving the kingdom or state.

Necessaries Such things and articles furnished to a child as are useful and suitable to his state and condition of life, and not merely such as are requisite for bare subsistence.

Nisi prius A term used to denote the system of trial of issues of fact, in civil cases, before a jury, as distinguished from the argument of issues and questions of law before the court in bench.

Nisi prius court A court held for the trial of issues of fact, before a jury and a single presiding judge.

Non compos mentis Not in possession, or not having power of one's mind or mental faculties; of unsound mind or memory.

O

Obiter dictum An opinion of a judge delivered or expressed by the way, and not upon the point in question before him.

P

Parol evidence Oral or verbal evidence; that which is given by word of mouth; the ordinary kind of evidence given by a witness in court.

Parol promise A simple contract; a verbal promise.

Partial divorce *See* Divorce a mensa et thoro.

Particeps criminis A sharer, partner, participator, or accomplice in (of) crime. Applied to parties both in contracts and offenses.

Pendente lite Pending the suit; during the actual progress of a suit; during litigation.

Perjury False swearing; the making of a false oath; the breach of an oath.

Personal property That kind of property which usually consists of things temporary and movable, but includes all subjects of property not of a freehold nature, nor descendible to the heirs at law.

Plaintiff The complaining party in an action at law; the party bringing action, and so named on the record.

Plea An answer or allegation of fact which a defendant, in an action at law, opposes to the plaintiff's declaration.

Pleadings The individual allegations of the respective parties to an action at common law, proceeding from them alternately, in the order and under the distinctive names following: the plaintiff's declaration, the defendant's plea, the plaintiff's replication, the defend-

ant's rejoinder, the plaintiff's surrejoinder, the defendant's rebutter, the plaintiff's surrebutter, after which they have no distinctive names.

In equity the formal written allegation or statements of the respective parties in a suit, to maintain or defeat it. These are: the plaintiff's bill, the defendant's answer, and the plaintiff's replication.

Posthumous child A child born after the death of its father.

Power of attorney An instrument in writing, under seal, by which the party executing it appoints another to be his attorney, and empowers such attorney to act for him, either generally in all matters or business, or specially, to do some specified act or acts in his name and behalf.

Prima facie At the first view.

Prima facie evidence Evidence which, if not contradicted or unexplained, is sufficient to determine the matter at issue.

Privileged communication A communication made to a counsel, solicitor, or attorney, in professional confidence, which he is not permitted to divulge.

Propinquity The relationship which exists among members of a family or their descendants.

Q

Quitclaim The release or relinquishment of a claim. A deed by which some right, title, interest, or claim which one person has, or is supposed to have, in or to an estate held by another, is released or relinquished.

R

Rape The violation or carnal knowledge of a woman forcibly and against her will.

Recrimination A counteraccusation; an accusation made by an accused party against the accuser.

Res judicata or **adjudicata** A matter adjudged; a thing judicially acted upon or decided; a judgment.

Retainer The engagement by a client of an attorney, solicitor, or counsel to act in his behalf; as to institute or to defend a suit, to try a cause, or the like.

Retaining fee A fee given to a counsel to secure his services, or rather, as it has been said, to prevent the opposite side from engaging him.

Return day The day on which a writ is appointed or required to be returned.

S

Seduction The offense of inducing a woman to consent to unlawful intercourse.

Separate maintenance The maintenance of a woman by her husband, after an agreement to live separately.

Sodomy Carnal copulation between human beings, or between man and beast, contrary to nature.

Subpoena or **sub poena** A writ commanding the attendance or appearance of a witness or party in court, or before a judicial officer, under a penalty.

T

Tenancy in common The holding of an estate in lands by several persons, by several and distinct titles, but by unity of possession.

Tenant One who has temporary possession and use of that which is in reality the property of another; as a tenant for life or years.

Tenant by the curtesy One who, on the death of his wife seised of an estate of inheritance, after having by her issue born alive and capable of inheriting her estate, holds the lands and tenements for the term of his life. After the birth of the issue and before the death of the wife, he is called tenant by the curtesy initiate; after the death of the wife, tenant by the curtesy consummate.

Tenant in fee simple or **tenant in fee** One who has lands, tenements, or hereditaments, to hold to him and his heirs forever, generally, absolutely, and simply.

Tenant for life One who holds lands or tenements for the term of his own life.

Tenant by or **at sufferance** One who comes into the possession of land by lawful title, but holds over by wrong title, after the determination of his interest.

Tenant from year to year One who holds lands or tenements under a lease from year to year.

Tenant for years One who holds lands or tenements under a lease or demise from another, for the term of a certain number of years agreed upon; a lessee for years.

Testament A disposition of personal property, to take effect after the death of the person making it.

Testamentary Pertaining to a will or testament.

Testamentary causes Causes or matters relating to the probate of wills, the granting of administrations, and the suing for legacies.

Testate One who dies leaving a will; the opposite of intestate.

Testator One who makes or has made a testament or will.

Testimonium clause That clause of an instrument with which it concludes: "In witness whereof, the parties to these presents have hereunto set their hands and seals."

V

Valuable consideration A consideration which the law esteems an equivalent for a grant, such as money, marriage, or the like.

Void Of no force or effect, absolutely null; that which cannot be confirmed, or made effectual.

Voidable Not absolutely void, or void in itself; that which may be avoided or confirmed.

Voluntary conveyance A conveyance without valuable consideration, such as a deed or settlement in favor of a wife or children.

W

Wife's equity The equitable right or claim of a married woman to a reasonable and adequate provision, by way of settlements or otherwise, out of her choses in action, or out of any property of hers which is under the jurisdiction of the court of chancery, for the support of herself and her children.

Writ A judicial instrument by which a court commands some act to be done by the person to whom it is directed.

Index

Index

ABOUT THE AUTHOR

Samuel G. Kling is a man of many facets and accomplishments. He has been a practicing divorce lawyer in Baltimore for more than twenty-five years, he is a distinguished and successful marriage counselor, and he is a noted writer on legal subjects.

Born in New York City, he moved with his family to the stoney stoops of Baltimore when he was nine. He began writing seriously when he was a student at the University of Baltimore Law School, and his pen has been active since. His feature articles have appeared in the Baltimore *Sunday Sun*, he has frequently contributed reviews to the Sunday editions of *The New York Times* and the New York *Herald Tribune*, and he has had articles published in *Look, Better Homes and Gardens*, and many other magazines. *Your Marriage*, Mr. Kling's nationally syndicated column, appeared in the New York *World-Telegram*, the Chicago *Daily News*, and fifty-five other leading newspapers for eight years.

Two of Mr. Kling's previous books, *Your Legal Advisor*, a layman's handbook of law, and *The Encyclopedia for Home and Business*, have sold almost two million copies in Pocket Book editions.